THREE TREATISES

MARTIN LUTHER

FORTRESS PRESS

Philadelphia

Table of Contents

Foreword

The treatises of Luther included in this volume—*An Open Letter to the Christian Nobility, The Babylonian Captivity of the Church,* and *The Freedom of a Christian* —are sometimes referred to as his "primary works." All three were written in 1520 when the struggle between the Reformer and his opponents was at its height.

An Open Letter to the Christian Nobility is reprinted, with minor revisions, from the Philadelphia Edition of *The Works of Martin Luther,* translated by Charles M. Jacobs. *The Babylonian Captivity of the Church* is from the American Edition of *Luther's Works,* Vol. 36, translated by A. T. W. Steinhäuser and revised by Frederick C. Ahrens and Abdel Ross Wentz. *The Freedom of a Christian* is also from the American Edition, Vol. 31, translated by W. A. Lambert and revised by Harold J. Grimm.

LW refers to the American Edition of *Luther's Works, PE* refers to the Philadelphia Edition of *The Works of Martin Luther,* and *WA* refers to the German-language Weimar Ausgabe (Weimar Edition) of Luther's writings.

AN OPEN LETTER
TO
THE CHRISTIAN NOBILITY

Introduction

THE *Open Letter to the Christian Nobility of the German Nation* is closely related to the tract on *The Papacy at Rome: A Reply to the Celebrated Romanist at Leipzig.* In a letter to Spalatin dated before June 8, 1520, Luther says: "I shall assail that ass of an Alveld in such wise as not to forget the Roman pontiff, and neither of them will be pleased." In the same letter he writes, "I am minded to issue a broadside to Charles and the nobility of Germany against the tyranny and baseness of the Roman curia." The attack upon Alveld is the tract on *The Papacy at Rome;* the *schedu publica* grew into the *Open Letter.* At the time when the letter to Spalatin was written, the work on *The Papacy at Rome* must have been already in press, for it appeared in print on the 26th of the month, and the composition of the *Open Letter* had evidently not yet begun. On the 23rd Luther sent the manuscript of the *Open Letter* to Amsdorf, with the request that he read it and suggest changes. The two weeks immediately preceding the publication of the work *On the Papacy* must, therefore, have been the time when the *Open Letter* was composed.

⌐In the conclusion to the earlier work Luther had said: "Moreover, I should be truly glad if kings, princes, and all the nobles would take hold, and turn the knaves from Rome out of the country, and keep the appointments to bishoprics and benefices out of their hands. How has Roman avarice come to usurp all the foundations, bishoprics and benefices of our fathers? Who has ever read or heard of such monstrous robbery? Do we not also have the people who need them, while out of our poverty we must enrich the ass-drivers and stable-boys, nay, the harlots and knaves at Rome, who look upon us as nothing else but arrant fools, and make us the objects of their vile mockery? Oh, the pity, that kings and princes have so little reverence for Christ, and His honor concerns them so little that they allow such heinous abominations to gain the upper hand, and look on, while at Rome they think of nothing but to continue in their madness and to increase the abounding misery, until no hope is left on earth except in the temporal authorities. Of this I will say more anon, if this Romanist comes again; let this suffice for a beginning. May God help us at length to open our eyes. Amen."

This passage may fairly be regarded as the germ of the *Open Letter*. The ideas of the latter work are suggested with sufficient clearness to show that its materials are already at hand, and its plan already in the author's mind. The threat to write it is scarcely veiled. That Luther did not wait for that particular Romanist to "come again" may have been due to the intervention of another Romanist, none other than his old opponent, Sylvester Prierias. Before the 7th of June Luther had received a copy of Prierias' *Epitome of a Reply to Martin Luther*, which is the boldest and baldest possible assertion of the very theory of papal power which Luther had sought to demolish in his tract on *The Papacy*. In the preface to his reprint on the *Epitome*, Luther bids farewell to Rome: "Farewell, unhappy, hopeless, blasphemous Rome! The wrath of God hath come upon thee, as thou hast deserved! We have cared for Babylon, and she is not healed; let us, then, leave her, that she may be the habitation of dragons, spectres and witches, and true to her name of Babel, an everlasting confusion, a new pantheon of wickedness."

These words were written while the *Open Letter* was in

course of composition. The *Open Letter* is, therefore, Luther's first publication after the time when he recognized that the breach between him and the papal church was complete, and likely to be permanent. Meanwhile, the opposing party had come to the same conclusion. The verdict of the pope upon Luther had been long delayed, but on the 15th of June, midway between the letter to Spalatin, above mentioned, and the completion of the *Open Letter*, Leo X signed the bull of excommunication, though it was not published in Germany until later. Thus the *Open Letter* shows us the mind of Luther in the weeks when the permanent separation between him and Rome took place.

It was also the time when he had the highest hopes from the promised support of the German knights, who formed the patriotic party in Germany and are included in the "nobility" to whom the *Open Letter* is addressed.

The first edition of 4000 copies came off the press of Melchier Lotther in Wittenberg before the 18th of August. It is surmised that the earlier portion of the work was not contained in the orginal manuscript, but was added while it was in the printer's hands; perhaps it was added at the suggestion of Amsdorf. Less than a week later a second edition was in course of preparation. This "enlarged and revised edition" contained three passages not included in the first. They are indicated in the notes to the present edition.

He who would know the true Luther must read more than one of his writings; he must not by any chance omit to read the *Open Letter to the Christian Nobility of the German Nation*. In his other works we learn to know him as the man of God, or the prophet, or the theologian; in this treatise we meet Luther, *the German*. His heart is full of grief for the affliction of his people, and grief turns to wrath as he observes that this affliction is put upon them by the tyranny and greed of the pope and the cardinals and the

"Roman vermin." The situation is desperate; appeals and protests have been all in vain; and so, as a last resort, he turns to the temporal authorities — to Charles V. newly elected, but as yet uncrowned; to the territorial lords, great and small, who have a voice in the imperial diet and powers of jurisdiction in their own domains — reciting the abuses of "Roman tyranny," and pleading with them to intervene in behalf of the souls that are going to destruction "through the devilish rule of Rome." It is a cry out of the heart of Germany, a nation whose bent is all religious, but which, from that very circumstance, is all the more open to the insults and wrongs and deceptions of the Roman curia.

Yet it is no formless and incoherent cry, but an orderly recital of the ills of Germany. There are times when we feel in reading it that the writer is laying violent hands on his own wrath in the effort to be calm. For all its scathing quality, it is a sane arraignment of those who "under the holy name of Christ and St. Peter" are responsible for the nation's woes, and the remedies that are proposed are, many of them, practicable as well as reasonable.

The materials of the work are drawn from many sources — from hearsay, from personal observation, from such histories as Luther had at his command, from the proceedings of councils and of diets; there are passages which would seem to bear more than an accidental resemblance to similar passages in Hutten's *Vadiscus*. All was grist that *ground grain.* came to Luther's mill. But the spirit of the work is Luther's own.

For the general historian, who is concerned more with the practical than with the theoretical or theological aspects of the Reformation, the *Open Letter* is undoubtedly Luther's greatest work. Its frank outspokenness about the true condition of Germany, the number and variety of the subjects that it treats, the multiplicity of the sources from which the subject matter is drawn, and the point of view from which the whole is discussed make it a work of absorbing interest and priceless historical value. It shows, as does no other single work of the Reformation time, the things that were in men's minds and the variety of motives which led them to espouse the cause of the Protestant party. Doctrine, ethics, history, politics, economics, all have their place in the treatise. It is not only "a blast on the war-trumpet," but a connecting link between the thought of the Middle Ages and that of modern times, prophetic of the new age, but showing how closely the new is bound up with the old.

analagous to 95 theses on a grander scale.

AN OPEN LETTER

to the

CHRISTIAN NOBILITY of the GERMAN NATION

concerning

THE REFORM of the CHRISTIAN ESTATE

1520

To the
Esteemed and Reverend Master
NICHOLAS VON AMSDORF,
Licentiate of Holy Scripture and Canon at Wittenberg,
my special and kind friend;
Doctor Martin Luther.

The grace and peace of God be with thee, esteemed and reverend dear sir and friend.

The time to keep silence has passed and the time to speak is come, as Ecclesiastes says. I have followed out our intention and brought together some matters touching the reform of the Christian Estate, to be laid before the Christian Nobility of the German Nation, in the hope that God may deign to help His Church through the efforts of the laity, since the clergy, to whom this task more properly belongs, have grown quite indifferent. I am sending the whole thing to your Reverence, that you may pass judgment on it and, if necessary, improve it.

I know full well that I shall not escape the charge of presumption in that I, a despised monk, venture to address such high and great Estates on matters of such moment, and to give advice to people of such high intelligence. I shall offer no apologies, no matter who may chide me. Perchance I owe my God and the world another piece of folly, and I have now made up my mind honestly to pay that debt, if I can do so, and for once to become court-jester; if I fail, I still have one advantage — no one need buy me a cap or cut me my comb.[1] It is a question which one will put the bells on the other. I must fulfill the proverb, "Whatever the world does, a monk must be in it, even if he has to be painted in." More than once a fool has spoken wisely, and wise men often have been arrant fools, as Paul says, "If anyone will be wise, let him become a fool." Moreover since I am not only a fool, but also a sworn doctor of Holy Scripture, I am glad for the chance to fulfill my doctor's oath in this fool's way.

I pray you, make my excuses to the moderately intelligent, for I know not how to earn the grace and favor of the immoderately intelligent, though I have often sought to do so with great pains. Henceforth I neither desire nor regard their favor. God help us to seek not our own glory, but His alone! Amen.

Wittenberg, in the house of the Augustinians,
on the Eve of St. John the Baptist (June 23), in
the year 1520.

To
His Most Illustrious and Mighty Imperial Majesty,
and to
the Christian Nobility of the German Nation,
Doctor Martin Luther.

Grace and power from God, Most Illustrious Majesty, and most gracious and dear Lords.

It is not out of sheer frowardness or rashness that I, a

---

1. An ironical comparison of the monk's cowl and tonsure with the headgear of the jester.

single, poor man, have undertaken to address your worships. The distress and oppression which weigh down all the Estates of Christendom, especially of Germany, and which move not me alone, but everyone to cry out time and again, and to pray for help, have forced me even now to cry aloud that God may inspire some one with His Spirit to lend this suffering nation a helping hand. Ofttimes the councils[2] have made some pretense at reformation, but their attempts have been cleverly hindered by the guile of certain men and things have gone from bad to worse. I now intend, by the help of God, to throw some light upon the wiles and wickedness of these men, to the end that when they are known, they may not henceforth be so hurtful and so great a hindrance. God has given us a noble youth to be our head and thereby has awakened great hopes of good in many hearts,[3] wherefore it is meet that we should do our part and profitably use this time of grace.

In this whole matter the first and most important thing is that we take earnest heed not to enter on it trusting in great might or in human reason, even though all power in the world were ours; for God cannot and will not suffer a good work to be begun with trust in our own power or reason. Such works He crushes ruthless to earth, as it is written in the Thirty-third Psalm, "There is no king saved by the multitude of an host; a mighty man is not delivered by much strength." On this account, I fear, it came to pass of old that the good Emperors Frederick I[4] and II,[5] and many other German emperors were shamefully oppressed and trodden under foot by the popes, although all the world feared them. It may be that they relied on their

---

2. Councils of the Church, especially those of Constance (1414-18) and of Basel (1431-39).

3. Charles V was elected Emperor in 1519, when but twenty years of age.

4. Frederick Barbarossa (1152-90).

5. Frederick II (1212-50), grandson of Barbarossa and last of the great Hohenstaufen Emperors. He died under excommunication.

own might more than on God, and therefore they had to fall. In our own times, too, what was it that raised the bloodthirsty Julius II[6] to such heights? Nothing else, I fear, except that France, the Germans and Venice relied upon themselves. The children of Benjamin slew 42,000 Israelites[7] because the latter relied on their own strength.

That it may not so fare with us and our noble young Emperor Charles, we must be sure that in this matter we are dealing not with men, but with the princes of hell, who can fill the world with war and bloodshed, but whom war and bloodshed do not overcome. We must go at this work despairing of physical force and humbly trusting God; we must seek God's help with earnest prayer, and fix our minds on nothing else than the misery and distress of suffering Christendom, without regard to the deserts of evil men. Otherwise we may start the game with great prospect of success, but when we get well into it the evil spirits will stir up such confusion that the whole world will swim in blood, and yet nothing will come of it. Let us act wisely, therefore, and in the fear of God. The more force we use, the greater our disaster if we do not act humbly and in God's fear. The popes and the Romans have hitherto been able, by the devil's help, to set kings at odds with one another, and they may well be able to do it again, if we proceed by our own might and cunning, without God's help.

I. THE THREE WALLS OF THE ROMANISTS

The Romanists,[8] with great adroitness, have built three walls about them, behind which they have hitherto defended themselves in such wise that no one has been able to

---

6. Pope Julius II (1503-13). Nortorious among the popes for his unscrupulous pursuit of political power, he was continually involved in war with one and another of the European powers over the possession of territories in Italy.

7. Luther's recollection of the figures was faulty.

8. The term "Romanist" is applied by Luther to the champions of the extreme form of papal supremacy.

reform them and this has been the cause of terrible corruption throughout all Christendom.

① First, when pressed by the temporal power, they have made decrees and said that the temporal power has no jurisdiction over them, but, on the other hand, that the spiritual is above the temporal power. ② Second, when the attempt is made to reprove them out of the Scriptures, they raise the objection that the interpretation of the Scriptures belongs to no one except the pope. ③ Third, if threatened with a council, they answer with the fable that no one can call a council but the pope.

In this wise they have slyly stolen from us our three rods, that they may go unpunished, and have ensconced themselves within the safe stronghold of these three walls, that they may practice all the knavery and wickedness which we now see. Even when they have been compelled to hold a council they have weakened its power in advance by previously binding the princes with an oath to let them remain as they are. Moreover, they have given the pope full authority over all the decisions of the council, so that it is all one whether there are many councils or no councils — except that they deceive us with puppet-shows and sham battles. So terribly do they fear for their skin in a really free council! And they have intimidated kings and princes by making them believe it would be an offense against God not to obey them in all these knavish, crafty deceptions.

Now God help us, and give us one of the trumpets with which the walls of Jericho were overthrown, that we may blow down these walls of straw and paper, and may set free the Christian rods for the punishment of sin, bringing to light the craft and deceit of the devil, to the end that through punishment we may reform ourselves, and once more attain God's favor.

Against the *first wall* we will direct our first attack. *1st wall*

13

It is pure invention that pope, bishops, priests and monks are to be called the "spiritual estate"; princes, lords, artisans, and farmers the "temporal estate." That is indeed a fine bit of lying and hypocrisy. Yet no one should be frightened by it and for this reason — viz., that all Christians are truly of the "spiritual estate," and there is among them no difference at all but that of office, as Paul says in I Corinthians 12. We are all one body, yet every member has its own work, whereby it serves every other, all because we have one baptism, one Gospel, one faith, and are all alike Christians; for baptism, Gospel, and faith alone make us "spiritual" and a Christian people.

But that a pope or a bishop anoints, confers tonsures, ordains, consecrates, or prescribes dress unlike that of the laity — this may make hypocrites and graven images, but it never makes a Christian or "spiritual" man. Through baptism all of us are consecrated to the priesthood, as St. Peter says in I Peter 2, "Ye are a royal priesthood, a priestly kingdom," and the book of Revelation says, "Thou hast made us by thy blood to be priests and kings." For if we had no higher consecration than pope or bishop gives, the consecration by pope or bishop would never make a priest, nor might anyone either say mass or preach a sermon or give absolution. Therefore when the bishop consecrates it is the same thing as if he, in the place and stead of the whole congregation, all of whom have like power, were to take one out of their number and charge him to use this power for the others; just as though ten brothers, all king's sons and equal heirs, were to choose one of themselves to rule the inheritance for them all — they would all be kings and equal in power, though one of them would be charged with the duty of ruling.

To make it still clearer. If a little group of pious Christian laymen were taken captive and set down in a wilderness, and had among them no priest consecrated by a bishop, and if there in the wilderness they were to agree in choosing one of themselves, married or unmarried, and were to charge him with the office of baptizing, saying mass, absolving and preaching, such a man would be as truly a priest as though all bishops and popes had consecrated him. That is why in cases of necessity anyone can baptize and give absolution,[9] which would be impossible unless we were all priests. This great grace and power of baptism and of the Christian Estate they have well-nigh destroyed and caused us to forget through the canon law.[10] It was in the manner aforesaid that Christians in olden days chose from their number bishops and priests, who were afterwards confirmed by other bishops, without all the show which now obtains. It was thus that Sts. Augustine, Ambrose, and Cyprian became bishops.

Since, then, the temporal authorities are baptized with the same baptism and have the same faith and Gospel as we, we must grant that they are priests and bishops, and count their office one which has a proper and a useful place in the Christian community. For whoever comes out of the water of baptism can boast that he is already consecrated priest, bishop, and pope, though it is not seemly that everyone should exercise the office. Nay, just because we are all in like manner priests, no one must put himself forward and undertake, without our consent and election, to do what is in the power of all of us. For what is common to all, no one dare take upon himself without the will and

9. Lay-baptism in view of imminent death is a practice as old as the Christian Church. The right of the laity to administer baptism in such cases was expressly recognized by the Council of Elvira, in the year 306, and the decree of that Council became a part of the law of the Church. The right of the laity to give absolution in such cases rests on the principle that in the absence of the appointed official of the Church any Christian can do for any other Christian the things that are absolutely necessary for salvation, for "necessity knows no law."

10 The canon law, called by Luther throughout this treatise and elsewhere, the "spiritual law," is a general name for the decrees of councils and decisions of the popes, collected in the so-called *Corpus juris canonici.*

the command of the community; and should it happen that one chosen for such an office were deposed for malfeasance, he would then be just what he was before he held office. Therefore a priest in Christendom is nothing else than an office-holder. While he is in office, he has precedence; when deposed, he is a peasant or a townsman like the rest. Beyond all doubt, then, a priest is no longer a priest when he is deposed. But now they have invented *characteres indelebiles*,[11] and prate that a deposed priest is nevertheless something different from a mere layman. They even dream that a priest can never become a layman, or be anything else than a priest. All this is mere talk and man-made law.

From all this it follows that there is really no difference between laymen and priests, princes and bishops, "spirituals" and "temporals," as they call them, except that of office and work, but not of "estate"; for they are all of the same estate[12]—true priests, bishops and popes—though they are not all engaged in the same work, just as all priests and monks have not the same work. This is the teaching of St. Paul in Romans 12 and I Corinthians 12, and of St. Peter in I Peter 2, as I have said above, viz., that we are all one body of Christ, the Head, all members one of another. Christ has not two different bodies, one "temporal," the other "spiritual." He is one Head, and He has one body.

Therefore, just as those who are now called "spiritual" — priests, bishops, or popes — are neither different from other Christians nor superior to them, except that they are

---

11. The *character indelebilis*, or "indelible mark," received authoritative statement in the bull *Exultate Deo* (1439). The Council of Trent defined the correct Roman teaching as follows: "Since in the sacrament of orders, as in baptism and confirmation, a character is impressed which cannot be destroyed or taken away, the Holy Synod justly condemns the opinion of those who assert that the priests of the New Testament have only temporary power, and that those once rightly ordained can again be made laymen, if they do not exercise the ministry of the Word of God."

12. i.e., They are all Christians, among whom there can be no essential difference.

charged with the administration of the Word of God and the sacraments, which is their work and office, so it is with the temporal authorities — they bear sword and rod with which to punish the evil and to protect the good. A cobbler, a smith, a farmer, each has the work and office of his trade, and yet they are all alike consecrated priests and bishops, and everyone by means of his own work or office must benefit and serve every other, that in this way many kinds of work may be done for the bodily and spiritual welfare of the community, even as all the members of the body serve one another.

See, now, how Christian is the decree which says that the temporal power is not above the "spiritual estate" and may not punish it.[13] That is as much as to say that the hand shall lend no aid when the eye is suffering. Is it not unnatural, not to say unchristian, that one member should not help another and prevent its destruction? Verily, the more honorable the member, the more should the others help. I say then, since the temporal power is ordained of God to punish evil-doers and to protect them that do well, it should therefore be left free to perform its office without hindrance through the whole body of Christendom without respect of persons, whether it affect pope, bishops, priests, monks, nuns, or anybody else. For if the mere fact that the temporal power has a smaller place among the Christian offices than has the office of preachers or confessors, or of the clergy, then the tailors, cobblers, masons, carpenters, pot-boys, tapsters, farmers, and all the

---

13. The sharp distinction which the Roman Church drew between clergy and laity found practical application in the contention that the clergy should be exempt from the jurisdiction of the civil courts. It was further claimed that the government of the clergy and the administration of Church property must be entirely in the hands of the Church authorities, and that no lay rulers might either make or enforce laws which in any way affected the Church.

17

secular tradesmen, should also be prevented from providing pope, bishops, priests and monks with shoes, clothing, houses, meat and drink, and from paying them tribute. But if these laymen are allowed to do their work unhindered, what do the Roman scribes mean by their laws, with which they withdraw themselves from the jurisdiction of the temporal Christian power, only so that they may be free to do evil and to fulfill what St. Peter has said: "There shall be false teachers among you, and through covetousness shall they with feigned words make merchandise of you."

On this account the Christian temporal power should exercise its office without let or hindrance, regardless whether it be pope, bishop, or priest whom it affects; whoever is guilty, let him suffer. All that the canon law has said to the contrary is sheer invention of Roman presumption. For St. Paul says to all Christians: "Let every soul (I take that to mean the pope's soul also) be subject unto the higher powers; for they bear not the sword in vain, but are the ministers of God for the punishment of evildoers, and for the praise of them that do well." St. Peter also says: "Submit yourselves unto every ordinance of man for the Lord's sake, for so is the will of God." He has also prophesied that such men shall come as will despise the temporal authorities, and this has come to pass through the canon law.

So then, I think this first paper wall is overthrown, since the temporal power has become a member of the body of Christendom, and is of the "spiritual estate," though its work is of a temporal nature. Therefore its work should extend freely and without hindrance to all the members of the whole body; it should punish and use force whenever guilt deserves or necessity demands, without regard to pope, bishop and priests — let them hurl threats and bans as much as they will.

This is why guilty priests, if they are surrendered to the

temporal law,[14] are first deprived of their priestly dignities, which would not be right unless the temporal sword had previously had authority over them by divine right.

Again, it is intolerable that in the canon law so much importance is attached to the freedom, life, and property of the clergy, as though the laity were not also as spiritual and as good Christians as they, or did not belong to the Church. Why are your life and limb, your property and honor so free, and mine not? We are all alike Christians, and have baptism, faith, Spirit, and all things alike. If a priest is killed, the land is laid under interdict[15] — why not when a peasant is killed? Whence comes this great distinction between those who are equally Christians? Only from human laws and inventions!

Moreover, it can be no good spirit who has invented such exceptions and granted to sin such license and impunity. For if we are bound to strive against the works and words of the evil spirit, and to drive him out in whatever way we can, as Christ commands and His Apostles, ought we, then, to suffer it in silence when the pope or his satellites are bent on devilish words and works? Ought we for the sake of men to allow the suppression of divine commandments and truths which we have sworn in baptism to support with life and limb? Of a truth we should then have to answer for all the souls that would thereby be abandoned and led astray.

It must therefore have been the very prince of devils who said what is written in the canon law: "If the pope

---

14. It was the contention of the Church authorities that priests charged with infraction of the laws of the state first be tried in the ecclesiastical courts. If found guilty, they were degraded from the priesthood and handed over to the state authorities for punishment.

15. The interdict is the prohibition of the administration of the sacraments and of the other rites of the Church within the territory upon which the interdict is laid. Its use was not uncommon in the Middle Ages, and during the time that the power of the popes was at its height it proved an effective means of bringing refractory rulers to terms. A famous instance is the interdict laid upon the Kingdom of England by Innocent III in 1208.

were so scandalously bad as to lead souls in crowds to the devil, yet he could not be deposed." [16] On this accursed and devilish foundation they build at Rome, and think that we should let all the world go to the devil, rather than resist their knavery. If the fact that one man is set over others were sufficient reason why he should escape punishment, then no Christian could punish another, since Christ commands that every man shall esteem himself the lowliest and the least.

Where sin is, there is no escape from punishment; as St. Gregory [17] also writes that we are indeed all equal, but guilt puts us in subjection one to another. Now we see how they whom God and the Apostles have made subject to the temporal sword deal with Christendom, depriving it of its liberty by their own wickedness, without warrant of Scripture. It is to be feared that this is a game of Antichrist [18] or a sign that he is close at hand.

2nd wall The *second wall* is still more flimsy and worthless. They wish to be the only Masters of the Holy Scriptures, [19] even though in all their lives they learn nothing from them. They assume for themselves sole authority, and with insolent juggling of words they would persuade us that the pope, whether he be a bad man or a good man, cannot err in matters of faith, [20] and yet they cannot prove a single letter

---

16. Prierias, an opponent of Luther, had quoted this canon as follows: "A *Pontifex indubitatus* (i. e., a pope who is not accused of heresy or schism) cannot lawfully be deposed or judged either by a council or by the whole world, even if he is so scandalous as to lead people with him by crowds into the possession of hell." Luther's comment is: "Be astonished, O heaven; shudder, O earth! Behold, O Christians, what Rome is!"

17. Gregory the Great, pope 590-604.

18. Antichrist, the incarnation of all that is hostile to Christ and His Kingdom. His appearance is prophesied in 2 Thess. 2:3-10 (the "man of sin, sitting in the temple of God"); 1 John 2:18,22; 4:3; and Rev. 13.

19. According to academic usage, the holder of a Master's degree was authorized to expound the subject named in the degree.

20. The doctrine of papal infallibility was never officially sanctioned in the Middle Ages, but the claim of infallibility was repeatedly made by the champions of the more extreme view of papal power.

20

of it. Hence it comes that so many heretical and unchristian, nay, even unnatural ordinances have a place in the canon law, of which, however, there is no present need to speak. For since they think that the Holy Spirit never leaves them, be they never so unlearned and wicked, they make bold to decree whatever they will. And if it were true, where would be the need or use of the Holy Scriptures? Let us burn them, and be satisfied with the unlearned lords at Rome, who are possessed of the Holy Spirit — although He can possess only pious hearts! Unless I had read it myself, I could not have believed that the devil would make such clumsy pretensions at Rome, and find a following.

But not to fight them with mere words, we will quote the Scriptures. St. Paul says in I Corinthians 14: "If to anyone something better is revealed, though he be sitting and listening to another in God's Word, then the first, who is speaking, shall hold his peace and give place." What would be the use of this commandment, if we were only to believe him who does the talking or who has the highest seat? Christ also says in John 6 that all Christians shall be taught of God. Thus it may well happen that the pope and his followers are wicked men, and no true Christians, not taught of God, not having true understanding. On the other hand, an ordinary man may have true understanding; why then should we not follow him? Has not the pope erred many times? Who would help Christendom when the pope errs, if we were not to believe another, who had the Scriptures on his side, more than the pope?

Therefore it is a wickedly invented fable, and they cannot produce a letter in defense of it, that the interpretation of Scripture or the confirmation of its interpretation belongs to the pope alone. They have themselves usurped this power; and although they allege that this power was given to Peter when the keys were given to him, it is plain enough that the keys were not given to Peter alone, but to the whole community. Moreover, the keys were not ordained for doctrine or government, but only for the binding and loosing of sin, and whatever further power of the keys they arrogate to themselves is mere invention. But Christ's word to Peter, "I have prayed for thee that thy faith fail not," cannot be applied to the pope, since the majority of the popes have been without faith, as they must themselves confess. Besides, it is not only for Peter that Christ prayed, but also for all Apostles and Christians, as he says in John 17: "Father, I pray for those whom thou hast given me, and not for these only, but for all who believe on me through their word." Is not this clear enough?

Only think of it yourself! They must confess that there are pious Christians among us, who have the true faith, Spirit, understanding, word, and mind of Christ. Why, then, should we reject their word and understanding and follow the pope, who has neither faith nor Spirit? That would be to deny the whole faith and the Christian Church. Moreover, it is not the pope alone who is always in the right, if the article of the Creed is correct: "I believe one holy Christian Church"; otherwise the prayer must run: "I believe in the pope at Rome," and so reduce the Christian Church to one man — which would be nothing else than a devilish and hellish error.

Besides, if we are all priests, as was said above, and all have one faith, one Gospel, one sacrament, why should we not also have the power to test and judge what is correct or incorrect in matters of faith? What becomes of the words of Paul in I Corinthians 2: "He that is spiritual judgeth all things, yet he himself is judged of no man," and II Corinthians 4: "We have all the same Spirit of faith"? Why, then, should not we perceive what squares with faith and what does not, as well as does an unbelieving pope?

All these and many other texts should make us bold and free, and we should not allow the Spirit of liberty, as Paul calls Him, to be frightened off by the fabrications of the popes, but we ought to go boldly forward to test all that they do or leave undone, according to our interpretation of the Scriptures, which rests on faith, and compel them to follow not their own interpretation, but the one that is better. In the olden days Abraham had to listen to his Sarah, although she was in more complete subjection to him than we are to anyone on earth. Balaam's ass, also, was wiser than the prophet himself. If God then spoke by an ass against a prophet, why should He not be able even now to speak by a righteous man against the pope? In like manner St. Paul rebukes St. Peter as a man in error. Therefore it behooves every Christian to espouse the cause of the faith, to understand and defend it, and to rebuke all errors.

3rd wall.

The *third wall* falls of itself when the first two are down. For when the pope acts contrary to the Scriptures, it is our duty to stand by the Scriptures, to reprove him, and to constrain him, according to the word of Christ in Matthew 18: "If thy brother sin against thee, go and tell it him between thee and him alone; if he hear thee not, then take with thee one or two more; if he hear them not, tell it to the Church; if he hear not the Church, consider him a heathen." Here every member is commanded to care for every other. How much rather should we do this when the member that does evil is a ruling member, and by his evil-doing is the cause of much harm and offense to the rest! But if I am to accuse him before the Church, I must bring the Church together.

They have no basis in Scripture for their contention that it belongs to the pope alone to call a council or confirm its actions; for this is based merely upon their own laws, which are valid only in so far as they are not injurious to Christendom or contrary to the laws of God. When the pope deserves punishment, such laws go out of force, since it is injurious to Christendom not to punish him by means of a council.

Thus we read in Acts 15 that it was not St. Peter who called the Apostolic Council, but the Apostles and elders. If, then, that right had belonged to St. Peter alone, the council would not have been a Christian council, but a heretical *conciliabulum*.[21] Even the Council of Nicaea — the most famous of all — was neither called nor confirmed by the Bishop of Rome, but by the Emperor Constantine,[22] and many other emperors after him did the like, yet these councils were the most Christian of all.[23] But if the pope alone had the right to call councils, then all these councils must have been heretical. Moreover, if I consider the councils which the pope has created, I find that they have done nothing of special importance.

Therefore, when necessity demands, and the pope is an offense to Christendom, the first man who is able should, as a faithful member of the whole body, do what he can to bring about a truly free council.[24] No one can do this so well as the temporal authorities, especially since now they also are fellow-Christians, fellow-priests, "fellow-spirituals," fellow-lords over all things, and whenever it is needful or profitable, they should give free course to the office and work in which God has put them above every man. Would it not be an unnatural thing, if a fire broke out in a city, and everybody were to stand by and let

---

21. i.e., A mere gathering of people.
22. The Council of Nicaea, the first of the great councils of the Church, assembled in 325 for the settlement of the Orian controversy. Luther's statement that it was called by the Emperor Constantine, and that its decisions did not derive their validity from any papal confirmation, is historically correct.
23. Luther is here referring to the earlier so-called "ecumenical" councils.
24. i.e., A council which will not be subject to the pope.

it burn on and on and consume everything that could burn, for the sole reason that nobody had the authority of the burgomaster, or because, perhaps, the fire broke out in the burgomaster's house? In such case is it not the duty of every citizen to arouse and call the rest? How much more should this be done in the spiritual city of Christ, if a fire of offense breaks out, whether in the papal government, or anywhere else? In the same way, if the enemy attacks a city, he who first rouses the others deserves honor and thanks; why then should he not deserve honor who makes known the presence of the enemy from hell, and awakens the Christians, and calls them together? *Is Luther refering to himself?*

But all their boasts of an authority which dare not be opposed amount to nothing after all. No one in Christendom has authority to do injury, or to forbid the resisting of injury. There is no authority in the Church save for edification. Therefore, if the pope were to use his authority to prevent the calling of a free council, and thus became a hindrance to the edification of the Church, we should have regard neither for him nor for his authority; and if he were to hurl his bans and thunderbolts, we should despise his conduct as that of a madman, and relying on God, hurl back the ban on him, and coerce him as best we could. For this presumptuous authority of his is nothing; he has no such authority, and he is quickly overthrown by a text of Scripture; for Paul says to the Corinthians, "God has given us authority not for the destruction, but for the edification of Christendom." Who is ready to overlap this text? It is only the power of the devil and of Antichrist which resists the things that serve for the edification of Christendom; it is, therefore, in no wise to be obeyed, but is to be opposed with life and goods and all our strength.

Even though a miracle were to be done in the pope's behalf against the temporal powers, or though someone were to be stricken with a plague — which they boast has sometimes happened — it should be considered only the work of the devil, because of the weakness of our faith in God. Christ Himself prophesied in Matthew 24: "There shall come in my name false Christs and false prophets, and do signs and wonders, so as to deceive even the elect," and Paul says in II Thessalonians 2, that Antichrist shall, through the power of Satan, be mighty in lying wonders.

Let us, therefore, hold fast to this: No Christian authority can do anything against Christ; as St. Paul says, "We can do nothing against Christ, but for Christ." Whatever does aught against Christ is the power of Antichrist and of the devil, even though it were to rain and hail wonders and plagues. Wonders and plagues prove nothing, especially in these last evil times, for which all the Scriptures prophesy false wonders. Therefore we must cling with firm faith to the words of God, and then the devil will cease from wonders.

Thus I hope that the false, lying terror with which the Romans have this long time made our conscience timid and stupid, has been allayed. They, like all of us, are subject to the temporal sword; they have no power to interpret the Scriptures by mere authority, without learning; they have no authority to prevent a council or, in sheer wantonness, to pledge it, bind it, or take away its liberty; but if they do this, they are in truth the communion of Antichrist and of the devil, and have nothing at all of Christ except the name.

II. ABUSES TO BE DISCUSSED IN COUNCILS

We shall now look at the matters which should be discussed in the councils, and with which popes, cardinals, bishops and all the scholars ought properly to be occupied day and night if they loved Christ and His Church. But if they neglect this duty, then let the laity and the temporal authorities see to it, regardless of bans and thunders; for an unjust ban is better than ten just releases, and an unjust release worse than ten just bans. Let us, therefore, awake, dear Germans, and fear God rather than men, that we may not share the fate of all the poor souls who are so lamentably lost through the shameful and devilish rule of the Romans, in which the devil daily takes a larger and larger place — if, indeed, it were possible that such a hellish rule could grow worse, a thing I can neither conceive nor believe.

1. It is a horrible and frightful thing that the ruler of Christendom, who boasts himself vicar of Christ and successor of St. Peter, lives in such worldly splendor that in this regard no king nor emperor can equal or approach him, and that he who claims the title of "most holy" and "most spiritual" is more worldly than the world itself. He wears a triple crown, when the greatest kings wear but a single crown;[25] if that is like the poverty of Christ and of St. Peter, then it is a new kind of likeness. When a word is said against it, they cry out "Heresy!" but that is because they do not wish to hear how unchristian and ungodly such a practice is. I think, however, that if the pope were with tears to pray to God, he would have to lay aside these crowns, for our God can suffer no pride; and his office is nothing else than this: daily to weep and pray for Christendom, and to set an example of all humility.

However that may be, this splendor of his is an offense, and the pope is bound on his soul's salvation to lay it aside, because St. Paul says, "Abstain from all outward shows, which give offense," and in Romans 12, "We should provide good, not only in the sight of God, but also in the sight of all men." An ordinary bishop's crown would be enough for the pope; he should be greater than others in wisdom

---

25. The papal crown dates from the eleventh century; the triple crown, or tiara, from the beginning of the fourteenth. It was intended to signify that very superiority of the pope to the rulers of this world, of which Luther here complains

and holiness, and leave the crown of pride to Antichrist, as did his predecessors several centuries ago. They say he is a lord of the world; that is a lie; for Christ, whose vicar and officer he boasts himself to be, said before Pilate, "My kingdom is not of this world"; and no vicar's rule can go beyond his lord's. Moreover he is not the vicar of the glorified, but of the crucified Christ, as Paul says, "I was willing to know nothing among you save Christ, and him only as the Crucified"; and in Philippians 2, "So think of yourselves as ye see in Christ, who emptied himself and took upon him the appearance of a servant"; and again in I Corinthians 1, "We preach Christ, the Crucified." Now they make the pope a vicar of the glorified Christ in heaven, and some of them have allowed the devil to rule them so completely that they have maintained that the pope is above the angels in heaven, and has authority over them. These are indeed the very works of the very Antichrist.

2. What is the use in Christendom of those people who are called the cardinals? I shall tell you. Italy and Germany have many rich monasteries, foundations, benefices, and livings. No better way has been discovered to bring all these to Rome than by creating cardinals and giving them the bishoprics, monasteries, and prelacies, and so overthrowing the worship of God. For this reason we now see Italy a very wilderness — monasteries in ruins, bishoprics devoured, the prelacies and the revenues of all the churches drawn to Rome, cities decayed, land and people laid waste, because there is no more worship or preaching. Why? The cardinals must have the income. No Turk could have so devastated Italy and suppressed the worship of God.

Now that Italy is sucked dry, they come into Germany, and begin oh, so gently. But let us beware, or Germany will soon become like Italy. Already we have some cardinals; what the Romans seek by that the "drunken Germans" are not to understand until we have not a bishopric.

a monastery, a living, a benefice, a mite or a penny left. Antichrist must take the treasures of the earth, as it was prophesied. So it goes on. They skim the cream off the bishoprics, monasteries, and benefices, and because they do not yet venture to turn them all to shameful use, as they have done in Italy, they only practice for the present the sacred trickery of coupling together ten or twenty prelacies and taking a yearly portion from each of them, so as to make a tidy sum after all. The priory of Würzburg yields a thousand gulden; that of Bamberg, something; Mainz, Trier, and the others, something more; and so from one to ten thousand gulden might be got together, in order that a cardinal might live at Rome like a rich king.

"After they are used to this, we will create thirty or forty cardinals in a day,[26] and give to one Mount St. Michael at Bamberg[27] and the bishopric of Würzburg to boot, hang on to these a few rich livings, until churches and cities are waste, and after that we will say, 'We are Christ's vicars and shepherds of Christ's sheep; the mad, drunken Germans must put up with it.'"

I advise, however, that the number of the cardinals be reduced, or that the pope be made to keep them at his own expense. Twelve of them would be more than enough, and each of them might have an income of a thousand gulden a year. How comes it that we Germans must put up with such robbery and such extortion of our property at the hands of the pope? If the Kingdom of France has prevented it,[28] why do we Germans let them make such fools and apes

26. The creation of new cardinals was a lucrative proceeding for the popes. On July 31, 1517, Leo X created thirty-one cardinals, and is said to have received from the new appointees about 300,000 ducats. Needless to say, the cardinals expected to make up the fees out of the income of their livings.

27. The famous Benedictine monastery just outside the city of Bamberg.

28. As early as the fourteenth century both England and France had enacted laws prohibiting the very practices of which Luther here complains. It should be noted, however, that these laws were enforced only occasionally, and never very strictly.

of us? It would all be more bearable if in this way they only stole our property; but they lay waste the churches and rob Christ's sheep of their pious shepherds, and destroy the worship and the Word of God. Even if there were not a single cardinal, the Church would not go under. As it is they do nothing for the good of Christendom; they only wrangle about the incomes of bishoprics and prelacies, and that any robber could do.

3. If ninety-nine parts of the papal court[29] were done away and only the hundredth part allowed to remain, it would still be large enough to give decisions in matters of faith. Now, however, there is such a swarm of vermin yonder in Rome, all boasting that they are "papal," that there was nothing like it in Babylon. There are more than three thousand papal secretaries alone; who will count the other offices, when they are so many that they scarcely can be counted? And they all lie in wait for the prebends and benefices of Germany as wolves lie in wait for the sheep. I believe that Germany now gives much more to the pope at Rome than it gave in former times to the emperors. Indeed, some estimate that every year more than three hundred thousand gulden find their way from Germany to Rome, quite uselessly and fruitlessly; we get nothing for it but scorn and contempt. And yet we wonder that princes, nobles, cities, endowments, land, and people are impoverished! We should rather wonder that we still have anything to eat!

Since we here come to the heart of the matter, we will pause a little, and let it be seen that the Germans are not

---

29. The papal court or curia consisted of all the officials of various sorts who were employed in the transaction of papal business, including those who were in immediate attendance upon the person of the pope, the so-called "papal family." In the sixteenth century reference is made to 949 offices, exclusive of those which had to do with the administration of the city of Rome and of the States of the Church, and not including the members of the pope's "family."

quite such gross tools as not to note or understand the sharp practices of the Romans. I do not now complain that at Rome God's command and Christian law are despised; for such is the state of Christendom, and particularly of Rome, that we may not now complain of such high matters. Nor do I complain that natural or temporal law and reason count for nothing. The case is worse even than that. I complain that they do not keep their own self-devised canon law, though it is, to be sure, mere tyranny, avarice, and temporal splendor, rather than law. Let us see!

In former times German emperors and princes permitted the pope to receive the annates from all the benefices of the German nation, i.e., the half of the first year's revenues from each benefice.[30] This permission was given, however, in order that by means of these large sums of money, the pope to receive the annates from all the benefices of the Turks and infidels in defense of Christendom, so that the burden of the war might not rest too heavily upon the nobility, but that the clergy also should contribute something toward it. This single-hearted devotion of the German nation the popes have so used that they have received this money for more than a hundred years, have now made of it a binding tax and tribute, and have not only accumulated no treasure, but have used the money to endow many orders and offices at Rome, and to provide these offices with salaries, as though the annates were a fixed rent.

When they pretend that they are about to fight against the Turks, they send out emissaries to gather money. Ofttimes they issue an indulgence on this same pretext of fighting the Turks, for they think the mad Germans are forever to remain utter and arrant fools, give them money

---

30. Early in their history, which dates from the beginning of the sixteenth century, the annates had become a fixed tax on all Church offices which fell vacant, and the complaint of extortion in their appraisement and collection was frequently raised.

without end, and satisfy their unspeakable greed; though we clearly see that not a mite of the annates or of the indulgence money or of all the rest is used against the Turks, but all of it goes into the bottomless bag. They lie and deceive, make laws and make agreements with us, and they do not intend to keep any of them. All this must be counted the work of Christ and St. Peter!

Now, in this matter the German nation, bishop, and princes should consider that they too are Christians, and should protect the people, whom they are set to rule and guard in things temporal and spiritual, against these ravening wolves who, in sheep's clothing, pretend to be shepherds and rulers; and, since the annates are so shamefully abused and the stipulated conditions are not fulfilled, they should not permit their land and people to be so sadly robbed and ruined, against all justice; but by a law of the emperor or of the whole nation, they should either keep the annates at home or else abolish them again. For since the Romans do not keep the terms of the agreement, they have no right to the annates. Therefore the bishops and princes are bound to punish or prevent such thievery and robbery, as the law requires.

In this they should aid the pope and support him, for he is perchance too weak to prevent such an abuse all by himself; or if he were to undertake to defend and maintain this practice, they ought resist him and fight against him as against a wolf and a tyrant, for he has no authority to do or to defend evil. Moreover, if it were ever desired to accumulate such a treasure against the Turks, we ought in the future to have sense enough to see that the German nation would be a better custodian for it than the pope; for the German nation has people enough for the fighting, if only the money is forthcoming. It is with the annates as it has been with many another Roman pretense.

Again, the year has been so divided between the pope

and the ruling bishops and canons,[31] that the pope has six months in the year—every other month—in which to bestow the benefices which fall vacant in his months.[32] In this way almost all the benefices are absorbed by Rome, especially the very best livings and dignities, and when once they fall into the hands of Rome, they never come out of them again, though a vacancy may never again occur in the pope's month. Thus the canons are cheated. This is a genuine robbery, which intends to let nothing escape. Therefore it is high time that the "papal months" be altogether abolished, and that everything which they have brought to Rome be taken back again. For the princes and nobles should take measures that the stolen goods be returned, the thieves punished, and those who have abused privilege be deprived of privilege. If it is binding and valid when the pope on the day after his election makes, in his chancery, rules and laws whereby our foundations and livings are robbed—a thing which he has no right to do—then it should be still more valid if the Emperor Charles on the day after his coronation were to make rules and laws that not another benefice or living in all Germany shall be allowed to come into the hands of Rome by means of the "papal months," and that the livings which have already fallen into its hands shall be released, and redeemed from the Roman robbers; for he has this right by virtue of his office and his sword.

But now the Roman See of Avarice and Robbery has not been able to await the time when all the benefices, one

---

31. The canons are the clergy attached to a cathedral church who constituted the "chapter" of that cathedral, and to whom the right to elect the bishop normally belonged.

32. This whole section deals with the abuse of the "right of reservation," i.e., the alleged right of the pope to appoint directly to vacant church positions. According to papal theory the right of appointment belonged absolutely to the pope, who graciously yielded the right to others under certain circumstances, reserving it to himself in other cases. The practice of reserving the appointments seems to date from the twelfth century, and was originally an arbitrary exercise of papal authority.

33

after another, would, by the "papal months," come into its power, but hastens, with insatiable appetite, to get possession of them all as speedily as possible; and so besides the annates and the "months" it has hit upon a device by which benefices and livings fall to Rome in three ways:

First, If anyone who holds a free[33] living dies at Rome or on the way to Rome, his living must forever belong to the Roman—I should rather say the robbing—See,[34] and yet they will not be called robbers, though they are guilty of such robbery as no one has ever heard or read about.

Second, In case anyone who belongs to the household of the pope or of the cardinals holds or takes over a benefice, or in case one who already holds a benefice afterward enters the "household" of the pope or of a cardinal. But who can count the "household" of the pope and of the cardinals, when the pope, if he only goes on a pleasure-ride, takes with him three or four thousand mule-riders, eclipsing all emperors and kings? Christ and St. Peter went on foot in order that their vicars might have the more pomp and splendor. Now avarice has cleverly thought out another scheme, and brings it to pass that even here many have the name of "papal servant," just as though they were in Rome; all in order that in every place the mere rascally little word "papal servant" may bring all benefices to Rome and tie them fast there forever. Are not these vexatious and devilish inventions? Let us beware! Soon Mainz, Magdeburg and Halberstadt will gently pass into the hands of Rome, and the cardinalate will be paid for dearly enough. "Afterwards we will make all the German bishops cardinals so that there will be nothing left outside."

Third, When a contest has started at Rome over a benefice. This I hold to be almost the commonest and widest

---

33. i.e., A living which has not hitherto been filled by papal appointment.
34. This rule, like that of the "papal months," is found in the Concordat of Vienna.

[handwritten annotation across top and right margin: "pope has far too much control over individual benefices and dioceses."]

road for bringing livings to Rome. For when there is no contest at home, unnumbered knaves will be found at Rome to dig up contests out of the earth and assail livings at their will. Thus many a good priest has to lose his living, or settle the contest for a time by the payment of a sum of money. Such a living rightly or wrongly contested must also belong forever to the Roman See. It would be no wonder if God were to rain from heaven fire and brimstone and to sink Rome in the abyss, as He did Sodom and Gomorrah of old. Why should there be a pope in Christendom, if his power is used for nothing else than such archknavery, and if he protects and practices it? O noble princes and lords, how long will you leave your lands and people naked to these ravening wolves!

Since even these practices were not enough, and Avarice grew impatient at the long time it took to get hold of all the bishoprics, therefore my Lord Avarice devised the fiction that the bishoprics should be nominally abroad, but that their land and soil should be at Rome, and no bishop can be confirmed unless with a great sum of money he buy the *pallium*,[35] and bind himself with terrible oaths to be the pope's servant.[36] This is the reason that no bishop ventures to act against the pope. That, too, is what the Romans

---

35. The *pallium* is a woolen shoulder-cape which is the emblem of the archbishop's office, and which must be secured from Rome. The bestowal of the *pallium* by the pope is a very ancient custom. The canon law prescribes that the archbishop-elect must secure the *pallium* from Rome within three months of his election; otherwise he is forbidden to discharge any of the duties of his office. It is regarded as the necessary complement of his election and consecration, conferring the "plenitude of the pontifical office," and the name of archbishop. Luther's charge that it had to be purchased "with a great sum of money" is substantiated by similar complaints from the twelfth century on, though the language of the canon law makes it evident that Luther's other contention is also correct, viz., that the *pallium* was originally bestowed gratis. The sum required from the different archbishops varied with the wealth of their sees, and was a fixed sum in each case.

36. The oath of allegiance to the pope was required before the pallium could be bestowed. The canon law describes this oath as one "of allegiance, obedience and unity."

were seeking when they imposed the oath, and thus the very richest bishoprics have fallen into debt and ruin. Mainz pays, as I hear, 20,000 gulden. These be your Romans! To be sure they decreed of old in the canon law that the *pallium* should be bestowed gratis, the number of papal servants diminished, the contests lessened, the chapters and bishops allowed their liberty. But this did not bring in money, and so they turned over a new leaf, and all authority was taken from the bishops and chapters; they are made ciphers, and have no office nor authority nor work, but everything is ruled by the archknaves at Rome; soon they will have in hand even the office of sexton and bell-ringer in all the churches. All contests are brought to Rome, and by authority of the pope everyone does as he likes.

What happened this very year? The Bishop of Strassburg wished to govern his chapter properly and to institute reforms in worship, and with this end in view made certain godly and Christian regulations. But my dear Lord Pope and the Holy Roman See, at the instigation of the priests, overthrew and altogether condemned this holy and spiritual ordinance. This is called "feeding the sheep of Christ"! Thus priests are to be encouraged against their own bishop, and their disobedience to divine law is to be protected! Antichrist himself, I hope, will not dare to put God to such open shame! There you have your pope after your own heart! Why did he do this? Ah! if one church were reformed, it would be a dangerous departure; Rome's turn too might come! Therefore it were better that no priest should be left at peace with another, that kings and princes should be set at odds, as has been the custom heretofore, and the world filled with the blood of Christians, only so the concord of Christians should not trouble the Holy Roman See with a reformation.

So far we have been getting an idea of how they deal

with livings which become vacant. But for tender-hearted Avarice the vacancies are too few, and so he brings his foresight to bear upon the benefices which are still occupied by their incumbents, so that they must be unfilled, even though they are not unfilled.[37] And this he does in many ways, as follows:

First, He lies in wait for fat prebends or bishoprics which are held by an old or a sick man, or by one with an alleged disability. To such an incumbent, without his desire or consent, the Holy See gives a *coadjutor,* i.e., an "assistant," for the coadjutor's benefit, because he is a "papal servant," or has paid for the position, or has earned it by some other ignoble service to Rome. In this case the rights of the chapter or the rights of him who has the bestowal of the living[38] must be surrendered, and the whole thing fall into the hands of Rome.

Second, There is a little word *commend,*[39] by which the pope entrusts the keeping of a rich, fat monastery or church to a cardinal or to another of his people, just as though I were to give you a hundred gulden to keep. This is not called the giving or bestowing of the monastery nor even its destruction, or the abolition of the worship of God, but only "giving it into keeping"; not that he to whom it is entrusted is to care for it, or build it up, but he is to drive out the incumbent, to receive the goods and revenues, and to install some apostate, renegade monk,[40] who accepts

---

37. i.e., The benefices are treated as though they were vacant.
38. In the case of certain endowed benefices the right to nominate the incumbent was vested in individuals, usually of the nobility, and was hereditary in their family.
39. *Commendation* was one of the practices by which the pope evaded the provision of the canon law which prescribed that the same man should not hold two livings with the cure of souls. The man who received an office *in commendum* was not required to fulfill the duties attached to the position and when a living or an abbacy was granted in this way during the incumbency of another, the recipient received its entire income during a subsequent vacancy. The practice was most common in the case of abbacies.
40. A monk who deserted his monastery was known as an "apostate."

five or six gulden a year and sits in the church all day selling pictures and images to the pilgrims, so that henceforth neither prayers nor masses are said there. If this were to be called destroying monasteries and abolishing the worship of God, then the pope would have to be called a destroyer of Christendom and an abolisher of God's worship, because this is his constant practice. That would be a hard saying at Rome, and so we must call it a *commend* or a "command to take charge" of the monastery. The pope can every year make *commends* out of four or more of these monasteries, a single one of which may have an income of more than six thousand gulden. This is the way the Romans increase the worship of God and preserve the monasteries. The Germans also are beginning to find it out.

Third, There are some benefices which they call *incompatibilia,* and which, according to the ordinances of the canon law, cannot be held by one man at the same time, as for instance, two parishes, two bishoprics and the like. In these cases the Holy Roman See of Avarice evades the canon law by making "glosses,"[41] called *unio* and *incorporatio,* i.e., by "incorporating" many *incompatibilia,* so that each becomes a part of every other and all of them together are looked upon as though they were one living. They are then no longer "incompatible," and the holy canon law is satisfied, in that it is no longer binding, except upon those who do not buy these "glosses"[42] from the pope or his

---

41. A gloss is a note explanatory of a word or passage of doubtful meaning. The glosses are the earliest form of commentary on the Bible. The glosses of the canon law are the more or less authoritative comments of the teachers, and date from the time when the study of the canon law became a part of the theological curriculum. Their aim is chiefly to show how the law applies to practical cases which may arise. The so-called *glossa ordinaria* had in Luther's time an authority almost equal to that of the *corpus juris* itself.

42. The thing which was bought was, of course, the dispensation, permission to avail oneself of the gloss.

datarius.[43] The *unio,* i.e., "uniting," is of the same nature. The pope binds many such benefices together like a bundle of sticks, and by virtue of this bond they are all regarded as one benefice. So there is at Rome one courtesan who holds, for himself alone, 22 parishes, 7 priories and 44 canonries besides—all by the help of that masterly "gloss," which holds that this is not illegal. What cardinals and other prelates have, everyone may imagine for himself. In this way the Germans are to have their purses eased and their itch cured.

Another of the "glosses" is the *administratio,* i.e., a man may have, besides his bishopric, an abbacy or a dignity, and possess all the property which goes with it, only he has no other title than that of "administrator." For at Rome it is sufficient that words are changed and not the things they stand for; as though I were to teach that a bawdy-house keeper should have the name of "burgomaster's wife," and yet continue to ply her trade. This kind of Roman rule St. Peter foretold when he said, in II Peter 2: "There shall come false teachers, who in covetousness with feigned words, shall make merchandise of you, to get their gains."

Again, dear Roman Avarice has invented the custom of selling and bestowing livings to such advantage that the seller or disposer retains reversionary rights upon them: to wit, if the incumbent dies, the benefice freely reverts to him who previously sold, bestowed or surrendered it. In this way they have made livings hereditary property, so that henceforth no one can come into possession of them, except the man to whom the seller is willing to dispose of them, or to whom he bequeaths his rights at death. Besides, there are many who transfer to others the mere title to a benefice from which those who get the title derive not a

---

43. *Dataria* is the name for that department of the curia which had to deal with the granting of dispensations and the disposal of benefices. *Datarius* is the title of the official who presided over this department.

mite of income. It is now an old custom, too, to give another man a benefice and to reserve a certain part out of the annual revenue.[44] In olden times this was simony.[45] Of these things there are so many more that they cannot all be counted. They treat livings more shamefully than the heathen beneath the cross treated the garments of Christ.

Yet all that has hitherto been said is ancient history and an everyday occurrence at Rome. Avarice has devised one thing more, which may, I hope, be his last morsel, and choke him. The pope has a noble little device called *reservation pectoralis*, i.e., his "mental reservation," and *proprius motus*, i.e., the "arbitrary will of his authority." It goes like this. When one man has gotten a benefice at Rome, and the appointment has been regularly signed and sealed, according to custom, and there comes another, who brings money, or has laid the pope under obligation in some other way, of which we will not speak, and desires of the pope the same benefice, then the pope takes it from the first man and gives it to the second. If it is said that this is unjust, then the Most Holy Father must make some excuse, that he may not be reproved for doing such open violence to the law, and says that in his mind and heart he had reserved that benefice to himself and his own plenary dis-

---

44. The complaint was made at Worms (1521) that it was impossible for a German to secure a clear title to a benefice at Rome unless he applied for it in the name of an Italian, to whom he was obliged to pay a percentage of the income, a yearly pension, or a fixed sum of money for the use of his name.

45. *Simony*—the sin of Simon Magus (Acts 8:18-20)—the sin committed by the sale or the purchase of an office or position which is formally conferred by a ritual act of the Church. In the ancient and earlier medieval Church the use of money to secure preferment was held to invalidate the title of the guilty party to the position thus secured, and the acceptance of money for such a purpose was an offense punishable by deposition and degradation. The "heresy of Simon" was conceived to be the greatest of all heresies. The traffic in Church offices, which became a flagrant abuse from the time of John XXII (1316-34), would have been regarded in earlier days as the most atrocious simony.

posal, although he had never before in his whole life either thought or heard of it. Thus he has now found a little "gloss" by which he can, in his own person, lie and deceive, and make a fool and an ape of anybody—all this he does brazenly and openly, and yet he wishes to be the head of Christendom, though with his open lies he lets the Evil Spirit rule him.

This arbitrary will and lying "reservation" of the pope creates in Rome a state of affairs which is unspeakable. There is buying, selling, bartering, trading, trafficking, lying, deceiving, robbing, stealing, luxury, harlotry, knavery, and every sort of contempt of God, and even the rule of Antichrist could not be more scandalous. Venice, Antwerp, Cairo[46] are nothing compared to this fair which is held at Rome and the business which is done there, except that in those other places they still observe right and reason. At Rome everything goes as the devil wills, and out of this ocean a like virtue flows into all the world. Is it a wonder that such people fear a reformation and a free council, and prefer to set all kings and princes at enmity rather than have them unite and bring about a council? Who could bear to have such knavery exposed if it were his own?

Finally, for all this noble commerce the pope has built a warehouse, namely, the house of the *datarius*, in Rome. Thither all must come who deal after this fashion in benefices and livings. From him they must buy their "glosses" and get the power to practice such archknavery. In former times Rome was generous, and then justice had either to be bought or else suppressed with money, but now she has become exorbitant, and no one dare be a knave unless with a great sum he has first bought the right. If that is not a brothel above all the brothels one can imagine, then I do not know what brothel means.

---

46. The three chief centers of foreign commerce in the fifteenth and the early sixteenth centuries.

If you have money in this house, then you can come by all the things I have said; and not only these, but all sorts of usury[47] are here made honest, for a consideration, and the possession of all property acquired by theft or robbery is legalized. Here vows are dissolved; here monks are granted liberty to leave their orders; here marriage is on sale to the clergy; here bastards can become legitimate; here all dishonor and shame can come to honor; all ill-repute and stigma of evil are here knighted and ennobled; here is permitted the marriage which is within the forbidden degrees or has some other defect.[48] Oh! what a taxing and a robbing rules there! It looks as though all the laws of the Church were made for one purpose only—to be nothing but so many money-snares, from which a man must extricate himself,[49] if he would be a Christian. Yea, here the devil becomes a saint, and a god to boot. What heaven and earth cannot, that this house can do! They call them *compositiones!*[50] "Compositions" indeed! rather "confusions"! Oh, what a modest tax is the Rhine-toll,[51] compared with the tribute taken by this holy house!

Let no one accuse me of exaggeration! It is all so open that even at Rome they must confess the evil to be greater and more terrible than anyone can say. I have not yet stirred up the hell-broth of personal vices, nor do I intend to do so. I speak of things which are common talk, and yet I have not words to tell them all. The bishops, the priests and, above all, the doctors in the universities, who draw their salaries for this purpose, should have done their duty and with common consent have written and cried out

---

47. The Church law forbade the taking of interest on loans of money.
48. During the Middle Ages all questions touching marriage and divorce, including, therefore, the question of the legitimacy of children, were governed by the laws of the Church, on the theory that marriage was a sacrament.
49. i.e., By buying dispensations.
50. The sums paid for special dispensations were so called.
51. The toll which the "robber-barons" of the Rhine levied upon merchants passing through their domains.

against these things, but they have done the very opposite.

There remains one last word, and I must say that too. Since boundless Avarice has not been satisfied with all these treasures, which three great kings might well think sufficient, he now begins to transfer this trade and sell it to Fugger of Augsburg[52] so that the lending and trading and buying of bishoprics and benefices, and the driving of bargains in spiritual goods, have now come to the right place, and spiritual and temporal goods have become one business. And now I would fain hear of a mind so lofty that it could imagine what this Roman Avarice might yet be able to do and has not already done; unless Fugger were to transfer or sell this combination of two lines of business to somebody else. I believe we have reached the limit.

As for what they have stolen in all lands and still steal and extort, by means of indulgences, bulls, letters of confession,[53] "butter-letters,"[54] and other *confessionalia*,[55]—all this I consider mere patchwork, and like casting a single devil more into hell. Not that they bring in little, for a mighty king could well support himself on their returns, but they are not to be compared with the streams of treasure above mentioned. I shall also say nothing at present of how this indulgence money has been applied. Another time

---

52. The Fuggers of Augsburg were the greatest of the German capitalists in the sixteenth century. They were international bankers, "the Rothschilds of the sixteenth century." Their control of large capital enabled them to advance large sums of money to the territorial rulers, who were in a chronic state of need. In return for these favors they received monopolistic concessions by which their capital was further increased. The spiritual, as well as the temporal lords, availed themselves regularly of the services of this accommodating firm. They were the pope's financial representatives in Germany.

53. Certificates entitling the holder to choose his own confessor and authorizing the confessor to absolve him from certain classes of "reserved" sins; referred to in the Ninety-five Theses as *confessionalia*.

54. Certificates granting their possessor permission to eat milk, eggs, butter and cheese on fast days.

55. The word is used here in the broad sense, and means dispensations of all sorts, including those just mentioned, relating to penance.

I shall inquire about that, for Campofiore[56] and Belvidere[57] and certain other places probably know something about it.

Since, then, such devilish rule is not only open robbery and deceit, and the tyranny of the gates of hell, but also ruins Christendom in body and soul, it is our duty to use all diligence in protecting Christendom against such misery and destruction. If we would fight the Turks, let us make a beginning here, where they are at their worst. If we justly hang thieves and behead robbers, why should we let Roman Avarice go free? For he is the greatest thief and robber that has come or can come into the world, and all in the holy Name of Christ and of St. Peter! Who can longer endure it or keep silence? Almost everything he owns has been gotten by theft and robbery; that is the truth, and all history shows it. The pope never got by purchase such great properties that from his *officia*[58] alone he can raise about a million ducats, not to mention the mines of treasure named above and the income of his lands. Nor did it come to him by inheritance from Christ or from St. Peter; no one ever loaned it or gave it to him; it has not become his by virtue of immemorial use and enjoyment. Tell me, then, whence he can have it? Learn from this what they have in mind when they send out legates to collect money for use against the Turks.

Sarcasm or
seriousness?

III. PROPOSALS FOR REFORM

Now, although I am too small a man to make propositions which might effect a reform in this dreadful state of things, nevertheless I may as well sing my fool's song to

56. The Campo di Fiore, a Roman market-place, restored and adorned at great expense by Eugenius IV (1431-47), and his successors.

57. A part of the Vatican palace notorious as the banqueting-hall of Alexander VI (1492-1503), turned by Julius II (1503-13) into a museum for the housing of his wonderful and expensive collection of ancient works of art. Luther is hinting that the indulgence money has been spent on these objects rather than on the maintenance of the Church.

58. i.e., The offices and positions in Rome which were for sale.

the end, and say, so far as I am able, what could and should be done by the temporal authorities or by a general council.

1. Every prince, nobleman, and city should boldly forbid their subjects to pay the annates to Rome and should abolish them entirely; for the pope has broken the compact, and made the annates a robbery, to the injury and shame of the whole German nation. He gives them to his friends, sells them for large amounts of money, and uses them to endow offices. He has thus lost his right to them, and deserves punishment. It is therefore the duty of the temporal authorities to protect the innocent and prevent injustice, as Paul teaches in Romans 13, and St. Peter in I Peter 2, and even the canon law in Case 16, Question 7, de *filiis*.[59] Thus it has come about that men are saying to the pope and his followers, *Tu ora*, "Thou shalt pray"; to the emperor and his followers, *Tu protege*, "Thou shalt guard"; to the common man, *Tu labora*, "Thou shalt work." Not, however, as though everyone were not to pray, guard, and work; for the man who is diligent in his calling is praying, guarding, and working in all that he does, but everyone should have his own special task.

2. Since the pope with his Roman practices—his commends, adjutories; reservations, *gratiae expectativae*,[60] papal months, incorporations, unions, *pallia*, rules in chancery,[61] and such like knavery—usurps all the German foundations without authority and right, and gives and sells them to foreigners at Rome, who do nothing in German

---

59. The passage is chapter 31, *Filiis vel nepotibus*. It provides that in case the income of endowments bequeathed to the Church is misused, and appeals to the bishop and archbishop fail to correct the misuse, the heirs of the testator may appeal to the royal courts. Luther wishes this principle applied to the annates.

60. i.e., Promises to bestow on certain persons livings not yet vacant.

61. Rules for the transaction of papal business, including such matters as appointments and the like. At Worms (1521) the Estates compain that these rules are made to the advantage of the "courtesans" and the disadvantage of the Germans.

lands to earn them; and since he thereby robs the ordinaries[62] of their rights, makes the bishops mere ciphers and figureheads, and acts against his own canon law, against nature and against reason, until it has finally gone so far that out of sheer avarice the livings and benefices are sold to gross, ignorant asses and knaves at Rome, while pious and learned folk have no profit of their wisdom and merit, so that the poor people of the German nation have to go without good and learned prelates and thus go to ruin:

Therefore, the Christian nobility should set itself against the pope as against a common enemy and destroyer of Christendom, and should do this for the salvation of the poor souls who must go to ruin through his tyranny. They should ordain, order, and decree, that henceforth no benefice shall be drawn into the hands of Rome, and that hereafter no appointment shall be obtained there in any manner whatsoever, but that the benefices shall be brought out and kept out from under this tyrannical authority; and they should restore to the ordinaries the right and office of ordering these benefices in the German nation as best they may. And if a "courtesan" were to come from Rome, he should receive a strict command either to keep his distance, or else to jump into the Rhine or the nearest river, and take the Roman ban, with its seals and letters, to a cold bath. They would then take note at Rome that the Germans are not always mad and drunken, but that they have really become Christians, and intend to permit no longer the mockery and scorn of the holy name of Christ, under which all this knavery and destruction of souls goes on, but have more regard to God and His glory than to the authority of men.

3. An imperial law should be issued, that no bishop's cloak[63] and no confirmation of any dignity whatsoever shall henceforth be secured from Rome, but that the ordinance

---

62. The local Church authorities, here equivalent to "the bishops."
63. The sign of the episcopal office; as regards archbishops, the *pallium*.

of the most holy and most famous Council of Nicaea[64] shall be restored, in which it is decreed that a bishop shall be confirmed by the two nearest bishops or by the archbishop. If the pope will break the statutes of this and of all other councils, what is the use of holding councils? or who has given him the authority thus to despise and break the rules of councils?

If he has this power then we should depose all bishops, archbishops, and primates[65] and make them mere parish priests, so that the pope alone may be over them, as he now is. He leaves to bishops, archbishops, and primates no regular authority or office, usurps everything for himself, and lets them keep only the name and empty title. It has gone so far that by his "exemptions"[66] the monasteries, the abbots, and the prelates are withdrawn from the regular authority of the bishops, so that there is no longer any order in Christendom. From this must follow what has followed — relaxation of discipline and license to do evil everywhere — so that I verily fear the pope can be called the "man of sin." [67] There is in Christendom no discipline, no rule, no order; and who is to blame except the pope? This usurped authority of his he applies strictly to all the prelates, and takes away their rods; and he is generous to all subjects, giving them or selling them their liberty.

Nevertheless, for fear he may complain that he is robbed of his authority, it should be decreed that when the primates

---

64. The first of the ecumenical councils (A.D. 325). The decree to which Luther here refers is Canon IV of that Council.

65. The primate is the ranking archbishop of a country.

66. "Exemption" was the practice by which monastic houses were withdrawn from the jurisdiction of the bishops and made directly subject to the pope. The practice seems to have originated in the tenth century with the famous monastery of Cluny (918), but it was almost universal in the case of the houses of the mendicant orders. The bishops made it a constant subject of complaint, and the Lateran Council (December 19, 1516) passed a decree abolishing all monastic exemptions, though the decree does not seem to have been effective.

67. i.e., Antichrist.

or archbishops are unable to settle a case, or when a controversy arises among themselves, such a case must be laid before the pope, but not every little matter.[68] Thus it was
done in olden times, and thus the famous Council of Nicaea
decreed. If a case can be settled without the pope, then
His Holiness should not be troubled with such minor matters, but give himself to that prayer, meditation, and care
for all Christendom, of which he boasts. This is what the
Apostles did. They said, "It is not meet that we should
leave the Word of God and serve tables, but we will keep
to preaching and prayer and set others over the work."
But now Rome stands for nothing else than the despising of
the Gospel and of prayer, and for the serving of "tables,"
i.e., of temporal affairs, and the rule of the Apostles and of
the pope agree as Christ agrees with Lucifer, heaven with
hell, night with day; yet he is called "Vicar of Christ and
Successor of the Apostles."

4. It should be decreed that no temporal matter shall
be taken to Rome,[69] but that all such cases shall be left to
the temporal authorities, as the Roman themselves decree
in that canon law of theirs, which they do not keep. For it
should be the duty of the pope, as the man most learned in
the Scriptures and most Holy, not in name only, but in
truth, to administer affairs which concern the faith and
holy life of Christians, to hold the primates and archbishops
to these things, and to help them in dealing with and caring
for these matters. So St. Paul teaches in I Corinthians 6,
and takes the Corinthians severely to task for their concern
with worldly things. For it works intolerable injury to all
lands that such cases are tried at Rome. It increases the

---

68. The papal interference in the conduct of the local Church courts was as
flagrant as in the appointments, of which Luther has heretofore spoken. At
Worms (1521) it was complained that cases were cited to Rome as a court
of first instance, and the demand was made that a regular course of
appeals should be re-established.

69. i.e., Appealed to Rome for decision.

48

costs, and moreover the judges do not know the manners, laws and customs of the various countries, so that they often do violence to the facts and base their decisions on their own laws and opinions, and thus injustice is inevitably done the contestants.

Moreover, the outrageous extortion practised by the *officiales*[70] must be forbidden in all the dioceses, so that they may attend to nothing else than matters of faith and good morals, and leave to the temporal judges the things that concern money, property, life and honor. The temporal authorities, therefore, should not permit sentences of ban or exile when faith or right life is not concerned. Spiritual authorities should have rule over spiritual goods, as reason teaches; but spiritual goods are not money, nor anything pertaining to the body, but they are faith and good works.

Nevertheless it might be granted that cases which concern benefices or livings should be tried before bishops, archbishops and primates. Therefore, in order to decide contests and contentions, it might be possible for the Primate of Germany to maintain a general consistory, with auditors and chancellors, which should have control over the *signaturae gratiae* and *signaturae justitiae*[71] that are now controlled at Rome, and which should be the final court of appeal for German cases. The officers of this consistory must not, however, be paid, as at Rome, by chance presents and gifts, and thereby acquire the habit of selling justice and injustice, which they now have to do at Rome because the pope gives them no remuneration, but allows them to fatten themselves on presents. For at Rome no

---

70. The judges in the bishops' courts. The complaint is that they interfere with the administration of justice by citing into their courts cases which properly belong in the lay courts, and enforce their verdicts (usually fines) by means of ecclesiastical censures.

71. The *signatura gratiae* and the *signatura justitiae* were the bureaus through which the pope regulated those matters of administration which belonged to his own special prerogative.

one cares what is right or not right, but only what is money or not money. This court might, however be paid out of the annates, or some other way might easily be devised, by those who are more intelligent and who have more experience in these matters than I. All I wish to do is to arouse and set to thinking those who have the ability and the inclination to help the German nation become once more free and Christian, after the wretched, heathenish, and unchristian rule of the pope.

5. No more reservations should be valid, and no more benefices should be seized by Rome, even if the incumbent dies, or there is a contest, or the incumbent is a "servant" of a cardinal or of the pope; and it should be strictly forbidden and prevented that any "courtesan" should institute a contest over any benefice, so as to cite pious priests to Rome, harass them and drive them into lawsuits. If, in consequence of this prohibition, there should come from Rome a ban or an ecclesiastical censure, it should be disregarded, just as though a thief were to lay a man under the ban because he would not let him steal. Indeed they should be severely punished because they so blasphemously misuse the ban and the name of God to support their robbery, and with falsely devised threats would drive us to endure and to praise such blasphemy of God's name and such abuse of Christian authority, and thus to become, in the sight of God, partakers in their rascality; it is our duty before God to resist it, for St. Paul, in Romans 1, reproves as guilty of death not only "those who do such things," but also those who consent to such things and allow them to be done. Most unbearable of all is the lying *reservatio pectoralis,* whereby Christendom is so scandalously and openly put to shame and scorn, because its head deals in open lies, and out of love for the accursed money, shamelessly deceives and fools everybody.

6. The *casus reservati*,[72] the "reserved cases," should also be abolished, for not only are they the means of extorting much money from the people, but by means of them the ravening tyrants ensnare and confuse many poor consciences, to the intolerable injury of their faith in God. This is especially true of the ridiculous and childish cases about which they make so much ado in the Bull *Coena Domini*,[73] and which are not worth calling daily sins, still less cases so grave that the pope may not remit them by any indulgence; as for example, hindering a pilgrim on his way to Rome, furnishing weapons to the Turks, or tampering with papal letters. With such gross, crazy, clumsy things do they make fools of us! Sodom and Gomorrah, and all the sins which are committed and can be committed against the commandments of God, are not reserved cases; but sins against what God has never commanded and what they have themselves devised, these must be reserved cases, solely that no one be hindered in bringing money to Rome, in order that, safe from the Turks, they may live in luxury and keep the world under their tyranny with their wanton, useless bulls and breves.[74]

All priests ought rightly to know, or else there should be a public ordinance to that effect, that no secret sin, of which a man has not been publicly accused, is a reserved case, and that every priest has the power to remit all sorts of sins, however they may be called, so long as they are secret; moreover that no abbot, bishop, or pope has the power to reserve any such case to himself. If they attempt it, their reservation does not hold and is not valid, and they should

72. i.e., The cases in which a priest was forbidden to give absolution. The reference here is to cases in which only the pope could absolve.

73. A papal bull published annually at Rome on Holy Thursday. It was directed against heretics, but to the condemnation of the heretics and their heresies was added a list of offenses which could receive absolution only from the pope, or by his authorization.

74. The breve is a papal decree, of equal authority with the bull, but differing from it in form, and usually dealing with matters of small importance.

be reproved, as men who without authority interfere in God's judgment, and without cause ensnare and burden poor, ignorant consciences. But if great public sins are committed, especially sins against God's commandments, then there is indeed a reason for reserved cases, but even then there should not be too many of them, and they should not be reserved arbitrarily and without cause; for Christ has set in His Church not tyrants, but shepherds, as St. Peter says.

7. The Roman See should also do away with the *officia,* and diminish the swarm of vermin at Rome, so that the pope's household can be supported by the pope's own purse. The pope should not allow his court to surpass in pomp and extravagance the courts of all kings, seeing that such a condition not only has never been serviceable to the cause of Christian faith, but the courtiers have been kept thereby from study and prayer, until they are scarce able to speak about the faith at all. This they proved quite plainly at the last Roman Council,[75] in which, amongst many other childish and frivolous things, they decreed that the soul of man is immortal and that every priest must say his prayers once a month on pain of losing his benefice. How shall matters which concern faith and the Church be decided by people so hardened and blinded by great avarice, wealth and worldly splendor, that they have only now decreed that the soul is immortal? It is no small shame to all Christians that at Rome they deal so disgracefully with the faith. If they had less wealth and pomp, they could pray and study better, and so become worthy and able to deal with matters of faith, as was the case in olden times when they were bishops, and did not presume to be kings over all kings.

8. The hard and terrible oaths should be abolished which the bishops are wrongfully compelled to render to

---

75. The Fifth Lateran Council (1512-17).

the pope, and by which they are bound like servants, as that worthless and unlearned chapter, *Significasti*[76] arbitrarily and most stupidly decrees. It is not enough that they burden us in body, soul and property with their many mad laws, by which faith is weakened and Christendom ruined; but they seize upon the person and office and work of the bishops, and now upon the investiture[77] also, which was in olden times the right of the German emperors, and in France and other kingdoms still belongs to the kings. On this point they had great wars and disputes with the emperors,[78] until at last, with impudent authority, they took the right and have kept it until now; just as though the Germans, above all the Christians on earth, had to be the puppets of the pope and the Roman See and do and suffer what no one else will do and suffer. Since, then, this is sheer violence and robbery, hindering the regular authority of the bishops and injuring poor souls, therefore the emperor and his nobles are in duty bound to prevent and punish such tyranny.

9. The pope should have no authority over the emperor, except that he anoints and crowns him at the altar, just as a bishop anoints and crowns a king;[79] and we should not henceforth yield to that devilish pride which compels the emperor to kiss the pope's feet or sit at his feet, or, as they claim, hold his stirrup or the bridle of his mule when he mounts for a ride; still less should he do homage and

---

76. It forbids the bestowing of the *pallium* on an archbishop elect, until he shall first have sworn allegiance to the Holy See.

77. The induction of Church officials into office. The term was used particularly of the greater offices — those of bishop and abbot. These offices carried with them the enjoyment of certain incomes, and the possession of certain temporal powers. For this reason the right of investiture was a bone of contention between popes and emperors during the Middle Ages.

78. Especially in the time of the Emperors Henry IV and V (1056-1125).

79. The German Empire was regarded during the Middle Ages as a continuation of the Roman Empire. The right to crown an emperor was held to be the prerogative of the pope; until the pope bestowed the imperial crown, the emperor bore the title, "King of the Romans."

swear faithful allegiance to the pope, as the popes have shamelessly ventured to demand as if they possessed that right. The chapter, *Solite*, in which the papal authority is raised above the imperial authority, is not worth a cent, nor are any of those who rest upon it or fear it; for it does nothing else than force the holy words of God out of their true meaning, and wrest them to human dreams, as I have showed in a Latin treatise.

Such extravagant, overpresumptuous, and more than wicked doings of the pope have been devised by the devil, in order that under their cover he may in time bring in Antichrist, and raise the pope above God, as many are already doing and have done. It is not proper for the pope to exalt himself above the temporal authorities, save only in spiritual offices such as preaching and absolving. In other things he is to be subject, as Paul and Peter teach, in Romans 13, and I Peter 3, and as I have said above.

He is not vicar of Christ in heaven, but of Christ as He walked on earth. For Christ in heaven, in the form of a ruler, needs no vicar, but He sits and sees, does, and knows all things, and has all power. But He needs a vicar in the form of a servant, in which He walked on earth, toiling, preaching, suffering, and dying. Now they turn it around, take from Christ the heavenly form of ruler and give it to the pope, leaving the form of a servant to perish utterly. He might almost be the "Counter-christ" whom the Scriptures call Antichrist, for all his nature, work and doings are against Christ, for the destruction of Christ's nature and work.

It is also ridiculous and childish that the pope, with such perverted and deluded reasoning, boasts in his decretal *Pastoralis*,[80] that he is rightful heir to the Empire, in case

---

80. A decree of Pope Clement V of 1313, incorporated subsequently in the canon law.

of a vacancy. Who has given him this right? Did Christ, when He said, "The princes of the Gentiles are lords, but ye shall not be so"? Did St. Peter will it to him? It vexes me that we must read and learn such shameless, gross, crazy lies in the canon law, and must even hold them for Christian doctrine, when they are devilish lies.

Of the same sort is also that unheard-of lie about the "Donation of Constantine." [81] It must have been some special plague of God that so many people of understanding have let themselves be talked into accepting such lies as these, which are so manifest and clumsy that I should think any drunken peasant could lie more adroitly and skilfully. How can a man rule an empire and at the same time continue to preach, pray, study and care for the poor? Yet these are the duties which properly and peculiarly belong to the pope, and they were imposed by Christ in such earnest that He even forbade His disciples to take with them cloak or money, since these duties can scarcely be performed by one who has to rule even a single household. Yet the pope would rule an empire and continue to be pope! This is a device of the knaves who would like, under the pope's name, to be lords of the world, and by means of the pope and the name of Christ, to restore the Roman Empire to its former state.

10. The pope should restrain himself, take his fingers out of the pie, and claim no title to the Kingdom of Naples

---

81. A forged document of the eighth century, professing to come from the hand of the Emperor Constantine (306-37). The Donation conveyed to the pope title to the city of Rome (the capital had been removed to Constantinople), certain lands in Italy and "the islands of the sea." It was used by the popes of the Middle Ages to support their claims to worldly power, and its genuineness was not disputed. In 1440, however, Laurentius Valla, an Italian humanist, published a work in which he proved that the Donation was a forgery. This work was republished in Germany by Ulrich von Hutten in 1517, and seems to have come to Luther's attention in the early part of 1520, just before the composition of the present treatise.

and Sicily.[82] He has exactly as much right to that kingdom as I have, and yet he wishes to be its overlord. It is plunder got by violence, like almost all his other possessions. The emperor, therefore, should not grant him this fief, and if it has been granted, he should no longer give his consent to it, and should point him instead to the Bible and the prayer-books, so that he may preach and pray, and leave to temporal lords the ruling of lands and peoples, especially when no one has given them to him.

The same opinion should hold as regards Bologna, Imola, Vicenza, Ravenna and all the territories in the Mark of Ancona, in Romagna, and in other Italian lands, which the pope has taken by force and possesses without right.[83] Moreover, he has meddled in these things against all the commands of Christ and of St. Paul. For St. Paul says, "No one entangleth himself with worldly affairs, whose business it is to wait upon the divine knighthood." [84] Now the pope should be the head and front of this knighthood, yet he meddles in worldly affairs more than any emperor or king. Why then he must be helped out of them and allowed to attend to his knighthood. Christ also, whose vicar he boasts

---

82. The papal claim to temporal sovereignty over this little kingdom, which comprised the island of Sicily and certain territories in Southern Italy, goes back to the eleventh century, and was steadily asserted during the whole of the later Middle Ages. It was one of the questions at issue in the conflict between the Emperor Frederick II (1200-1260) and the popes, and played an important part in the history of the stormy times which followed the fall of the Hohenstaufen. The popes claimed the right to award the kingdom to a ruler who would swear allegiance to the Holy See. The right to the kingdom was at this time contested between the royal houses of France and of Spain, of which latter house the Emperor Charles V was the head.

83. The popes claimed temporal sovereignty over a strip of territory in Italy, beginning at Rome and stretching in a northeasterly direction across the peninsula to a point on the Adriatic south of Venice, including the cities and lands which Luther mentions. This formed the so-called "States of the Church." The attempt to consolidate the States and make the papal sovereignty effective involved Popes Alexander VI (1492-1503) and Julius II (1503-13) in war and entangled them in political alliances with the European powers and petty Italian states. It resulted at last in actual war between Pope Clement VII and the Emperor Charles V (1526-27).

84. A free translation of the Vulgate.

himself to be, was never willing to have aught to do with temporal rule; indeed, to one who asked of Him a decision respecting his brother, He said, "Who made me a judge over you?" But the pope rushes in unbidden, and boldly takes hold of everything as though he were a god, until he no longer knows what Christ is, whose vicar he pretends to be.

11. The kissing of the pope's feet[85] should take place no more. It is an unchristian, nay, an antichristian thing for a poor sinful man to let his feet be kissed by one who is a hundred times better than himself. If it is done in honor of his authority, why does not the pope do the same to others in honor of their holiness? Compare the two — Christ and the pope! Christ washed His disciples' feet and dried them, and the disciples never washed His feet; the pope, as though he were higher than Christ, turns things around and, as a great favor, allows people to kiss his feet, though he ought properly to use all his power to prevent it, if anyone wished to do it; like Paul and Barnabas, who would not let the people of Lystra pay them divine honor, but said, "We are men like you." But our sycophants have gone so far as to make for us an idol, and now no one fears God so much as he fears the pope, no one pays Him such ceremonious honor. That they can endure! What they cannot endure is that a hair's-breadth should be taken away from the proud estate of the pope. Now if they were Christians, and held God's honor above their own, the pope would never be happy while he knew that God's honor was despised and his own exalted, and he would let no man pay him honor until he saw that God's honor was again exalted and was greater than his own.

[86][It is another piece of the same scandalous pride, that

---

85. The kissing of the pope's feet was a part of the "adoration" which he claimed as his right.
86. The three paragraphs enclosed in brackets were added by Luther to the second edition.

the pope is not satisfied to ride or to be driven in a vehicle, but although he is strong and in good health, he has himself borne by men, with unheard-of splendor, like an idol. How pray, does such satanic pride agree with the example of Christ, who went on foot, as did all His disciples? Where has there ever been a worldly monarch who went about in such worldly glory as he who wishes to be the head of all those who are to despise and flee worldly glory, i.e., of Christians? Not that this in itself should give us very much concern, but we should rightly fear the wrath of God, if we flatter this kind of pride and do not show our indignation. It is enough that the pope should rant and play the fool in this wise; but that we should approve it and tolerate it, this is too much.

For what Christian heart can or ought to take pleasure in seeing that when the pope wishes to receive the communion, he sits quiet, like a gracious lord, and has the sacrament passed to him on a golden rod by a bowing cardinal on bended knee? As though the holy sacrament were not worthy that a pope, a poor stinking sinner, should rise to show God honor, when all other Christians, who are much more holy than the Most Holy Father, the pope, receive it with all reverence! Would it be a wonder if God were to send a plague upon us all because we suffer such dishonor to be done Him by our prelates, and approve it, and by our silence or our flattery make ourselves partakers of such damnable pride?

It is the same way when he carries the sacrament in procession. He must be carried, but the sacrament is set before him, like a can of wine on the table. In short, at Rome Christ counts for nothing, the pope counts for everything; and yet they would compel us with threats to approve, and praise and honor such antichristian sins, though this is against God and against all Christian doctrine. Now God help a free Council to teach the pope that he too is a man, and is not more than God, as he presumes to be.]

12. Pilgrimages to Rome should either be abolished, or else no one should be allowed to make such a pilgrimage out of curiosity or because of a pious impulse, unless it is first recognized by his parish priest, his town authorities or his overlord, that he has good and sufficient reason for it. I say this not because pilgrimages are bad, but because they are at this time ill-advised. For men see at Rome no good example, but only that which offends; and they have themselves made the proverb, "The nearer Rome, the worse Christians." [87] Men bring back with them contempt for God and His commandments. It is said: "The first time one goes to Rome he seeks a rascal, the second time he finds him, the third time he brings him home with him." [88] Now, however, they have become so clever that they make the three journeys at once, and they have verily brought back from Rome such pretty things that it were better never to have seen or known Rome.

Even if this reason did not exist, there is still another and a better: to wit, that by these pilgrimages men are led away into a false conceit and a misunderstanding of the divine commandments; for they think that this going on pilgrimage is a precious, good work, and this is not true. It is a very small good work, oftentimes an evil, delusive work, for God has not commanded it. But He has commanded that a man shall care for his wife and children, and look after such other duties as belong to the married state, and besides this, to serve and help his neighbor. Now it comes to pass that a man makes a pilgrimage to Rome when no one has commanded him to do so, spends fifty or a hundred gulden, more or less, and leaves his wife and child, or

---

87. Cf. the Italian proverb, "God is everywhere except at Rome; there He has a vicar."

88 Cf. Hutten's saying in *Vadiscus:* "Three things there are which those who go to Rome usually bring home with them, a bad conscience, a ruined stomach and an empty purse."

at least his neighbor, at home to suffer want. Yet the foolish fellow thinks to gloss over such disobedience and contempt of the divine commandments with his self-willed pilgriming, when it is really only curiosity or devilish delusion whish leads him to it. The popes have helped this along with their false, feigned, foolish, "golden years,"[89] by which the people are excited, stirred up, torn away from God's commandments, and drawn toward their own deluded undertakings. Thus they have accomplished the very thing they should have forbidden; but it has brought in money and strengthened false authority, therefore it has had to continue, though it is against God and the salvation of souls.

In order to destroy in simple Christians this false, seductive faith, and to restore a true understanding of good works, all pilgrimages should be given up; for there is in them nothing good — no commandment, no obedience — but on the contrary, numberless occasions for sin and for the despising of God's commandments. Hence come the many beggars, who by this pilgriming carry on endless knaveries and learn the habit of begging when they are not in want. Hence, too, come vagabondage, and many other ills which I shall not now recount.

If anyone, now, wishes to go on pilgrimage or take a pilgrim's vow, he should first show his reasons to his parish priest or to his lord. If it turns out that he wishes to do it for the sake of the good work, the priest or lord should boldly tread the vow and good work under foot, as though it were a lure of the devil, and show him how to apply the money and labor necessary for the pilgrimage to the keeping of God's commandments and to works a thousandfold

---

89. The "golden" or "jubilee years" were the years when special rewards were attached to worship at the shrines of Rome. The custom was instituted by Boniface VIII in 1300, and it was the intention to make every hundredth year a jubilee. In 1343 the interval between jubilees was fixed at fifty, in 1389 at thirty-three, in 1473 at twenty-five years.

better, viz., by spending it on his own family or on his poor neighbors. But if he wishes to make the pilgrimage out of curiosity, to see new lands and cities, he may be allowed to do as he likes. If, however, he has made the vow while ill, then such vows ought to be forbidden and canceled, and the commandments of God exalted, and he ought to be shown that he should henceforth be satisfied with the vow he made in baptism, to keep the commandments of God. And yet, in order to quiet his conscience, he may be allowed this once to perform his foolish vow. No one wants to walk in the straight and common path of God's commandments; everyone makes himself new roads and new vows, as though he had fulfilled all the commandments of God.

13. Next we come to that great crowd who vow much and keep little. Be not angry, dear lords! Truly, I mean it well. It is the truth, and bitter-sweet, and it is this: the building of mendicant-houses[90] should no more be permitted. God help us, there are already far too many of them! Would to God they were all done away, or at least given over to two or three orders! Wandering about the land has never brought any good, and never will bring any good. It is my advice, therefore, to put together ten of these houses, or as many as may be necessary, and out of them all to make one house, which will be well provided and need no more begging. It is much more important to consider what the common people need for their salvation, than what St. Francis, St. Dominic, St. Augustine,[91] or any other man has decreed; especially since things have not turned out as they expected.

---

90. The houses, or monasteries, of the mendicant or "begging" orders — the "friars." The members of these orders were sworn to support themselves on the alms of the faithful.

91. The three leading mendicant orders were the Franciscan (the Minorites, or "little brothers"), founded by St. Francis of Assisi (died 1226), the Dominican (the "preaching brothers"), founded by St. Dominic (died 1221), and the Augustinian Hermits, to which Luther himself belonged, and which claimed foundation by St. Augustine (died 430).

The mendicants should also be relieved of preaching and hearing confession, except when they are called to this work by the express desire of bishops, parishes, congregations, or the temporal authorities. Out of their preaching and shriving there has come nothing but hatred and envy between priests and monks, and great offense and hindrance to the common people. For this reason it should properly and deservedly cease, because it can well be dispensed with.[92] It looks suspicious as though it were not for nothing that the Holy Roman See has increased this army, so that the priests and bishops, tired of its tyranny, might not sometime become too strong for it and begin a reformation which would not be to the liking of His Holiness.

At the same time the manifold divisions and differences within one and the same order should be abolished. These divisions have at times arisen for small reason and maintained themselves for still smaller, combating one another with unspeakable hatred and envy.[93] Nevertheless the Christian faith, which can well exist without any of these distinctions, is lost by both sides, and a good Christian life is valued and sought after only in outward laws, works and forms; and this results only in the devising of hypocrisy and the destruction of souls, as everyone may see with his own eyes.

The pope must also be forbidden to found and confirm any more of these orders; nay, he must be commanded to abolish some of them and reduce their number, since the faith of Christ, which is alone the highest good and which exists without any orders, is in no small danger, because these many different works and forms easily mislead men

---

92. The interference of the friars in the duties of the parish clergy was a continual subject of complaint through this period.
93. By the middle of the fifteenth century there were eight distinct sects within the Franciscan order alone, and Luther had himself taken part in a vigorous dispute between two parties in the Augustinian order.

into living for them instead of giving heed to the faith. Unless there are in the monasteries wise prelates, who preach and who concern themselves with faith more than with the rules of the orders, the order cannot but harm and delude simple souls who think only of works.

In our days, however, the prelates who have had faith and who founded the orders have almost all passed away. Just as in olden days among the children of Israel, when the fathers, who knew God's works and wonders, had passed away, the children, from ignorance of God's works and of faith, immediately became idolatrous and set up their own human works; so now, alas! these orders have lost the understanding of God's works and of faith, and only torture themselves pitifully, with labor and sorrow, in their own rules, laws, and customs, and withal never come to a right understanding of a good spiritual life, as the Apostle declared when he said, in II Timothy 3: "They have the appearance of a spiritual life, yet there is nothing back of it; they are ever and ever learning, but they never come to a knowledge of what a true spiritual life is." There should be no monastery unless there were a spiritual prelate, learned in the Christian faith, to rule it, for no other kind of prelate can rule without injury and ruin, and the holier and better he appears to be in his outward works and life, the more injury and ruin he causes.

To my way of think it would be a necessary measure, especially in these perilous times of ours, that all foundations and monasteries should be re-established as they were at the first, in the days of the Apostles and for a long time afterwards, when they were all open to every man, and every man might remain in them as long as he pleased. For what were the foundationss and monasteries except Christian schools in which the Scriptures and Christian living were taught, and people were trained to rule and to preach?

So we read that St. Agnes[94] went to school, and we still see the same practice in some of the nunneries, like that at Quedlinburg[95] and others elsewhere. And in truth all monasteries and convents ought to be so free that God is served in them with free will and not with forced avarice. Afterward, however, they hedged them about with vows and turned them into a lifelong prison, so that these vows are thought to be of more account than the vows of baptism. What sort of fruit this has borne, we see, hear, read, and learn more and more every day.

I suppose this advice of mine will be regarded as the height of foolishness; but I am not concerned about that just now. I advise what I think best; let him reject it who will! I see how the vows are kept, especially the vow of chastity, which has become so universal through these monasteries and yet is not commanded by Christ; on the contrary, it is given to very few to keep it, as He himself says, and St. Paul. I would have all men to be helped, and not have Christian souls caught in human, self-devised customs and laws.

14. We also see how the priesthood has fallen, and how many a poor priest is overburdened with wife and child, and his conscience troubled, yet no one does anything to help him though he might easily be helped. Though pope and bishops may let things go as they go, and let them go to ruin if they will, I will save my conscience and open my mouth freely, whether it vex pope, bishops, or anyone else. Wherefore I say that according to the institution of Christ and the Apostles every city should have a priest or bishop, as St. Paul clearly says in Titus 1; and this priest should not be compelled to live without a wedded wife, but should be permitted to have one, as St. Paul says in I Timothy 3,

---

94. St. Agnes the Martyr, put to death in the beginning of the fourth century, one of the favorite saints of the Middle Ages.
95. One of the most famous of the German convents, founded in 936.

and Titus 1, "A bishop should be a man who is blameless, and the husband of but one wedded wife, whose children are obedient and virtuous," etc. For with St. Paul a bishop and a priest are one and the same thing, as witness also St. Jerome.[96] But of bishops as they now are, the Scriptures know nothing; they have been appointed by the ordinance of the Christian Church, that one of them may rule over many priests.

So then we clearly learn from the Apostle that it should be the custom for every town to choose out of the congregation[97] a learned and pious citizen, entrust to him the office of the ministry, and support him at the expense of the community, leaving him free choice to marry or not. He should have with him several priests or deacons, who might also be married or not, as they chose, to help him rule the people of the community[98] by means of preaching and the sacraments, as is still the practice in the Greek Church. At a later time,[99] when there were so many persecutions and controversies with heretics, there were many holy fathers who of their own accord abstained from matrimony, to the end that they might the better devote themselves to study and be prepared at any time for death or for controversy. Then the Roman See interfered, out of sheer wantonness, and made a universal commandment forbidding priests to marry.[100] This was done at the bidding of the devil, as St. Paul declares in I Timothy 4, "There shall come teachers who bring doctrines of devils, and forbid to marry." From this has arisen so much untold misery, occasion was given for the withdrawal of the Greek Church, and division, sin, shame, and scandal were increased without end —

---

96. The celebrated Church Father (died 420).
97. Or "community" (*Gemeine*).
98. Or "congregation."
99. i.e., At a time later than that of the Apostles.
100. The first absolute prohibition of marriage to the clergy is contained in a decree of Pope Siricius and dated 385.

things which are the result of everything the devil does.[101]

What, then, shall we do about it? My advice is that matrimony be again made free, and that everyone be left free choice to marry or not to marry. In that case, however, there must be a very different government and administration of Church property, the whole canon law must go to pieces and not many benefices find their way to Rome.[102] I fear that greed has been a cause of this wretched unchaste chastity, and as a result of greed every man has wished to become a priest and everyone wants his son to study for the priesthood, not with the idea of living in chastity, for that could be done outside the priesthood, but of being supported in temporal things without care or labor, contrary to the command of God in Genesis 3, "In the sweat of thy face shalt thou eat thy bread." They have construed this to mean that their labor was to pray and say mass.

I am not referring here to popes, bishops, canons, and monks. God has not instituted these offices. They have taken burdens on themselves; let them bear them. I would speak only of the ministry which God has instituted[103] and which is to rule a congregation by means of preaching and sacraments, whose incumbents are to live and be at home among the people. Such ministers should be granted liberty by a Christian council to marry, for the avoidance of temptation and sin. For since God has not bound them, no one else ought to bind them or can bind them, even though he were an angel from heaven, still less if he be only a pope, and everything that the canon law decrees to the contrary is mere fable and idle talk.

Furthermore, I advise that henceforth neither at his consecration to the priesthood nor at any other time shall any-

---

101. The priests of the Greek Church are required to marry, and the controversy over celibacy was involved in the division between the Greek and Roman Churches.
102. i.e., Lie in Roman appointment.
103. i.e., The ministry in the congregation.

one under any circumstances promise the bishop to live in celibacy, but shall declare to the bishop that he has no authority to demand such a vow, and that to demand it is the devil's own tyranny.

But if anyone is compelled to say or wishes to say, as do some, "so far as human frailty permits," let everyone frankly interpret these words negatively, to mean "I do not promise chastity."[104] For human frailty does not permit a chaste life, but only angelic power and celestial might. Thus he should keep his conscience free from all vows.

On the question whether those who are not yet married should marry or remain unmarried, I do not care to give advice either way. I leave that to common Christian order and to everyone's better judgment. But as regards the wretched multitude who now sit in shame and heaviness of conscience because their wives are called "priests' harlots" and their children "priests' children" I will not withhold my faithful counsel nor deprive them of the comfort which is their due. I say this boldly by my jester's right.[105]

You will find many a pious priest against whom no one has anything to say except that he is weak and has come to shame with a woman, though both parties may be minded with all their heart to live always together in wedded love and troth, if only they could do it with a clear conscience, even though they might have to bear public shame. Two such persons are certainly married before God. And I say that where they are thus minded, and so come to live together, they should boldly save their consciences; let him take and keep her as his wedded wife, and live honestly with her as her husband, caring nothing whether the pope will have it so or not, whether it be against canon law or human law. The salvation of your soul is of more importance than tyrannical, arbitrary, wicked laws, which are not

---

104. i.e., Celibacy.
105. The court-jester was allowed unusual freedom of speech.

necessary for salvation and are not commanded by God. You should do like the children of Israel, who stole from the Egyptians the hire they had earned, or like a servant who steals from his wicked master the wages he has earned. In like manner steal thou from the pope thy wife and child! Let the man who has faith enough to venture this, boldly follow me; I shall not lead him astray. Though I have not the authority of a pope, I have the authority of a Christian to advise and help my neighbor against sins and temptations; and that not without cause and reason.

First, Not every priest can do without a woman, not only on account of the weakness of the flesh, but much more because of the necessities of the household. If he, then, may have a woman, and the pope grants him that, and yet may not have her in marriage—what is that but leaving a man and a woman alone and forbidding them to fall? It is as though one were to put fire and straw together and command that it shall neither smoke nor burn.

Second, The pope has as little power to command this, as he has to forbid eating, drinking, the natural movement of the bowels or growing fat. No one, therefore, is bound to keep it, but the pope is responsible for all the sins which are committed against this ordinance, for all the souls which are lost thereby, for all the consciences which are thereby confused and tortured; and therefore he has long deserved that someone should drive him out of the world, so many wretched souls has he strangled with this devil's snare; though I hope that there are many to whom God has been more gracious at their last hour than the pope has been in their life. Nothing good has ever come out of the papacy and its laws, nor ever will.

Third, Although the law of the pope is against it, nevertheless, when the estate of matrimony has been entered against the pope's law, then his law is at an end, and is no longer valid; for the commandment of God, which decrees *pope should not have right to divorce*

because of god's law concerning matri-

that no one shall put man and wife asunder, takes precedence of the law of the pope; and the commandments of *money*
God must not be broken and neglected for the sake of the
pope's commandment, though many mad jurists, in the
papal interest, have devised "impediments"[106] and have
prevented, destroyed, and confused the estate of matrimony,
until by their means God's commandment has been altogether destroyed. To make a long story short, there are
not in the whole "spiritual" law of the pope two lines which
could be instructive to a pious Christian, and there are,
alas! so many mistaken and dangerous laws that the best
thing would be to make a bonfire of it.[107]

But if you say that this[108] would give offense, and the
pope must first grant dispensation, I reply that whatever
offense is in it, is the fault of the Roman See, which has
established such laws without right and against God; before
God and the Scriptures it is no offense. Moreover, if the
pope can grant dispensations from his avaricious and tyrannical laws for money's sake, then every Christian can grant
dispensations from them—for the sake of God and the salvation of souls. For Christ has set us free from all human
laws, especially when they are opposed to God and the salvation of souls, as St. Paul teaches in Galatians 5 and I
Corinthians 11.

15. Nor must I forget the poor convents! The evil spirit,
who by human laws now confuses all estates in life, and
has made them unbearable, has taken possession of certain

---

106. The laws governing marriage were entirely the laws of the Church. The
canon law prohibited marriage of blood-relatives as far as the seventh
degree of consanguinity. In 1204 the prohibition was restricted to the first
four degrees; lawful marriage within these degrees was possible only by
dispensation, which was not all too difficult to secure, especially by those
who were willing to pay for it. The relation of god-parents to god-chil-
dren was also held to establish a "spiritual consanguinity" which might
serve as a bar to lawful marriage.

107. This Luther actually did. When he burned the papal bull of excommunication (Dec. 10, 1520) a copy of the canon law was also given to the
flames.

108. i.e., The marriage of the clergy.

abbots, abbesses and prelates also, and causes them so to govern their brethren and sisters as to send them the more speedily to hell, and make them lead a wretched life even here; for such is the lot of all the devil's martyrs. That is to say, they have reserved to themselves in confession, all, or at least some, of the mortal sins which are secret, so that no brother, on his obedience and on pain of the ban, can absolve another from these sins. Now we do not always find angels everywhere, but we find also flesh and blood, which suffers all bannings and threatenings rather than confess secret sins to the prelates and the appointed confessors. Thus they go to the sacrament with such consciences that they become "irregular"[109] and all sorts of other terrible things. O blind shepherds! O mad prelates! O ravening wolves!

To this I say: If a sin is public or notorious, then it is proper that the prelate alone should punish it, and of these sins only and no others he may make exceptions, and reserve them to himself; over secret sins he has no authority, even though they were the worst sins that are or ever can be found, and if the prelate makes exceptions of these sins, he is a tyrant, for he has no such right and is interfering in the judgment of God.

And so I advise these children, brethren and sisters: If your superiors are unwilling to grant you permission to confess your secret sins to whomever you wish, then take them to whatever brother or sister you will and confess them, receive absolution, and then go and do whatever you wish and ought to do; only believe firmly that you are absolved, and nothing more is needed. And do not allow yourself to be troubled by ban, "irregularity," or any of the

---

109. "Irregularity" is the condition of any member of a monastic order who has violated the prescriptions of the order and been deprived, in consequence, of the benefits enjoyed by those who live under the *regula*, viz., the rule of the order.

other things they threaten; these things are valid only in the case of public or notorious sins which one is unwilling to confess; they do not affect you at all. Why do you try by your threatenings, O blind prelate, to prevent secret sins? Let go what you cannot publicly prove, so that God's judgment and grace may also have its work in your subjects! He did not give them so entirely into your hands as to let them go entirely out of His own! Nay, what you have under your rule is but the smaller part. Let your statutes be statutes, but do not exalt them to heaven, to the judgment-seat of God.

16. It were also necessary to abolish all anniversary, mortuary, and "soul" masses,[110] or at least to diminish their number, since we plainly see that they have become nothing but a mockery, by which God is deeply angered, and that their only purpose is money-getting, gorging, and drunkenness. What kind of pleasure should God have in such a miserable gabbling of wretched vigils and masses, which is neither reading nor praying, and even when prayed,[111] they are performed not for God's sake and out of willing love, but for money's sake and because they are a bounden duty. Now it is not possible that any work not done out of willing love can please God or obtain anything from Him. And so it is altogether Christian to abolish, or at least diminish, everything which we see growing into an abuse, and which angers rather than reconciles God. It would please me more—nay, it would be more acceptable to God and far better—that a foundation, church, or monastery should put all its anniversary masses and vigils together, and on one day, with hearty sincerity, devotion, and faith, hold a true vigil and mass for all its benefactors,

---

110. The three kinds of masses are really but one thing, viz., masses for the dead, celebrated on certain fixed days in each year, in consideration of the enjoyment of certain incomes, received either out of bequeathed endowments or from the heirs of the supposed beneficiaries.

111. i.e., Even when the mass is decently said.

rather than hold them by the thousand every year, for each benefactor a special mass, without this devotion and faith. O dear Christians! God cares not for much praying, but for true praying! Nay, He condemns the many and long prayers, and says in Matthew 6, they will only earn more punishment thereby. But avarice, which cannot trust God, brings such things to pass, fearing that otherwise it must die of hunger!

17. Certain of the penalties or punishments of the canon law should also be abolished, especially the interdict, which is, beyond all doubt, an invention of the evil Spirit. Is it not a devil's work to try to atone for one sin with many greater sins? And yet, to put God's Word and worship to silence, or to do away with them, is a greater sin than strangling twenty popes at once, and far greater than killing a priest or keeping back some Church property. This is another of the tender virtues taught in the "spiritual law." For one of the reasons why this law is called "spiritual" is because it comes from the Spirit; not, however, from the Holy Spirit, but from the evil spirit.

The ban is to be used in no case except where the Scriptures prescribe its use, i.e., against those who do not hold the true faith, or who live in open sin; it is not to be used for the sake of temporal possessions. But now it is the other way around. Everyone believes and lives as he pleases, most of all those who use the ban to plunder and defame other people, and all the bans are now laid only on account of temporal possessions, for which we have no one to thank but the holy "spiritual lawlessness." Of this I have previously said more in the Discourse.[112]

The other punishments and penalties—suspension, irregularity, aggravation, reaggravation, deposition, lightnings, thunderings, cursings, damnings and the rest of these

112. The *Treatise Concerning the Ban.*

devices—should be buried ten fathoms deep in the earth, so that there should be neither name nor memory of them left on earth. The evil spirit, who has been let loose by the "spiritual law," has brought this terrible plague and misery into the heavenly kingdom of the holy Church, and has accomplished by it nothing else than the destruction and hindrance of souls, so that the word of Christ may well be applied to them[113]: "Woe unto you scribes! Ye have taken upon you the authority to teach, and ye shut up the kingdom of heaven against men. Ye go not in yourselves, and ye suffer not them that are entering."

18. All festivals[114] should be abolished, and Sunday alone retained. If it were desired, however, to retain the festivals of Our Lady and of the greater saints, they should be transferred to Sunday, or observed only by a morning mass, after which all the rest of the day should be a working-day. The reason is this: The feast-days are now abused by drinking, gaming, idleness, and all manner of sins, so that on the holy days we anger God more than on other days, and have altogether turned things around; the holy days are not holy and the working days are holy, and not only is no service done to God and His saints by the many holy days, but rather great dishonor. There are, indeed, some mad _prel-_ _ates_ who think they are doing a good work if they make a festival in honor of St. Ottilia or St. Barbara or some other saint, according to the promptings of their blind devotion; but they would be doing a far better work if they honored the saint by turning a saint's-day into a working-day.

Over and above the spiritual injury, the common man receives two material injuries from this practice, i.e., he neglects his work and he spends more than at other times; nay, he also weakens his body and unfits it for work. We see this every day, yet no one thinks to make it better. We

113. i.e., To those who teach and enforce the canon law.
114. Luther means the saint's-days and minor religious holidays.

ought not to consider whether or not the pope has instituted the feasts, and whether we must have dispensation and permission to omit them. If a thing is opposed to God, and harmful to man in body and soul, any community,[115] council[116] or government has not only the right to abolish it and put a stop to it, without the will or knowledge of pope or bishop, but they are bound on their souls' salvation to prevent it, even against the will of pope and bishop, though these ought to be themselves the first to forbid it.

Above all, we ought utterly to abolish the consecration days,[117] since they have become nothing else than taverns, fairs, and gaming places,[118] and serve only to the increase of God's dishonor and to the damnation of souls. All the pretense about the custom having had a good beginning and being a good work is of no avail. Did not God Himself set aside His own law, which He had given from heaven, when it was perverted and abused? And does He not still daily overturn what He has appointed and destroy what He has made, because of such perversion and abuse? As it is written of Him in Psalm 18, "With the perverted thou wilt show thyself perverse."

19. The grades or degrees within which marriage is forbidden should be changed, as, for instance, the sponsorships and the third and fourth degrees, and if the pope can grant dispensation in these matters for money and for the sake of his shameful traffic, then every parish priest may give the same dispensations gratis and for the salvation of souls. Yea, would to God that all the things which we must buy at Rome to free ourselves from that money-snare, the canon law — such things as indulgences, letters of indulgence,

---

115. Or "congregation."

116. i.e., City council.

117. *Kirchweihen,* i.e., the anniversary celebration of the consecration of a church. These days had become feast days for the parish, and were observed in anything but a spiritual fashion.

118. i.e., Occasions for drunkenness, gain and gambling.

74

"butter-letters," "mass-letters,"[119] and all the rest of the *confessionalia* and knaveries for sale at Rome, with which the poor folk are deceived and robbed of their money—would to God, I say, that any priest could, without payment, do and omit all these things! For if the pope has the authority to sell his snares for money and his spiritual nets (I should say laws),[120] surely any priest has much more authority to rend his nets and for God's sake to tread them under foot. But if he has not this right, neither has the pope the right to sell them at his shameful fair.[121]

This is the place to say too that the fasts should be matters of liberty, and all sorts of food made free, as the Gospel makes them. For at Rome they themselves laugh at the fasts, making us foreigners eat the oil with which they would not grease their shoes, and afterwards selling us liberty to eat butter and all sorts of other things; yet the holy Apostle says that in all these things we already have liberty through the Gospel. But they have caught us with their canon law and stolen our rights from us, so that we may have to buy them back with money. Thus they have made our consciences so timid and shy that it is no longer easy to preach about this liberty because the common people take such great offense, thinking it a greater sin to eat butter than to lie, to swear, or even to live unchastely. Nevertheless, what men have decreed, that is the work of man; put it where you will,[122] nothing good ever comes out of it.

20. The forest chapels and rustic churches[123] must be utterly destroyed: those, namely, to which the recent pil-

---

119. Letters entitling their holder to the benefits of the masses founded by the sodalities or confraternities.
120. The pun is untranslatable—*Netz, Gesetz solt ich sagen.*
121. What the pope sold was release from the "snares" and "nets," viz., dispensation.
122. i.e., Even into the law of the church.
123. i.e., Churches which are built in the country, where there are no congregations.

grimages have been direvted — Wilsnack,[124] Sternberg,[125] Trier,[126] the Grimmenthal,[127] and now Regensburg[128] and a goodly number of others. Oh, what a terrible and heavy account will the bishops have to render, who permit this devilish deceit and receive its profits![129] They should be the first to forbid it, and yet they think it a divine and holy thing, and do not see that it is the devil's doing, to strengthen avarice, to create a false, feigned faith, to weaken the parish churches, to multiply taverns and harlotry, to waste money and labor, and to lead the poor folk by the nose. If they had only read the Scriptures to as good purpose as they have read their damnable canon law, they would know well how to deal with this matter.

That miracles are done at these places does not help things, for the evil spirit can do miracles, as Christ has told us in Matthew 24. If they took the matter seriously and

---

124. A little town in East Prussia, where was displayed a sacramental wafer, said to have been miraculously preserved from a fire which destroyed the church in 1383. It was alleged that at certain times this wafer exuded drops of blood, reverenced as the blood of Christ, and many miracles were said to have been performed by it. Wilsnack early became a favorite resort for pilgrims. In 1412 the archbishop of Prague, at the instigation of John Huss, forbade the Bohemians to go there. Despite the protests of the Universities of Leipzig and Erfurt, Pope Eugenius IV in 1446 granted special indulgences for this pilgrimage, and the popularity of the shrine was undiminished until the time of the Reformation.

125. In Mecklenburg, where another relic of "the Holy Blood" was displayed after 1491.

126. The "Holy Coat of Trier" was believed by the credulous to be the seamless coat of Christ, which the soldiers did not rend. It was first exhibited in 1512, but was said to have been presented to the cathedral church of Trier by the Empress Helena, mother of Constantine the Great.

127. Pilgrimage to the Grimmenthal in Meiningen began in 1499. An image of the Virgin, declared to have been miraculously created, was displayed there and was alleged to work wonderful cures, especially of syphilis.

128. The "Fair Virgin of Regensburg" was an image of the Virgin similar to that exhibited in the Grimmenthal. The shrine was opened March 25, 1519, and within a month 50,000 pilgrims are said to have worshiped there.

129. The pilgrimages were a source of large revenue, derived from the sale of medals which were worn as amulets, the fees for masses at the shrines, and the free-will offerings of the pilgrims. A large part of this revenue accrued to the bishop of the diocese, though the popes never overlooked the profits which the sale of indulgences for worship at these shrines could produce.

forbade this sort of thing, the miracles would quickly come to an end; on the other hand, if the thing were of God their prohibition would not hinder it. And if there were no other evidence that it is not of God, this would be enough—that people run to these places in excited crowds, as though they had lost their reason, like herds of cattle; for this cannot possibly be of God. Moreover, God has commanded nothing of all this; there is neither obedience nor merit in it; the bishops, therefore, should boldly step in and keep the folk away. For what is not commanded—and is concerned for self rather than for the commands of God—that is surely the devil himself. Then, too, the parish churches receive injury, because they are held in smaller honor. In short, these things are signs of great unbelief among the people; if they truly believed, they would have all that they need in their own churches, for to them they are commanded to go.

But what shall I say? Everyone[130] plans only how he may establish and maintain such a place of pilgrimage in his diocese and is not at all concerned to have the people believe and live aright; the rulers are like the people; one blind man leads another. Nay, where pilgrimages are not successful, they begin to canonize saints,[131] not in honor of the saints—for they are sufficiently honored without canonization—but in order to draw crowds and bring in money. Pope and bishop help along, it rains indulgences; there is always money enough for that. But for what God has commanded no one provides; no one runs after these things; there is no money for them. Alas, that we should be so blind! We not only give the devil his own way in his tricks, but we even strengthen him in his wantonness

---

130. i.e., Every bishop.
131. The possession of a saint gave a church a certain reputation and distinction, which was sufficiently coveted to make local Church authorities willing to pay roundly for the canonization of a departed bishop or other local dignitary.

and increase his pranks. I would that the dear saints were left in peace, and the poor folk not led astray! What spirit has given the pope the authority to canonize the saints? Who tells him whether they are saints or not? Are there not already sins enough on earth, that we too must tempt God, interfere in His judgment and set up the dear saints as lures for money?

Therefore I advise that the saints be left to canonize themselves. Yea, it is God alone who should canonize them. And let every man stay in his own parish, where he finds more than in all the shrines of pilgrimage, even though all the shrines were one. Here we find baptism, the sacrament, preaching, and our neighbor, and these are greater things than all the saints in heaven, for it is by God's Word and sacrament that they have all been made saints. So long as we despise such great things God is just in the wrathful judgment by which He appoints the devil to lead us hither and thither, to establish pilgrimages, to found churches and chapels, to secure the canonization of saints, and to do other such fool's-works, by which we depart from true faith into new, false misbelief. This is what he did in olden times to the people of Israel, when he led them away from the temple at Jerusalem to countless other places, though he did it in the name of God and under the plausible guise of holiness, though all the prophets preached against it and were persecuted for so doing. But now no one preaches against it, perhaps for fear that pope, priests and monks would persecute him also. In this way St. Antoninus of Florence[132] and certain others must now be made saints and canonized, that their holiness, which would otherwise have served only for the glory of God and as a good example, may serve to bring in fame and money.

---

132. Archbishop of Florence (died 1459). He was canonized, May 31, 1523, by Pope Hadrian VI. When Luther wrote this the process of canonization had already begun.

Although the canonizing of saints may have been good in olden times, it is not good now; just as many other things were good in olden times and are now scandalous and injurious, such as feast-days, church treasures and church adornment. For it is evident that through the canonizing of saints neither God's glory nor the improvement of Christians is sought, but only money and glory, in that one church wants to be something more and have something more than others, and would be sorry if another had the some thing and its advantage were common property. So entirely, in these last, evil days, have spiritual goods been misused and applied to the gaining of temporal goods, that everything, even God Himself, has been forced into the service of avarice. And even these special advantages lead only to dissensions, divisions and pride, in that the churches, differing from one another, hold each other in contempt, and exalt themselves one above another, though all the gifts which God bestows are the common and equal property of all churches and should only serve the cause of unity. The pope, too, is glad for the present state of affairs; he would be sorry if all Christians were equal and were at one.

This is the place to speak of the church licenses, bulls, and other things which the pope sells at his flaying-place in Rome. We should either abolish them or disregard them, or at least make them the common property of all churches. For if he sells or gives away licenses and privileges, indulgences, graces, advantages, faculties[133] to Wittenberg, to Halle, to Venice and, above all, to his own Rome, why does he not give these things to all churches alike? Is he not bound to do for all Christians, gratis and for God's sake, everything that he can, and even to shed his blood for them? Tell me, then, why he gives or sells to one church and not to another? Or must the accursed money make, in the eyes of His Holiness, so great a difference among Christians, who

_____
133. *Indulta,* i.e., grants of special privilege.

all have the same baptism, Word, faith, Christ, God, and all things? Are we to be blind while we have eyes to see, fools while we have our reason, that they expect us to worship such greed, knavery, and humbug? He is a shepherd — yes, so long as you have money, and no longer! And yet they are not ashamed of their knavery, leading us hither and yon with their bulls! Their one concern is the accursed money, and nothing else!

My advice is this: If such fool's-work cannot be abolished, then every pious Christian man should open his eyes, and not be misled by the hypocritical Roman bulls and seals, stay at home in his own church and be content with his baptism, his Gospel, his faith, his Christ, and with God, who is everywhere the same; and let the pope remain a blind leader of the blind. Neither angel nor pope can give you as much as God gives you in your parish church. Nay, the pope leads you away from the gifts of God, which you have without pay, to his gifts, which you must buy; and he gives you lead[134] for gold, hide for meat, the string for the purse, wax for honey, words for goods, the letter for the spirit. You see this before your very eyes, but you are unwilling to notice it. If you are to ride to heaven on his wax and parchment, your chariot will soon go to pieces, and you will fall into hell, not in God's name!

Let this be your fixed rule: What you must buy from the pope is neither good nor of God; for what is from God, to wit, the Gospel and the works of God, is not only given without money, but the whole world is punished and damned because it has not been willing to receive it as a free gift. We have deserved of God that we should be so deceived, because we have despised His holy Word and the grace of baptism, as St. Paul says: "God shall send a strong

---

134. "Lead," the leaden seal attached to the bull; "hide," the parchment on which it is written; "the string," the ribbon or silken cord from which the seals depend, "wax," the seal holding the cord to the parchment.

delusion upon all those who have not received the truth to their salvation, to the end that they may believe and follow after lies and knavery," which serves them right.

21. One of our greatest necessities is the abolition of all begging throughout Christendom. Among Christians no one ought to go begging! It would also be easy to make a law, if only we had the courage and the serious intention, to the effect that every city should provide for its own poor, and admit no foreign beggars by whatever name they might be called, whether pilgrims or mendicant monks. Every city could support its own poor, and if it were too small, the people in the surrounding villages also should be exhorted to contribute, since in any case they have to feed so many vagabonds and knaves in the guise of mendicants. In this way, too, it could be known who were really poor and who not.

There would have to be an overseer or warden who knew all the poor and informed the city council or the priests what they needed; or some other better arrangement might be made. In my judgment there is no other business in which so much knavery and deceit are practiced as in begging, and yet it could all be easily abolished. Moreover, this free and universal begging hurts the common people. I have considered that each of the five or six mendicant orders[135] visits the same place more than six or seven times every year; besides these there are the common beggars, the "stationaries" [136] and the palmers,[137] so that it has been

---

135. Franciscans, Dominicans, Augustinians, Carmelites, and Servites.

136. *Botschaften,* interpreted as a reference to the *stationarii.* They were wandering beggars who, for an alms, would enroll the contributor in the list of beneficiaries of their patron saint, an alleged insurance against disease, accident, etc. They were classified according to the names of their patron saints, St. Anthony, St. Hubert, St. Valentine, etc. Protests against their operations were raised at the Diets of Worms (1521) and Nuernberg (1523). Included in these protests are the *terminarii,* i.e., the collectors of alms sent out by the mendicant orders.

137. *Wallbrueder,* the professional pilgrims who spent their lives in wandering from one place of pilgrimage to another and subsisted on the alms of the faithful.

reckoned that every town is laid under tribute about sixty times a year, not counting what is given to the government in taxes, imposts and assessments, what is stolen by the Roman See with its wares, and what is uselessly consumed. Thus it seems to me one of God's greatest miracles that we can continue to support ourselves.

To be sure, some think that in this way the poor would not be so well provided for and that not so many great stone houses and monasteries would be built. This I can well believe. Nor is it necessary. He who wishes to be poor should not be rich; and if he wishes to be rich, let him put his hand to the plow and seek his riches in the earth! It is enough if the poor are decently cared for, so that they do not die of hunger or of cold. It is not fitting that one man should live in idleness on another's labor, or be rich and live comfortably at the cost of another's discomfort, according to the present perverted custom; for St. Paul says, "If a man will not work, neither shall he eat." God has not decreed that any man shall live from another's goods save only the priests, who rule and preach, and these because of their spiritual labor, as Paul says in I Corinthians 9, and Christ also says to the Apostles, "Every laborer is worthy of his hire."

22. It is also to be feared that the many masses which are endowed in the foundations and monasteries are not only of little use, but greatly arouse the wrath of God. It would therefore be profitable not to endow any more, but rather to abolish many that are already endowed, since we see that they are regarded only as sacrifices and good works, though they are really sacraments, just like baptism and penance,[138] which profit only those who receive them, and no others. But now the custom has crept in that masses are said for the living and the dead, and all hopes are built

---

138. In the *Babylonian Captivity* Luther definitely excludes penance from the number of sacraments.

upon them; for this reason so many of them have been founded and the present state of affairs has come about.

My proposal is perhaps too novel and daring, especially for those who fear that through the discontinuance of these masses their trade and livelihood may be destroyed, and so I must refrain from saying more about it until we have come back to a correct understanding of what the mass is and what it is good for. These many years, alas, it has been made a trade practiced for a temporal livelihood, so that I would henceforth advise a man to become a shepherd or to seek some other trade rather than become a priest or a monk, unless he first knows well what it is to celebrate mass.

I am not speaking, however, of the old foundations and cathedrals, which were doubtless established in order that the children of the nobility (since, according to the customs of the German nation not all of them can become heirs or rulers), might be provided for in these foundations, and there be free to serve God, to study, to become scholars and to make scholars. But I am speaking of the new foundations, which have been established only for the saying of prayers and masses; for after their example, even the old foundations have been burdened with like prayers and masses, so that they are of little or no profit; though it is also of God's grace that they too come at last, as they deserve, to the dregs, i.e., to the wailing of organs and of choral singers, and to dead, cold masses, by which the incomes of the worldly endowments are gotten and spent. Such things pope, bishops, and doctors should examine and proscribe; but now it is they who are most given to them. They let everything pass, if only it brings in money; one blind man is always leading another. This is the work of avarice and of the spiritual law.

Again, no one person should be allowed any longer to hold more than one canonry or prebend. He must be content with a modest position, that someone else may also have something. This would do away with the excuses of those who say that they must hold more than one such office to "maintain a proper station." A "proper station" might be so broadly interpreted that a whole land would not be enough to maintain it! Moreover avarice and veiled distrust of God assuredly go with it, so that what is alleged to be the need of "a proper station" is often nothing else than avarice and distrust.

23. Sodalities,[139] indulgences, letters of indulgence, "butter-letters," mass-letters, dispensations, and everything else of the sort, are to be drowned and destroyed. There is nothing good in them. If the pope has the power to grant you dispensation to eat butter and to absent yourself from mass, then he ought also be able to leave this power to the priests, from whom, indeed, he has no right to take it. I speak especially of those fraternities in which indulgences, masses, and good works are portioned out. Dear friend, in your baptism you entered into a fraternity with Christ, all the angels, saints, and Christians on earth. Hold to this fraternity and live up to its demands, and you have fraternities enough. The others — let them glitter as they will — are but as counters compared with *guldens*. But if there were a fraternity which contributed money to feed the poor or to help somebody in some other way, such a one would be good, and would have its indulgence and its merit in heaven. Now, however, they have all become excuses

---

139. The sodalities ("fraternities," "confraternities"), still an important institution in the Roman Church, flourished especially in the sixteenth century. They are associations for devotional purposes. The members of the sodalities are obligated to the recitation of certain prayers and the attendance upon certain masses at stipulated times. By virtue of membership in the association each member is believed to participate in the benefits accruing from these "good works" of all the members. In the case of most of the sodalities membership entitled the member to the enjoyment of certain indulgences. In 1520 Wittenberg boasted of 20 such fraternities, Cologne of 80, Hamburg of more than 100.

for every kind of gluttony and for drunkenness as well.[140]

Above all, we should drive out of German lands the papal legates with their "faculties," [141] which they sell us for large sums of money, though that is sheer knavery. For example, in return for money they legalize unjust gains, dissolve oaths, vows and agreements, break and teach men to break the faith and fealty which they have pledged to one another; and they say the pope has the authority to do this. It is the evil spirit who bids them say this. Thus they sell us a doctrine of devils, and take money for teaching us sin and leading us to hell.

If there were no other evil wiles to prove the pope the true Antichrist, yet this one thing were enough to prove it. Hearest thou this, O pope, not most holy, but most sinful? O that God from heaven would soon destroy thy throne and sink it in the abyss of hell! Who hath given thee authority to exalt thyself above thy God, to break and to loose His commandments, and to teach Christians, especially the German nation, praised in all history for its nobility, its constancy, and fidelity, to be inconstant, perjurers, traitors, profligates, faithless? God hath commanded to keep oath and faith even with an enemy, and thou undertakest to loose this His commandment, and ordainest in thine heretical, antichristian decretals that thou hast His power. Thus through thy throat and through thy pen the wicked Satan doth lie as he hath never lied before. Thou dost force and

---

140. The excesses committed at the feast of the religious societies were often a public scandal.

141. "Faculties" were extraordinary powers, usually for the granting of indulgences and of absolution in "reserved cases." They were bestowed by the pope and could be revoked by him at any time. Sometimes they were given to local Church officials, but were usually held by the legates or commissaries sent from Rome. Complaints were made at the Diets of Worms (1520) and Nuernberg (1523) that the papal commissaries and legates interfered with the ordinary methods of ecclesiastical jurisdiction and appointment.

wrest the Scriptures to thy fancy. O Christ, my Lord, look down, let the day of Thy judgment break, and destroy the devil's nest at Rome! Here sitteth the man of whom St. Paul hath said that he shall exalt himself above Thee, sit in Thy Church and set himself up as God — the man of sin and the son of perdition! What else is the papal power than only the teaching and increasing of sin and evil, the leading of souls to damnation under Thy name and guise?

In olden times the children of Israel had to keep the oath which they had unwittingly been deceived into giving to their enemies, the Gibeonites, and King Zedekiah was miserably lost, with all his people, because he broke this oath to the king of Babylon. Even among us, a hundred years ago, that fine king of Hungary and Poland, Wladislav,[142] was slain by the Turk, with so many noble people, because he allowed himself to be deceived by the papal legate and cardinal, and broke the good and advantageous treaty which he had sworn with the Turk. The pious Emperor Sigismund had no good fortune after the Council of Constance, when he allowed the knaves to break the safe-conduct which had been given to John Huss and Jerome,[143] and all the trouble between us and the Bohemians was the consequence. Even in our own times, God help us! how much Christian blood has been shed over the oath and alliance which Pope Julius made between the Emperor

---

142. Wladislav I forced the Sultan to sue for peace in 1443. At the instigation of the papal legate, Cardinal Caesarini, who represented that the treaty had not been approved by the pope, and absolved the king from the fulfillment of its conditions, he renewed the war in 1444. At the battle of Varna, November 10, 1444, the Hungarians were decisively defeated, and Wladislav and Caesarini both killed.

143. John Huss and Jerome of Prague were convicted of heresy by the Council of Constance and burned at the stake, the former July 6, 1415, the latter May 30, 1416. Huss had come to Constance under the safe-conduct of the Emperor Sigismund. Luther is in error when he assumes that Jerome had a similar safe-conduct. In September, 1415, the Council passed a decree which asserted that "neither by natural, divine or human law was any promise to be observed to the prejudice of the catholic faith."

Maximilian and King Louis of France,[144] and afterwards broke? How could I tell all the troubles which the popes have stirred up by the devilish presumption with which they annul oaths and vows which have been made between great princes, making a jest of these things, and taking money for it. I have hopes that the judgment day is at the door; nothing can possibly be worse than the Roman See. He suppresses God's commandment, he exalts his own commandment over it; if he is not Antichrist, then let someone else tell who he can be! But more of this another time, and better.

24. It is high time that we seriously and honestly consider the case of the Bohemians,[145] and come into union with them so that the terrible slander, hatred, and envy on both sides may cease. As befits my folly, I shall be the first *Luther's* to submit an opinion on this subject, with due deference to *charac.* everyone who may understand the case better than I.

First, We must honestly confess the truth, stop justifying ourselves, and grant the Bohemians that John Huss and Jerome of Prague were burned at Constance in violation of the papal, Christian, imperial safe-conduct and oath; whereby God's commandment was sinned against and the Bohemians were given ample cause for bitterness; and although they ought to have been perfect and to have patiently endured this great injustice and disobedience of God

---

144. The League of Cambray, negotiated in 1508 for war against Venice. In 1510 Venice made terms with the pope and detached him from the alliance, and the result was war between the pope and the King of France.
145. i.e., The Hussites. After the martyrdom of Huss his followers maintained for a time a strong organization in Bohemia, and resisted with arms all attempts to force them into conformity with the Roman Church. The Council of Basel succeeded (1434) in reconciling the more moderate party among the Bohemians (the Calixtines) by allowing the administration of the cup to the laity. The more extreme party, however, refused to subscribe the *Compactata* of Basel. Though they soon ceased to be a factor in the political situation, they remained outside the Church and perpetuated the teachings of Huss in sectarian organizations. The most important of these, the so-called Bohemian Brethren, had extended into Poland and Prussia before Luther's time.

on our part, nevertheless they were not bound to approve of it and to acknowledge that it was well done. Nay, even today they should give up life and limb rather than confess that it is right to violate an imperial, papal, Christian safe-conduct, and faithlessly to act contrary to it. So then, although it is the impatience of the Bohemians which is at fault, yet the pope and his followers are still more to blame for all the trouble, error and loss of souls that have followed upon that council.

I have no desire to pass judgment at this time upon John Huss' articles or to defend his errors, though I have not yet found any errors in his writings, and I am quite prepared to believe that it was neither fair judgment nor honest condemnation which was passed by those who, in their faithless dealing, violated a Christian safe-conduct and a commandment of God. Beyond doubt they were possessed rather by the evil spirit than by the Holy Spirit. No one will doubt that the Holy Spirit does not act contrary to the commandment of God; and no one is so ignorant as not to know that the violation of faith and of a safe-conduct is contrary to the commandment of God, even though they had been promised to the devil himself, still more when the promise was made to a mere heretic. It is also quite evident that such a promise was made to John Huss and the Bohemians and was not kept, but that he was burned in spite of it. I do not wish, however, to make John Huss a saint or a martyr, as do some of the Bohemians, though I confess that injustice was done him, and that his books and doctrines were unjustly condemned; for the judgments of God are secret and terrible, and no one save God alone should undertake to reveal or utter them.

All I wish to say is this: though he were never so wicked a heretic, nevertheless he was burned unjustly and against God's commandment, and the Bohemians should not be forced to approve of such conduct, or else we shall never come into unity. Not obstinacy but the open admission of truth must make us one. It is useless to pretend, as was done at that time, that a safe-conduct given to a heretic need not be kept. That is as much as to say that God's commandments are not to be kept to the end that God's commandments may be kept. The devil made them mad and foolish, so that they did not know what they were saying or doing. God has commanded that a safe-conduct shall be kept. This commandment we should keep though the world fall. How much more, when it is only a question of freeing a heretic! We should vanquish heretics with books, not with burning; for so the ancient fathers did. If it were a science to vanquish the heretics with fire, then the hangmen would be the most learned doctors on earth; we should no longer need to study, but he who overcame another by force might burn him at the stake.

Second, The emperor and the princes should send to the Bohemians some pious and sensible bishops and scholars; but by no means a cardinal or papal legate or inquisitor, for those people are utter ignoramuses as regards things Christian; they seek not the welfare of souls, but, like all the pope's hypocrites, only their own power, profit and glory; indeed, they were the prime movers in this miserable business at Constance. The men thus sent into Bohemia should inform themselves about the faith of the Bohemians, and whether it be possible to unite all their sects. Then the pope should, for their souls' sake, lay aside his supremacy for the time being, and, according to the decree of the most Christian Council of Nicaea, allow the Bohemians to choose one of their number to be Archbishop of Prague,[146] and he should be confirmed by the bishop of Olmütz in Moravia, or the bishop of Gran in Hungary, or the bishop of Gnesen in Poland, or the bishop of Magdeburg in Germany.[147] It

do not condemn Bohemians— try to help them

146. The Archbishop of Prague was primate of the Church in Bohemia.
147. The dioceses of these bishops were contiguous to that of the Archbishop of Prague.

will be enough if he is confirmed by one or two of these, as was the custom in the time of St. Cyprian.[148] The pope has no right to oppose such an arrangement, and if he does oppose it, he becomes a wolf and a tyrant; no one should follow him and his ban should be met with a counter-ban.

If, however, it were desired, in honor of the See of St. Peter, to do this with the pope's consent, I should be satisfied, provided it does not cost the Bohemians a penny and the pope does not bind them at all nor make them subject to his tyrannies by oaths and obligations, as he does all other bishops, in despite of God and of justice. If he will not be satisfied with the honor of having his consent asked, then let them not bother any more about him and his rights, laws, and tyrannies; let the election suffice, and let the blood of all the souls which are endangered cry out against him, for no one should consent to injustice; it is enough to have offered tyranny an honor. If it cannot be otherwise, then an election and approval by the common people can even now be quite as valid as a confirmation by a tyrant; but I hope this will not be necessary. Some of the Romans or the good bishops and scholars will sometime mark and oppose papal tyranny.

I would also advise against compelling them to abolish both kinds in the sacrament,[149] since that is neither unchristian nor heretical, but they should be allowed to retain their own practice, if they wish. Yet the new bishop should be careful that no discord arise because of such a practice, but should kindly instruct them that neither practice is wrong;[150] just as it ought not to cause dissension that the clergy differ from the laity in manner of life and in dress.

---

148. Bishop of Carthage, A.D. 249-58.
149. One of the chief points of controversy between the Roman Church and the Hussites. The Roman Church administered to the laity only the bread, the Hussites used both elements.
150. Luther had not yet reached the conviction that the administration of the cup to the laity was a necessity.

In like manner if they were unwilling to receive the Roman canon law, they should not be forced to do so, but we should first make sure that they live in accordance with faith and with the Scriptures. For Christian faith and life can well exist without the intolerable laws of the pope, nay, they cannot well exist unless there be fewer of these Roman laws, or none at all. In baptism we have become free and have been made subject to God's Word only; why should any man ensnare us in his words? As St. Paul says, "Ye have become free, be not servants of men," i.e., of those who rule with man-made laws.

If I knew that the Picards[151] held no other error touching the sacrament of the altar except that they believe that the bread and wine are present in their true nature, but that the body and blood of Christ are truly present under them, then I would not condemn them, but would let them enter the obedience of the bishop of Prague. For it is not an article of faith that bread and wine are not essentially and naturally in the sacrament, but this is an opinion of St. Thomas[152] and the pope. On the other hand, it is an article of faith that in the natural bread and wine the true natural body and blood of Christ are present.[153] And so we should tolerate the opinions of both sides until they come to an agreement, because there is no danger in believing that bread is there or is not there. For we have to endure many practices and ordinances so long as they are not harmful to faith. On the other hand, if they had a different faith,[154] I would rather have them outside the Church; yet I would teach them the truth.

Whatever other errors and schisms might be discovered

Occam-ism [margin note]

---

151. The Bohemian Brethren, who are here distinguished from the Hussites.
152. St. Thomas Aquinas, the great Dominican theologian of the thirteenth century (1225-74), whose influence is still dominant in Roman theology.
153. The view of the sacramental presence adopted by William of Occam.
154. i.e., If they did not believe in the real presence of the body and blood of Christ in the Lord's Supper.

in Bohemia should be tolerated until the archbishop had been restored and had gradually brought all the people together again in one common doctrine. They will assuredly never be united by force, nor by defiance, nor by haste; it will take time and forbearance. Had not even Christ to tarry with His disciples a long while and bear with their unbelief, until they believed His resurrection? If they but had again a regular bishop and church order, without Roman tyranny, I could hope that things would soon be better.

The restoration of the temporal goods which formerly belonged to the Church should not be too strictly demanded, but since we are Christians and each is bound to help the rest, it is in our power, for the sake of unity, to give them these things and let them keep them in the sight of God and men. For Christ says, "Where two are at one with each other on earth, there am I in the midst of them." Would to God that on both sides we were working toward this unity, offering our hands to one another in brotherly humility, and not standing stubbornly on our powers or rights! Love is greater and more necessary than the papacy at Rome, for there can be papacy without love and love without papacy.

With this counsel I shall have done what I could. If the pope or his followers hinder it, they shall render an account for seeking their own things rather than the things of their neighbor, contrary to the love of God. The pope ought to give up his papacy and all his possessions and honors, if he could by that means save one soul; but now he would let the world go to destruction rather than yield a hair's-breadth of his presumptuous authority. And yet he would be the "most holy"! Here my responsibility ends.

25. The universities also need a good, thorough reformation — I must say it no matter whom it vexes — for everything which the papacy has instituted and ordered is

directed only towards the increasing of sin and error. What else are the universities, if their present condition remains unchanged, than as the book of Maccabees says, "Places for training youth in Greek glory," in which loose living prevails, the Holy Scriptures and the Christian faith are little taught, and the blind, heathen master Aristotle[155] rules alone, even more than Christ? In this regard my advice would be that Aristotle's *Physics, Metaphysics, On the Soul, Ethics,* which have hitherto been thought his best books, should be altogether discarded, together with all the rest of his books which boast of treating the things of nature, although nothing can be learned from them either of the things of nature or the things of the Spirit. Moreover no one has so far understood his meaning, and many souls have been burdened with profitless labor and study, at the cost of much precious time. I venture to say that any potter has more knowledge of nature than is written in these books. It grieves me to the heart that this damned, conceited, rascally heathen has with his false words deluded and made fools of so many of the best Christians. God has sent him as a plague upon us for our sins.

Why, this wretched man, in his best book, *On the Soul,* teaches that the soul dies with the body, although many have tried with vain words to save his reputation. As though we had not the Holy Scriptures, in which we are abundantly instructed about all things, and of them Aristotle had not the faintest inkling! And yet this dead heathen has conquered and obstructed and almost suppressed the books of the living God, so that when I think of this miserable business I can believe nothing else than that the evil spirit has introduced the study of Aristotle.

---

155. The philosophy of Aristotle dominated the medieval universities. It not only provided the forms in which theological and religious truth came to expression, but it was the basis of all scientific study in every department. The man who did not know Aristotle was an ignoramus.

Again, his book on *Ethics* is the worst of all books. It flatly opposes divine grace and all Christian virtues, and yet it is considered one of his best works. Away with such books! Keep them away from all Christians! Let no one accuse me of exaggeration, or of condemning what I do not understand! My dear friend, I know well whereof I speak. I know my Aristotle as well as you or the likes of you. I have lectured on him[156] and heard lectures on him, and I understand him better than do St. Thomas or Scotus.[157] This I can say without pride, and if necessary I can prove it. I care not that so many great minds have wearied themselves over him for so many hundred years. Such objections do not disturb me as once they did; for it is plain as day that other errors have remained for even more centuries in the world and in the universities.

I should be glad to see Aristotle's books on *Logic, Rhetoric,* and *Poetics* retained or used in an abridged form; as textbooks for the profitable training of young people in speaking and preaching. But the commentaries and notes should be abolished, and as Cicero's *Rhetoric* is read without commentaries and notes, so Aristotle's *Logic* should be read as it is, without such a mass of comments. But now neither speaking nor preaching is learned from it, and it has become nothing but a disputing and a weariness to the flesh.

Besides this there are the languages—Latin, Greek, and Hebrew—the mathematical disciplines and history. But all this I give over to the specialists, and, indeed, the reform would come of itself, if we were only seriously bent upon it. In truth, much depends upon it; for it is here that the Christian youth and the best of our people, with whom the future of Christendom lies, are to be educated and

---

156. Or, "I have read him."
157 Duns Scotus, died 1308. In the fifteen and sixteenth centuries he was regarded as the rival of Thomas Acquinas for first place among the theological teachers of the Church.

trained. Therefore I consider that there is no work more worthy of pope or emperor than a thorough reformation of the universities, and there is nothing worse or more worthy of the devil than unreformed universities.

The medical men I leave to reform their own faculties; the jurists and theologians I take as my share, and I say, in the first place, that it were well if the canon law, from the first letter to the last, and especially the decretals, were utterly blotted out. The Bible contains more than enough directions for all our living, and so the study of the canon law only stands in the way of the study of the Holy Scriptures, moreover, it smacks for the most part of mere avarice and pride. Even though there were much in it that is good, it might as well be destroyed, for the pope has taken the whole canon law captive and imprisoned it in the "chamber of his heart," so that the study of it is henceforth a waste of time and a farce. At present the canon law is not what is in the books, but what is in the sweet will of the pope and his flatterers. Your cause may be thoroughly established in the canon law; still the pope has his *scrinium pectoris*,[158] and all law and the whole world must be guided by that. Now it is ofttimes a knave, and even the devil himself, who rules this *scrinium,* and they boast that it is ruled by the Holy Spirit! Thus they deal with Christ's unfortunate people. They give them many laws and themselves keep none of them, but others they compel either to keep them or else to buy release.

Since, then, the pope and his followers have suspended the whole canon law, and since they pay no heed to it, but regard their own wanton will as a law exalting them above all the world, we should follow their example and for our part also reject these books. Why should we waste our time studying them? We could never discover the whole

---

158. i.e., "The chamber of his heart." Boniface VIII (1294-1303) had decreed, "the Roman pontiff has all laws in the chamber of his heart."

arbitrary will of the pope, which has now become the canon law. The canon law has arisen in the devil's name, let it fall in the name of God, and let there be no more *doctores decretorum*[159] in the world, but only *doctores scrinii papalis*, that is, "hypocrites of the pope"! It is said that there is no better temporal rule anywhere than among the Turks, who have neither spiritual nor temporal law, but only their Koran; and we must confess that there is no more shameful rule than among us, with our spiritual and temporal law, so that there is no estate which lives according to the light of nature, still less according to Holy Scripture.

The temporal law—God help us! what a wilderness it has become![160] Though it is much better, wiser and more rational than the "spiritual law" which has nothing good about it except the name, still there is far too much of it. Surely the Holy Scriptures and good rulers would be law enough; as St. Paul says in 1 Corinthians 6, "Is there no one among you can judge his neighbor's cause, that ye must go to law before heathen courts?" It seems just to me that territorial laws and territorial customs should take precedence of the general imperial laws, and the imperial laws be used only in case of necessity. Would to God that as every land has its own peculiar character, so it were ruled by its own brief laws, as the lands were ruled before these imperial laws were invented, and many lands are still

---

159. *Doctores decretorum*, "Doctor of Decrees," an academic degree occasionally given to professors of Canon Law; *doctor scrinii papalis*, "Doctor of the Papal Heart."

160. The introduction of Roman law into Germany, as the accepted law of the empire, had begun in the twelfth century. With the decay of the feudal system and the increasing desire of the rulers to provide their government with some effective legal system, its application became more widespread, until by the end of the fifteenth century it was the accepted system of the empire. The attempt to apply this ancient law to conditions utterly different from those of the time when it was formulated, and the continual conflict between the Roman law, the feudal customs and the remnants of Germanic legal ideas, naturally gave rise to a state of affairs which Luther could justly speak of as "a wilderness."

ruled without them! These diffuse and far-fetched laws are only a burden to the people, and hinder causes more than they help them. I hope, however, that others have given this matter more thought and attention than I am able to do.

My friends the theologians have spared themselves pains and labor; they leave the Bible in peace and read the Sentences. I should think that the Sentences[161] ought to be the first study of young students in theology and the Bible ought to be the study for the doctors. But now it is turned around; the Bible comes first, and is put aside when the bachelor's degree is reached, and the Sentences come last. They are attached forever to the doctorate, and that with such a solemn obligation that a man who is not a priest may indeed read the Bible, but the Sentences a priest must read. A married man, I observe, could be a Doctor of the Bible, but under no circumstances a Doctor of the Sentences. What good fortune can we expect if we act so perversely and in this way put the Bible, the holy Word of God, so far to the rear? Moreover the pope commands, with many severe words, that his laws are to be read and used in the schools and the courts, but little is said of the Gospel. Thus it is the custom that in the schools and the courts the Gospel lies idle in the dust under the bench, to the end that the pope's harmful laws may rule alone.

If we are called by the title of teachers[162] of Holy Scripture, then we ought to be compelled, in accordance with our name, to teach the Holy Scriptures and nothing else, although even this title is too proud and boastful and no one ought to be proclaimed and crowned teacher of Holy Scripture. Yet it might be suffered, if the work justified the name; but now, under the despotism of the Sentences, we find among the theologians more of heathen and human

---

161. "Sentences" was the title of the textbooks in theology. Theological instruction was largely by way of comment on the most famous book of Sentences, that of Peter Lombard.
162. i.e., Doctors.

opinion than of the holy and certain doctrine of Scripture. What, then, are we to do? I know of no other way than humbly to pray God to give us Doctors of Theology. Pope, emperor, and universities may make Doctors of Arts, of Medicine, of Laws, of the Sentences; but be assured that no one will make a Doctor of Holy Scripture, save only the Holy Ghost from heaven, as Christ says in John 6, "They must all be taught of God Himself." Now the Holy Ghost does not concern Himself about red or brown birettas[163] or other decorations, nor does He ask whether one is old or young, layman or priest, monk or secular, virgin or married; nay He spake of old by an ass, against the prophet who rode upon it. Would God that we were worthy to have such doctors given us, whether they were laymen or priests, married or virgin. True, they now try to force the Holy Ghost into pope, bishops and doctors, although there is no sign or indication whatever that He is in them.

The number of theological books must also be lessened, and a selection made of the best of them. For it is not many books or much reading that makes men learned; but it is good things, however little of them, often read, that make men learned in the Scriptures and make them godly too. Indeed the writings of all the holy fathers should be read only for a time, in order that through them we may be led to the Holy Scriptures. As it is, however, we read them only to be absorbed in them and never come to the Scriptures. We are like men who study the sign-posts and never travel the road. The dear fathers wished, by their writings, to lead us to the Scriptures, but we so use them as to be led away from the Scriptures, though the Scriptures alone are our vineyard in which we ought all to work and toil.

Above all, the foremost and most general subject of study, both in the higher and the lower schools, should be the Holy Scriptures, and for the young boys the Gospel. And

---

163. The headdress of the doctors.

would to God that every town had a girls' school also, in which the girls were taught the Gospel for an hour each day in either German or Latin. Indeed the schools, monasteries, and nunneries began long ago with that end in view, and it was a praiseworthy and Christian purpose, as we learn from the story of St. Agnes and other of the saints. That was the time of holy virgins and martyrs, and then it was well with Christendom; but now they[164] have come to nothing but praying and singing. Ought not every Christian at his ninth or tenth year to know the entire holy Gospel from which he derives his name[165] and his life? A spinner or a seamstress teaches her daughter the trade in her early years; but now even the great, learned prelates and bishops themselves do not know the Gospel.

O how unjustly we deal with these poor young people who are committed to us for direction and instruction. We must give a terrible accounting for our neglect to set the Word of God before them. They fare as Jeremiah says in Lamentations 2: "Mine eyes are grown weary with weeping, my bowels are terrified, my liver is poured out upon the ground, because of the destruction of the daughter of my people, for the youth and the children perish in all the streets of the whole city; they said to their mothers, Where is bread and wine? and they swooned as the wounded in the streets of the city and gave up the ghost in their mothers' bosom." This pitiful evil we do not see—how even now the young folk in the midst of Christendom languish and perish miserably for want of the Gospel, in which we ought to be giving them constant instruction and training.

Moreover, if the universities were diligent in the study of Holy Scripture, we should not send everybody there, as we do when all we ask is numbers, and everyone wishes to have a doctor's degree; but we should send only the best

164. i.e., The monasteries and nunneries.
165. i.e., The name of Christian.

qualified students, who have previously been well trained in the lower schools. A prince or city council ought to see to this, and permit only the well qualified to be sent. But where the Holy Scriptures do not rule, there I advise no one to send his son. Everyone not unceasingly busy with the Word of God must become corrupt; that is why the people who are in the universities and who are trained there are the kind of people they are. For this no one is to blame but the pope, the bishops and the prelates, who are charged with the training of the youth. For the universities ought to turn out only men who are experts in the Holy Scriptures, who can become bishops and priests, leaders in the fight against heretics, the devil and all the world. But where do you find this true? I greatly fear that the universities are wide gates of hell, if they do not diligently teach the Holy Scriptures and impress them on the youth.

26. [166][I know full well that the Roman crowd will make pretensions and great boasts about how the pope took the Holy Roman Empire from the Greek Emperor[167] and bestowed it on the Germans, for which honor and benevolence he is said to have justly deserved and obtained from the Germans submission and thanks and all good things. For this reason they will, perhaps, undertake to throw to the winds all attempts to reform them, and will not allow us to think about anything but the bestowal of the Roman Empire. For this cause they have heretofore persecuted and oppressed many a worthy emperor so arbitrarily and

---

166. This section did not appear in the first edition.
167. Charles the Great, King of the Franks, was crowned Roman Emperor by Pope Leo III in the year A.D. 800. He was a German, but regarded himself successor to the line of emperors who had ruled at Rome. The fiction was fostered by the popes, and the German kings, after receiving the papal coronation, were called Roman Emperors. From this came the name of the German Empire of the Middle Ages, "the Holy Roman Empire of the German Nation." The popes of the later Middle Ages claimed that the bestowal of the imperial dignity lay in the power of the pope, and Pope Clement V (1313) even claimed that in the event of a vacancy the pope was the possessor of the imperial power.

arrogantly that it is pity to tell of it, and with the same adroitness they have made themselves overlords of all the temporal powers and authorities, contrary to the Holy Gospel. Of this too I must therefore speak.

There is no doubt that the true Roman Empire, which the writings of the prophets foretold in Numbers 24 and in Daniel, has long since been overthrown and brought to an end, as Balaam clearly prophesied in Numbers 24, when he said: "The Romans shall come and overthrow the Jews; and afterward they also shall be destroyed." That was brought to pass by the Goths,[168] but especially when the Turkish Empire arose almost a thousand years ago;[169] then in time Asia and Africa fell away, and finally Venice arose, and there remained to Rome nothing of its former power.

Now when the pope could not subdue to his arrogant will the Greeks and the emperor at Constantinople, who was hereditary Roman emperor,he bethought himself of this device, viz., to rob him of his empire and his title and turn it over to the Germans, who were at that time warlike and of good repute, so as to bring the power of the Roman Empire under his control and give it away as a fief. So too it turned out. It was taken away from the emperor at Constantinople and its name and title were given to us Germans. Thereby we became the servants of the pope, and there is now a second Roman Empire, which the pope has built upon the Germans; for the other, which was first, has long since fallen, as I have said.

So then the Roman See has its will. It has taken possession of Rome, driven out the German emperor, and bound him with oaths not to dwell at Rome. He is to be Roman emperor, and yet he is not to have possession of Rome, and besides he is at all times to be dependent upon the caprice

---

168. The city of Rome was sacked by the Visigoths in 410.
169. Luther is characteristically careless about his chronology. By the "Turkish Empire" he means the Mohammedan power.

of the pope and his followers, so that we have the name and they have the land and cities. They have always abused our simplicity to serve their own arrogance and tyranny, and they call us mad Germans, who let ourselves be made apes and fools at their bidding.

Ah well! For God the Lord it is a small thing to toss empires and principalities to and fro! He is so generous with them that once in a while He gives a kingdom to a knave and takes it from a good man, sometimes by the treachery of wicked, faithless men and sometimes by heredity, as we read of the kingdoms of Persia and Greece, and of almost all kingdoms; and Daniel 2 and 4 says: "He who ruleth over all things dwelleth in heaven, and it is he alone who changeth kingdoms, tosseth them to and fro, and maketh them." Since, therefore, no one can think it a great thing to have a kingdom given him, especially if he is a Christian, we Germans too cannot be puffed up because a new Roman Empire bestowed on us; for in His eyes it is a trifling gift, which He often gives to the most unworthy, as Daniel 4 says: "All who dwell upon the earth are in his eyes as nothing, and he has power in all the kingdoms of men, to give them to whomsoever he will."

But although the pope unjustly and by violence robbed the true emperor of his Roman Empire, or of its name, and gave it to us Germans, it is certain, nevertheless, that in this matter God has used the pope's wickedness to give such an empire to the German nation, and after the fall of the first Roman Empire, to set up another, which still exists. And although we gave no occasion to this wickedness of the popes, and did not understand their false aims and purposes, nevertheless, through this papal trickery and roguery, we have already paid too dearly for our empire, with incalculable bloodshed, with the suppression of our liberty, with the risk and robbery of all our goods, especially the goods of the churches and canonries, and with the suffering of unspeakable deception and insult. We have the name of the empire, but the pope has our wealth, honor, body, life, soul, and all that is ours. So we Germans are to be cheated in the trade. What the popes sought was to be emperors, and since they could not manage that, they at least succeeded in setting themselves over the emperors.

Because then, the empire has been given us without our fault, by the providence of God and the plotting of evil men, I would not advise that we give it up, but rather that we rule it wisely and in the fear of God, so long as it shall please Him. For, as has been said, it matters not to Him where an empire comes from; it is His will that it shall be ruled. Though the popes took it dishonestly from others, nevertheless we did not get it dishonestly. It is given us by the will of God through evil-minded men; and we have more regard for God's will than for the treacherous purpose of the popes, who, in bestowing it, wished to be emperors themselves, and more than emperors, and only to fool and mock us with the name. The king of Babylon also seized his empire by robbery and force; yet it was God's will that it should be ruled by the holy princes, Daniel, Hananiah, Azariah, and Mishael; much more then is it His will that this empire be ruled by the Christian princes of Germany, regardless whether the pope stole it, or got it by robbery, or made it anew. It is all God's ordering, which came to pass before we knew of it.

Therefore the pope and his followers may not boast that they have done a great favor to the German nation by the bestowal of this Roman Empire. First, because they did not mean it for our good, but were rather taking advantage of our simplicity in order to strengthen themselves in their proud designs against the Roman emperor at Constantinople, from whom the pope godlessly and lawlessly took this empire, a thing which he had no right to do. Second, because the pope's intention was not to give us the empire, but to get it for himself, that he might bring all our power, our freedom, wealth, body and soul into subjection to himself and use us (if God had not prevented) to subdue all the world. He clearly says so himself in his decretal, and he has attempted it, by many evil wiles, with a number of the German emperors. How beautifully we Germans have been taught our German! When we thought to be lords, we became slaves of the most deceitful tyrants, we have the name, title, and insignia of the empire, but the pope has its treasures, its authority, its law, and its liberty. So the pope gobbles the kernel, and we play with the empty hulls.

Now may God, who by the wiles of tyrants has tossed this empire into our lap, and charged us with the ruling of it, help us to live up to the name, title and insignia, to rescue our liberty, and to show the Romans, for once, what it is that we, through them, have received from God! They boast that they have bestowed on us an empire. So be it, then! If it is true, then let the pope give us Rome and everything else which he has got from the empire; let him free our land from his intolerable taxing and robbing, and give us back our liberty, authority, wealth, honor, body and soul; let the empire be what an empire should be, and let his words and pretensions be fulfilled!

If he will not do that, then why all this shamming, these false and lying words and juggler's tricks? Is he not satisfied with having so rudely led this noble nation by the nose these many hundred years without ceasing? It does not follow that the pope must be above an emperor because he makes or crowns him. The prophet Samuel at God's command anointed and crowned Kings Saul and David, and yet he was their subject; and the prophet Nathan anointed King Solomon, but was not set over him on that account, Elisha too had one of his servants anoint Jehu king of Israel, and yet they remained obedient and subject to him. Except in the case of the pope, it has never happened in all the world's history that he who consecrated or crowned the king was over the king. He lets himself be crowned pope by three cardinals, who are under him, and he is nevertheless their superior. Why then should he, contrary to the example which he himself sets, and contrary to the custom and teaching of all the world and of the Scriptures, exalt himself above temporal authorities, or the empire, simply because he crowns or consecrates the emperor? It is enough that he should be the emperor's superior in divine things, to wit, in preaching, teaching and administering the sacraments, in which things, indeed, any bishop or priest is over every other man, as St. Ambrose in his See was over the emperor Theodosius, and the prophet Nathan over David, and Samuel over Saul. Therefore, let the German emperor be really and truly emperor, and let not his authority or his sword be put down by this blind pretension of papal hypocrites, as though they were to be excepted from his dominion and themselves direct the temporal sword in all things.]

27. Enough has now been said about the failings of the clergy, though more of them can and will be found if these are properly considered. We would say something too about the failings of the temporal estate.

1. There is great need of a general law and decree of the German nation against the extravagance and excess in dress, by which so many nobles and rich men are impoverished. God has given to us, as to other lands, enough wool, hair, flax, and everything else which properly serves for the seemly and honorable dress of every rank, so that we do not need to spend and waste such enormous sums for silk and velvet and golden ornaments and other foreign wares. I believe that even if the pope had not robbed us Germans with his intolerable exactions, we should still have our hands more than full with these domestic robbers, the silk and velvet merchants. In the matter of clothes, as we see, everybody wants to be equal to everybody else, and pride

and envy are aroused and increased among us, as we deserve. All this and much more misery would be avoided if our curiosity would only let us be thankful, and be satisfied with the goods which God has given us.

2. In like manner it is also necessary to restrict the spice traffic[170] which is another of the great ships in which money is carried out of German lands. There grows among us, by God's grace, more to eat and drink than in any other land, and just as choice and good. Perhaps the proposals that I make may seem foolish and impossible and give the impression that I want to suppress the greatest of all trades, that of commerce; but I am doing what I can. If reforms are not generally introduced, then let everyone who is willing reform himself. I do not see that many good customs have ever come to a land through commerce, and in ancient times God made His people of Israel dwell away from the sea on this account, and did not let them engage much in commerce.

3. But the greatest misfortune of the German nation is certainly the traffic in annuities.[171] If that did not exist many a man would have to leave unbought his silks, velvets, golden ornaments, spices, and ornaments of every sort. It has not existed much over a hundred years, and has already brought almost all princes, cities, endowed institutions, nobles, and their heirs to poverty, misery, and ruin; if it shall continue for another hundred years Germany cannot possibly have a penny left and we shall certainly have to devour one another. The devil invented the practice, and the pope, by confirming it,[172] has injured the whole world.

---

170. Spices were one of the chief articles of foreign commerce in the sixteenth century. The discovery of the cape route to India had given the Portuguese a practical monopoly of this trade.

171. The *Zinskauf* or *Rentenkauf* was a means for evading the prohibition of usury. The buyer purchased an annuity, but the purchase price was not regarded as a loan, for it could not be recalled, and the annual payments could not therefore be called interest.

172. The practice was legalized by the Lateran Council, 1512.

Therefore I ask and pray that everyone open his eyes to see the ruin of himself, his children and his heirs, which not only stands before the door, but already haunts the house, and that emperor, princes, lords, and cities do their part that this trade be condemned as speedily as possible, and henceforth prevented, regardless whether or not the pope, with all his law and unlaw, is opposed to it, and whether or not benefices or church foundations are based upon it. It is better that there should be in a city one living based on an honest freehold or revenue than a hundred based on an annuity; indeed a living based on an annuity is worse and more grievous than twenty based on freeholds. In truth this traffic in rents must be a sign and symbol that the world, for its grievous sins, has been sold to the devil, so that both temporal and spiritual possessions must fail us, and yet we do not notice it at all.

Here, too, we must put a bit in the mouth of the Fuggers and similar corporations.[173] How is it possible that in the lifetime of a single man such great possessions, worthy of a king, can be piled up, and yet everything be done legally and according to God's will?[174] I am not a mathematician, but I do not understand how a man with a hundred gulden can make a profit of twenty gulden in one year, nay, how with one gulden he can make another; and that, too, by an-

173. The sixteenth century was the heyday of the great trading companies, among which the Fuggers of Augsburg easily took first place. The effort of these companies was directed toward securing monopolies in the staple articles of commerce, and their ability to finance large enterprises made it possible for them to gain practical control of the home markets. The sharp rise in the cost of living which took place in the first half of the sixteenth century was laid at their door. The Diet of Cologne (1512) had passed a stringent law against monopolies, which had, however, failed to suppress them.

174. The profits of the trading companies were enormous. The 9 per cent annually of the Welser pales into insignificance beside the 1634 per cent by which the fortune of the Fuggers grew in twenty-one years. In 1511 a certain Bartholomew Rem invested 900 gulden in the Hochstetter company of Augsburg; by 1517 he claimed 33,000 gulden profit. The company was willing to settle at 26,000, and the resulting litigation caused the figures to become public.

other way than agriculture or cattle-raising, in which increase of wealth depends not on human wits, but on God's blessing, I commend this to the men of affairs. I am a theologian, and find nothing to blame in it except its evil and offending appearance, of which St. Paul says, "Avoid every appearance or show of evil." This I know well, that it would be much more pleasing to God if we increased agriculture and diminished commerce, and that they do much better who, according to the Scriptures, till the soil and seek their living from it, as was said to us and to all men in Adam, "Accursed be the earth when thou laborest therein, it shall bear thee thistles and thorns, and in the sweat of thy face shalt thou eat thy bread." There is still much land lying untilled.

4. Next comes the abuse of eating and drinking which gives us Germans a bad reputation in foreign lands, as though it were our special vice. Preaching cannot stop it; it has become too common, and has got too firmly the upper hand. The waste of money which it causes would be a small thing, were it not followed by other sins—murder, adultery, stealing, irreverence, and all the vices. The temporal sword can do something to prevent it; or else it will be as Christ says: "The last day shall come like a secret snare, when they shall be eating and drinking, marrying and wooing, building and planting, buying and selling." It is so much like that now that I verily believe the judgment day is at the door; though men are thinking least of all about it.

5. Finally, is it not a pitiful thing that we Christians should maintain among us open and common houses of prostitution, though all of us are baptized unto chastity? I know very well what some say to this, to wit, that it is not the custom of any one people, that it is hard to break up, that it is better that there should be such houses than that married women, or maidens, or those of more honorable estate should be outraged. But should not the temporal, Christian government consider that in this heathen way the

evil is not to be controlled? If the people of Israel could exist without such an abomination, why could not Christian people do as much? Nay, how do many cities, towns, and villages exist without such houses? Why should not great cities also exist without them?

In this, and in the other matters above mentioned, I have tried to point out how many good works the temporal government could do, and what should be the duty of every government, to the end that everyone may learn what an awful responsibility it is to rule, and to have high station. What good would it do that an overlord were in his own life as holy as St. Peter, if he have not the purpose diligently to help his subjects in these matters? His very authority will condemn him! For it is the duty of the authorities to seek the highest good of their subjects. But if the authorities were to consider how the young people might be brought together in marriage, the hope of entering the married state would greatly help everyone to endure and to resist temptation.

But now every man is drawn to the priesthood or the monastic life, and among them, I fear, there is not one in a hundred who has any other reason than that he seeks a living, and doubts that he will ever be able to support himself in the estate of matrimony. Therefore they live wildly enough beforehand, and wish, as they say, to "wear out their lust," but rather wear it in, as experience shows. I find the proverb true, "Despair makes most of the monks and priests"; and so things are as we see them.

My faithful counsel is that, in order to avoid many sins which have become very common, neither boy nor maid should take the vow of chastity, or of the "spiritual life," before the age of thirty years. It is, as St. Paul says, a peculiar gift. Therefore let him whom God does not constrain put off becoming a cleric and taking the vows. Nay, I will go farther and say, If you trust God so little that you are not willing to support yourself as a married man, and wish to become a cleric only because of this distrust, then for the sake of your own soul, I beg of you not to become a cleric, but rather a farmer, or whatever else you please. For if to obtain your temporal support you must have one measure of trust in God, you must have ten measures of trust to continue in the life of a cleric. If you do not trust God to support you in the world, how will you trust him to support you in the Church? Alas, unbelief and distrust spoil everything and lead us into all misery, as we see in every estate of life!

Much could be said of this miserable condition. The young people have no one to care for them. They all do as they please, and the government is of as much use to them as if it did not exist; and yet this should be the chief concern of pope, bishops, lords and councils. They wish to rule far and wide, and yet to help no one. O, what a rare bird will a lord and ruler be in heaven just on this account, even though he build a hundred churches for God and raise up all the dead!

[Let this suffice for this time! Of what the temporal powers and the nobility ought to do, I think I have said enough in the little book, *On Good Works*. There is room for improvement in their lives and in their rule, and yet the abuses of the temporal power are not to be compared with those of the spiritual power, as I have there shown.][175]

I think too that I have pitched my song in a high key, have made many propositions which will be thought impossible, and have attacked many things too sharply. But what am I to do? I am in duty bound to speak. If I were able, these are the things I should wish to do. I prefer the wrath of the world to the wrath of God; they can do no more than take my life. Many times heretofore I have made overtures of peace to my opponents; but as I now

---

175. These sentences did not appear in the first edition.

see, God has through them compelled me to open my mouth wider and wider and give them enough to say, bark, shout, and write, since they have nothing else to do. Ah well, I know another little song about Rome and about them![176] If their ears itch for it I will sing them that song too, and pitch the notes to the top of the scale. Understandest thou, dear Rome, what I mean?

I have many times offered my writings for investigation and judgment, but it has been of no use. To be sure, I know that if my cause is just, it must be condemned on earth, and approved only by Christ in heaven; for all the Scriptures show that the cause of Christians and of Christendom must be judged by God alone. Such a cause has never yet been approved by men on earth, but the opposition has always been too great and strong. It is my greatest care and fear that my cause may remain uncondemned, by which I should know for certain that it was not yet pleasing to God.

Therefore let them boldly go to work—pope, bishop, priest, monk, and scholar! They are the right people to persecute the truth, as they have ever done.

God give us all a Christian mind, and especially to the Christian nobility of the German nation a right spiritual courage to do the best that can be done for the poor Church. Amen.

---

176. This "little song" is the *Prelude on the Babylonian Captivity of the Church.*

THE

BABYLONIAN CAPTIVITY

OF THE CHURCH

1520

*Translated by A. T. W. Steinhäuser and
revised by Frederick C. Ahrens and
Abdel Ross Wentz*

Introduction

The primary importance of this treatise for the present-day reader of Luther lies in its courageous interpretation of the sacraments. But it is important also for its place in Luther's progressive assault upon the total position of the Romans. In *An Open Letter to the Christian Nobility*[1] Luther demolished the three walls behind which Rome sat entrenched in her spiritual-temporal power. Now in *The Babylonian Captivity of the Church* he enters and takes her central stronghold and sanctuary—the sacramental system by which she accompanied and controlled her members from the cradle to the grave. Only then could he set forth, in language of almost lyrical rapture, *The Freedom of a Christian.*[2]

Luther was thinking of such a treatise long before it was written. In the first of the reformatory treatises of 1520, as they have been called, we read at the close: "I know another little song about Rome, and if their ears itch to hear it, I will sing it for them and I will pitch it in a high key. Dost thou take my meaning, beloved Rome?"[3] In this book on the "Babylonian Captivity," later that year, he fulfills his promise and the "little song" becomes a veritable "prelude."

Luther intends his book to be only an introduction to his major engagement on this theme of the sacraments. He expects that after this "Prelude" the Romans will gird themselves for battle and attack him in force, but he intends to

1. *PE* 2, 55-164.
2. *LW* 31, 327-377.
3. *PE* 2, 164.

keep one step ahead of them and lead them on. In fact, he fully expects a papal bull against him threatening him with the most dire consequences if he does not recant, and in the closing paragraphs of this treatise he explains in bitter irony that he intends this document to be the beginning or prelude of his "recantation." If he is to recant or rechant or unsing what he has been singing hitherto, he will not really "change his tune," but will only "pitch it in a higher key."

This book is therefore only a skirmish preliminary to the main engagement, or, as a musician might say, a mere prelude introducing the main theme of the suite. It is a promise of more complete and more positive treatises on the sacraments in the future. And this promise was fulfilled. For that reason this "Prelude" is presented first among the treatises in this volume on the sacraments.

The theme that is presented by the Prelude Luther calls "The Babylonian Captivity of the Church." The reference is clear from the contents of the document: just as the Jews were carried away from Jerusalem into captivity under the tyranny of the Babylonian Empire, so in Europe the Christians have been carried away from the Scriptures and made subject to the tyranny of the papacy. This tyranny has been exercised by the misuse of the sacraments, chiefly the sacrament of the Lord's Supper.

After Luther had promised in his first reformatory treatise of 1520 that he would "sing another little song about Rome if their ears itch to hear it," he found that some ears were itching to hear the new song. This was brought home to him especially by two writings. One of these appeared in the summer of 1520; the other had been published the previous autumn but had not reached Wittenberg until some months later. The first came from the pen of Augustinus Alveld, that "celebrated Romanist of Leipzig," against whom Luther had fulminated in *The Papacy at Rome,* promising further disclosures if "Alveld came again."

He did come again, this time with a *Tractatus de communione sub utraque specie* [*Treatise Concerning Communion in Both Kinds*]. It was dedicated June 23, 1520. "The Leipzig ass has set up a fresh braying against me, full of blasphemies"; thus Luther describes it in a letter to Spalatin, July 22, 1520.

The other work was the anonymous tract of a "certain Italian friar of Cremona," who has only recently been identified as Isidoro Isolani, a Dominican hailing from Milan, who taught theology in various Italian cities, wrote a number of controversial works, and died in 1528. The title of the tract is *Revocatio Martini Lutheri Augustiniani ad sanctam sedem* [*The Recantation of the Augustinian Martin Luther before the Holy See*]. Its date is November 22, 1519, at Cremona. It begins and ends with a letter, and one paragraph from each of these is translated in Preserved Smith, *Luther's Correspondence* (Philadelphia, 1913), Vol. I, No. 199.

These two writings may be regarded as the immediate occasion for the writing of *The Babylonian Captivity*, but the *Captivity* is in no sense a direct reply to either of them. "I will not reply to Alveld," Luther writes on August 5 to Spalatin, "but he will be the occasion of my publishing something by which the vipers will be more irritated than ever." [4] Indeed, he had promised some such work more than half a year before, in a letter to Spalatin of December 18, 1519: "There is no reason why you or anyone else should expect from me a treatise on the sacraments [besides baptism, the Lord's Supper, and penance] until I am taught by what text I can prove that they are sacraments. I regard none of the others as a sacrament, for there is no sacrament except where there is a direct divine promise, exercising our faith. We can have no intercourse with God except by the word of Him promising, and by the faith of man receiv-

---

4. Smith, *op. cit.*, No. 283.

ing. At another time you shall hear more about their fables of the seven sacraments."[5]

Thus the Prelude grows under his hand and assumes the form of an elaborate examination of the whole sacramental system of the church. He makes short work of his two opponents, and after a few pages of delicious irony, of which Erasmus was suspected in some quarters of being the author, he turns his back on them and addresses himself to a positive and constructive treatment of the larger theme, lenient toward all nonessentials, but inexorable toward everything truly essential, that is, scriptural.

Luther discusses each one of the seven sacraments of the Roman church, but devotes nearly half of the book to the Lord's Supper and Baptism. The worst tyranny of the papacy he finds in the sacrament of the Lord's Supper and to this he gives his chief attention. The first captivity is the withholding of the cup from the laity; the second is found in the doctrine of transubstantiation; and the third is the sacrifice of the mass. The Sacrament of the Altar is not a magical device by which the priest brings God down from heaven but God's own revelation of himself where he is. In his discussion of Baptism Luther repudiates monasticism and insists that no vow should ever be taken beyond the baptismal vow.

The other five ceremonies he rejects as sacraments. Penance he would retain in purified form, but not as a sacrament, because it lacks a visible sign appointed by God; however, he strongly rejects priestly absolution. Everywhere he repudiates the authority of the church to institute new means of grace or new promises of mercy, and everywhere he bases upon the Holy Scriptures his general conception of a sacrament and his understanding of the individual sacraments.

---

5. *Ibid.*, No. 206.

Passage after passage, often whole pages, from the *Explanations of the Ninety-five Theses*,[6] *A Treatise on Baptism*,[7] *A Discussion of Confession*,[8] *A Treatise on the New Testament that is the Holy Mass*[9] and *A Treatise Concerning the Blessed Sacrament*[10] are transferred bodily to this new and definitive work, and find in it the goal toward which they had been unconsciously tending.

The *Captivity* was written in Latin because it is a theological treatise and was not intended for the rank and file of the Christian congregation. In this respect the treatise stands in contrast with the other five treatises in this volume on the sacraments, all of which were written in German and were intended for the individual Christian, whether layman or theologian.

All in all, the Prelude was a deadly dagger aimed at the very heart of sacramentalism and clericalism and monasticism. It was the most devastating assault Luther had yet undertaken against Roman teaching and practice. It marked Luther's final and irrevocable break with the church of Rome. There is special significance in the fact that in the same letter to Spalatin (October 3) in which he mentions the arrival of Eck in Leipzig armed with the papal bull, he also announces the publication of his book on the captivity of the church for the following Saturday (October 6).[11]

Both sides of the controversy took the book very seriously. In ducal Saxony it was rigorously suppressed. Before the imperial council at Worms, the middle of December, 1520, and again at the imperial diet the following February, the papal nuncio Aleander bitterly assailed the *Captivity* as completely blasphemous because it questioned the authority

---

6. *LW* 31, 83-252.
7. *PE* 1, 56-71.
8. *Ibid.*, 81-101.
9. *Ibid.*, 294-326.
10. *PE* 2, 9-31.
11. Smith, *op. cit.*, No. 303.

of the pope. John Glapion, the father confessor of Charles V, declared that it shocked him from head to foot. Erasmus now saw that his efforts to restore peace in the church would be futile: "The breach is irreparable." The University of Paris promptly condemned the document. One of Luther's most bitter enemies, Thomas Murner, translated it into German, confident that it would expose Luther to the rank and file of the people as a radical heretic and dangerous foe of the church. Of special significance was the action of Henry VIII of England. Not content with ordering Luther's writings to be publicly burned in London, he also turned theologian and wrote a book of 78 quarto pages dedicated to the pope, denouncing Luther and defending the Catholic positions on the sacraments. Henry's book so pleased the pope that he issued a special bull declaring that it was written with the help of the Holy Spirit, granting an indulgence of ten years to everyone who would read it, and bestowing upon Henry and his successors the title "Defender of the Faith."

On the other hand, the *Captivity* cleared the atmosphere for many thoughtful people and brought Luther not a few new friends. The most outstanding example of this was John Bugenhagen, who had previously regarded Luther as a reckless heretic, but on reading through the *Captivity* was completely converted to the cause of the Reformation and became one of Luther's ablest co-workers in the movement.

Julius Köstlin, probably the most thorough among modern analysts of Luther's theological development, says of the treatise: "The whole treatment of the subject is earnest and dignified. It is based upon biblical principles and shows thorough insight into the meaning of the Bible. At the same time it shows thorough acquaintance with the positions of the opponents and uses a dialectic that is a match for all the arts of the scholastics. Among all the scientific works of Luther this one stands at the top, but it also presents with clarity and warmth the simple religious interest of the Christian soul. It is sharp in its attitude toward the errors and tyranny of Rome but conservative toward the past and considerate toward such external practices as cannot be abrogated at once without injury to human consciences."

This is the fourth published translation of this treatise into English. The first was made by Wace and Buchheim (London, 1896). The second was by A. T. W. Steinhäuser and is included in the second volume of the Philadelphia edition of Luther's works (1915). The third came from the facile pen of Bertram Lee Woolf (*Reformation Writings of Martin Luther:* Vol. I, The Basis of the Protestant Reformation) and was published by the Lutterworth Press of London in 1952.

This revision is based on Steinhäuser's translation, but in every word there has been careful comparison with the original text and with the other English translations. The result is in some measure a new translation. The English of the Steinhäuser text has been revised in order to bring it into accord with present-day usage. Effort has been made also to conform a bit more closely to Luther's words. Some changes have been made in the interest of greater readability. We have sought to limit the use of intolerably long sentences. Also, there is more frequent paragraphing. The quotations from the Bible have been changed to the Revised Standard Version, except in the few instances where the context requires the King James Version or the Vulgate. Several paragraphs in the original that were omitted by Steinhäuser have been included here. The footnotes in Steinhäuser have, for the most part, been reproduced here, and they have been supplemented a bit.

The original Latin text of the treatise is in WA 6, 497-573.

THE

BABYLONIAN CAPTIVITY

OF THE CHURCH

A Prelude of Martin Luther
On the Babylonian Captivity of the Church

JESUS

Martin Luther, Augustinian, to his friend, Hermann Tulich,[1] greeting.

Whether I wish it or not, I am compelled to become more learned every day, with so many and such able masters eagerly driving me on and making me work. Some two years ago I wrote on indulgences, but in such a way that I now deeply regret having published that little book.[2] At that time I still clung with a mighty superstition to the tyranny of Rome, and so I held that indulgences should not be altogether rejected, seeing that they were approved by the common consent of so many. No wonder, for at the time I was still engaged singlehanded in this Sisyphean task.

---

1. Tulich was born at Steinheim, near Paderborn, in Westphalia; graduated from Wittenberg (A.B., 1511); was a proofreader in Melchior Lotter's printing-house at Leipzig. He returned to Wittenberg in 1519 and received the doctorate in 1520; became professor of poetry at the university; rector of the same, 1525. He was a staunch supporter of Luther; rector of the school at Lüneberg from 1532 until his death in 1540.
2. Probably the *Explanations of the Ninety-five Theses* (1518). LW 31, 83-252.

Afterwards, thanks to Sylvester,[3] and aided by those friars who so strenuously defended indulgences, I saw that they were nothing but impostures of the Roman flatterers, by which they rob men of their money and their faith in God. Would that I could prevail upon the booksellers and persuade all who have read them to burn the whole of my booklets on indulgences, and instead of all that I have written on this subject adopt this proposition: INDULGENCES ARE WICKED DEVICES OF THE FLATTERERS OF ROME.

Next, Eck and Emser[4] and their fellow-conspirators undertook to instruct me concerning the primacy of the pope. Here too, not to prove ungrateful to such learned men, I acknowedge that I have profited much from their labors. For while I denied the divine authority of the papacy, I still admitted its human authority.[5] But after hearing and reading the super-subtle subtleties of these coxcombs,[6] with which they so adroitly prop up their idol (for my mind is not altogether unteachable in these matters), I now know for certain that the papacy is the kingdom of Babylon and the power of Nimrod, the mighty hunter [Gen. 10:8-9]. Once more, therefore, that all may turn out to my friends' advantage, I beg both the booksellers and my readers that after burning what I have published on this

3. Sylvester Prierias (more properly called Mazzolini), from Prierio in Piedmont (1456-1523), was a prior of the Dominicans. He became Grand Inquisitor and Censor of Books in 1515. He and others of the order (e.g., Tetzel and Hochstraten) had written against Luther.

4. Johann Eck (properly Maier) from Eck in the Allgäu (1486-1543), had become professor at Ingolstadt in 1510. His criticism of the Ninety-five Theses in his *Obelisci*, to which Luther replied with the *Asterisci* (WA 1, 281-314; St.L. 18, 536-589), culminated in their Leipzig disputation in 1519. Jerome Emser (1477-1527) had been a humanist professor at Erfurt during Luther's student days, and was later secretary to Duke George of Saxony in Dresden. Luther is referring to the treatises both men published against him as a consequence of the disputation.

5. *Resolutio Lutheriana super propositione sua decima tertia de potestate papae (per autorem locupletata)* (1519). WA 2, 180-240.

6. *Trossulorum*, originally a designation for Roman knights who had conquered the city Trossulum, later came to have the derogatory sense of a fop, someone who pretends to rank and authority. St.L. 19, 6 n. 1.

subject they hold to this proposition: THE PAPACY IS THE GRAND HUNTING OF THE BISHOP OF ROME. This is proved by the arguments of Eck, Emser, and the Leipzig lecturer on the Scriptures.[7]

Now they are making a game of schooling me concerning communion in both kinds and other weighty subjects: here I must take pains lest I listen in vain to these "eminent teachers"[8] of mine. A certain Italian friar of Cremona has written a "Recantation of Martin Luther before the Holy See,"[9] which is not that I revoke anything, as the words declare, but that he revokes me. This is the kind of Latin the Italians are beginning to write nowadays. Another friar, a German of Leipzig, that same lecturer, as you know, on the whole canon of Scripture [Alveld] has written against me concerning the sacrament in both kinds and is about to perform, as I understand, still greater and more marvelous things. The Italian [Isolani] was canny enough to conceal his name, fearing perhaps the fate of Cajetan[10] and Sylvester. The man of Leipzig, on the other hand, as becomes a fierce and vigorous German, boasts on his ample title page of his name, his life, his sanctity, his learning, his office, his fame, his honor, almost his very clogs.[11] From him I shall doubtless learn a great deal, since he writes his dedicatory epistle to the Son of God himself: so familiar

7. Augustinus Alveld, a Franciscan. This reference by Luther is his chief claim to fame. Cf. the Introduction.
8. *Cratippos.* Cratippus, a peripatetic philosopher of Mytilene, had taught Cicero's son at Athens and received the rights of Roman citizenship through the orator's efforts. In addition to instructing the youth of Athens, he wrote on divination and the interpretation of dreams.
9. *Revocatio Martini Lutheri Augustiniani ad sanctam sedem* by Isidoro Isolani. Cf. the Introduction. Cf. WA 6, 486-487.
10. Thomas Cajetan (1469-1534), Italian cardinal, general of the Dominican order and foremost authority on Thomistic theology, found himself unequal to the task of testing and refuting Luther at Augsburg. Cf. *Proceedings at Augsburg* (1518). *LW* 31, 253-292.
11. The title page of Alveld's treatise contained twenty-six lines. Luther's *Calopodia* (perhaps originally intended as *calcipodium*) may have been a reference to the wooden-soled sandals worn by Alveld's order.

are these saints with Christ who reigns in heaven! Here it seems three magpies are addressing me, the first in good Latin, the second in better Greek, the third in purest Hebrew. What do you think, my dear Hermann, I should do but prick up my ears? The matter is being dealt with at Leipzig by the "Observance" of the Holy Cross.[12]

Fool that I was, I had hitherto thought that it would be well if a general council were to decide that the sacrament should be administered to the laity in both kinds.[13] This view our more than learned friar would correct, declaring that neither Christ nor the apostles had either commanded or advised that both kinds be administered to the laity; it was therefore left to the judgment of the church what to do or not to do in this matter, and the church must be obeyed. These are his words.

You will perhaps ask, what madness has entered into the man, or against whom is he writing? For I have not condemned the use of one kind, but have left the decision about the use of both kinds to the judgment of the church. This is the very thing he attempts to assert, in order to attack me with this same argument. My answer is that this sort of argument is common to all who write against Luther: either they assert the very things they assail, or they set up a man of straw whom they may attack. This is the way of Sylvester and Eck and Emser, and of the men of Cologne and Louvain,[14] and if this friar had not been one of their kind, he would never have written against Luther.

This man turned out to be more fortunate than his fellows, however, for in his effort to prove that the use of

---

12. Concerning Alveld's lengthy title and his peculiar spelling, IHSVH, for Jesus, which he tried to justify by arguments involving an admixture of the three languages, cf. WA 6, 485. He was a member of the stricter Observantine Franciscans, at that time separate from the Conventuals.

13. *A Treatise Concerning the Blessed Sacrament* (1519). PE 2, 9-10.

14. The universities of Cologne and Louvain had ratified Eck's "victory" over Luther at Leipzig.

both kinds was neither commanded nor advised, but left to the judgment of the church, he brings forward the Scriptures to prove that the use of one kind for the laity was ordained by the command of Christ. So it is true, according to this new interpreter of the Scriptures, that the use of one kind was not commanded and at the same time was commanded by Christ! This novel kind of argument is, as you know, the one which these dialecticians of Leipzig are especially fond of using. Does not Emser profess to speak fairly of me in his earlier book,[15] and then, after I had convicted him of the foulest envy and shameful lies, confess, when about to confute me in his later book,[16] that both were true, and that he has written in both a friendly and an unfriendly spirit? A fine fellow, indeed, as you know!

But listen to our distinguished distinguisher of "kinds,"[17] to whom the decision of the church and the command of Christ are the same thing, and again the command of Christ and no command of Christ are the same thing. With such dexterity he proves that only one kind should be given to the laity, by the command of Christ, that is, by the decision of the church. He puts it in capital letters, thus: THE INFALLIBLE FOUNDATION. Then he treats John 6 [:35, 41] with incredible wisdom, where Christ speaks of the bread of heaven and the bread of life, which is He Himself. The most learned fellow not only refers these words to the Sacrament of the Altar, but because Christ says: "I am the living bread" [John 6:51] and not "I am the living cup," he actually concludes that we have in this passage the institution of the sacrament in only one kind

---

15. *De disputatione Lipsicensi* (1519).

16. *A venatione Luteriana Aegocerotis Assertio* (1519).

17. *speciosum speciatorem.* In this play on words, Luther coined the second word to hint at the *species* or elements in the sacrament, while at the same time connoting ironically someone who tries to make his case appear plausible and favorable. *St.L.* 19, 9 n. 1.

for the laity. But here follow the words: "For my flesh is food indeed, and my blood is drink indeed" [John 6:55] and, "Unless you eat the flesh of the Son of man and drink his blood" [John 6:53]. When it dawned upon the good friar that these words speak undeniably for both kinds and against one kind—presto! how happily and learnedly he slips out of the quandary by asserting that in these words Christ means to say only that whoever receives the sacrament in one kind receives therein both flesh and blood. This he lays down as his "infallible foundation" of a structure so worthy of the holy and heavenly "Observance."

I pray you now to learn along with me from this that in John 6 Christ commands the administration of the sacrament in one kind, yet in such a way that his commanding means leaving it to the decision of the church; and further that Christ is speaking in this same chapter only of the laity and not of the priests. For to the latter the living bread of heaven, that is the sacrament in our kind, does not belong, but perhaps the bread of death from hell! But what is to be done with deacons and subdeacons,[18] who are neither laymen nor priests? According to this distinguished writer they ought to use neither the one kind nor both kinds! You see, my dear Tulich, what a novel and "Observant" method of treating Scripture this is.

But learn this too: In John 6 Christ is speaking of the Sacrament of the Altar, although he himself teaches us that he is speaking of faith in the incarnate Word, for he says: "This is the work of God, that you believe in him whom he has sent" [John 6:29]. But we'll have to give him credit: this Leipzig professor of the Bible can prove anything he

18. These are the sixth and fifth of the seven grades through which clergy advanced to the priesthood. Some then-contemporary Catholic theologians (e.g., Cajetan and Durandus) doubted whether the Sacrament of Order was actually received by deacons. They were later overruled by the Council of Trent which decided that it was. *The Catholic Encyclopedia* (15 vols.), IV, 650.

pleases from any passage of Scripture he pleases. For he is
an Anaxagorian,[19] or rather an Aristotelian,[20] theologian
for whom nouns and verbs when interchanged mean the
same thing and any thing. Throughout the whole of his
book he so fits together the testimony of the Scriptures
that if he set out to prove that Christ is in the sacrament he
would not hesitate to begin thus: "The lesson is from the
book of the Revelation of St. John the Apostle." All his
quotations are as apt as this one would be, and the wise-
acre imagines he is adorning his drivel with the multitude
of his quotations. The rest I will pass over, lest I smother
you with the filth of this vile-smelling cloaca.

In conclusion, he brings forward I Cor. 11 [:23], where
Paul says that he received from the Lord and delivered to
the Corinthians the use of both the bread and the cup.
Here again our distinguisher of kinds, treating the Scriptures with his usual brilliance, teaches that Paul permitted,
but did not deliver, the use of both kinds. Do you ask where
he gets his proof? Out of his own head, as he did in the
case of John 6. For it does not behoove this lecturer to give
a reason for his assertions; he belongs to that order whose
members prove and teach everything by their visions.[21]
Accordingly we are here taught that in this passage the
apostle did not write to the whole Corinthian congregation,
but to the laity alone—and therefore gave no "permission"
at all to the clergy, but deprived them of the sacrament
altogether! Further, according to a new kind of grammar,
"I have received from the Lord" means the same as "it is
permitted by the Lord," and "I have delivered to you" is
the same as "I have permitted to you." I pray you, mark

---

19. Anaxagoras (*circa* 500-428 B.C.), a Greek philosopher, was accused of
   atheism by his contemporaries because of his new interpretation of the myths
   of the gods.
20. For Luther's opinion of Aristotle, cf. *An Open Letter to the Christian Nobility*.
   PE 2, 146-47.
21. The Franciscans. Perhaps an allusion to the seraphic vision of St. Francis.

this well. For by this method not only the church, but any worthless fellow, will be at liberty, according to this master, to turn all the universal commands, institutions, and ordinances of Christ and the apostles into mere "permission."

I perceive therefore that this man is driven by a messenger of Satan [II Cor. 12:7] and that he and his partners are seeking to make a name for themselves in the world through me, as men who are worthy to cross swords with Luther. But their hopes shall be dashed. In my contempt for them I shall never even mention their names, but content myself with this one reply to all their books. If they are worthy of it, I pray that Christ in his mercy may bring them back to a sound mind. If they are not worthy, I pray that they may never leave off writing such books, and that the enemies of truth may never deserve to read any others. There is truth and popular saying:

"This I know for certain—whenever I fight with filth, Victor or vanquished, I am sure to be defiled."[22]

And since I see that they have an abundance of leisure and writing paper, I shall furnish them with ample matter to write about. For I shall keep ahead of them, so that while they are triumphantly celebrating a glorious victory over one of my heresies (as it seems to them), I shall meanwhile be devising a new one. I too am desirous of seeing these illustrious leaders in battle decorated with many honors. Therefore, while they murmur that I approve of communion in both kinds, and are most happily engrossed with this important and worthy subject, I shall go one step further and undertake to show that all who deny communion in both kinds to the laity are wicked men. To do this more conveniently I shall compose *a prelude on the*

---

22. The saying was also used later (1530) in the explanation to the fable about the ass and the lion in Luther's little book on Aesop's Fables, which included his translation of 14 of the fables. *Luther's Werke*, ed. Arnold E. Berger, III, 113. Cf. *MA*[3] 2, 405-406.

captivity of the Roman church.[23] In due time, when the most learned papists have disposed of this book, I shall offer more.

I take this course, lest any pious reader who may chance upon this book should be offended by the filthy matter with which I deal and should justly complain that he finds nothing in it which cultivates or instructs his mind or which furnishes any food for learned reflection. For you know how impatient my friends are that I waste my time on the sordid fictions of these men. They say that the mere reading of them is ample confutation; they look for better things from me, which Satan seeks to hinder through these men. I have finally resolved to follow the advice of my friends and to leave to those hornets the business of wrangling and hurling invectives.

Of that Italian friar of Cremona [Isolani] I shall say nothing. He is an unlearned man and a simpleton, who attempts with a few rhetorical passages to recall me to the Holy See, from which I am not as yet aware of having departed, nor has anyone proved that I have. His chief argument in those silly passages[24] is that I ought to be moved by my monastic vows and by the fact that the empire has been transferred to the Germans.[25] Thus he does not seem to have wanted to write my "recantation" so much as the praise of the French people and the Roman pontiff. Let him attest his allegiance in this little book, such as it is. He does not deserve to be harshly treated, for he seems

---

23. We have retained the italics of the original for the most part where they serve the purpose of emphasis, or of pointing up the organizational structure of the treatise, or both.

24. Cf. p. 125 n. 9.

25. Cf. *An Open Letter to the Christian Nobility,* PE 2, 153 n. 2, and 153-58. Luther is probably referring to the fact that German kings, since Charles the Great in 800 A.D., had been called Roman Emperors after receiving papal coronation. Perhaps, though, he is referring to the election of the half-German Charles V on May 28, 1519, despite the papal agitation in favor of a French king. *Luther's Werke für das christliche Haus,* ed. Buchwald, *et al.* (Braunschweig, 1890) [hereinafter cited as Buchwald], II, 386 n. 1.

to have been prompted by no malice; nor does he deserve to be learnedly refuted, since all his chatter is sheer ignorance and inexperience.

To begin with, I must deny that there are seven sacraments, and for the present[26] maintain that there are but three: baptism, penance, and the bread.[27] All three have been subjected to a miserable captivity by the Roman curia, and the church has been robbed of all her liberty. Yet, if I were to speak according to the usage of the Scriptures, I should have only one single sacrament,[28] but with three sacramental signs, of which I shall treat more fully at the proper time.

Now concerning the sacrament of the bread first of all.[29]

I shall tell you now what progress I have made as a result of my studies on the administration of this sacrament. For at the time when I was publishing my treatise on the Eucharist,[30] I adhered to the common custom and did not concern myself at all with the question of whether the pope was right or wrong. But now that I have been challenged and attacked, nay, forcibly thrust into this arena, I shall freely speak my mind, whether all the papists laugh or weep together.

In the first place the sixth chapter of John must be entirely excluded from this discussion, since it does not refer

---

26. The "present" did not last very long as far as penance was concerned. Cf. p. 258.
27. Luther uses the commonly accepted designation for the Lord's Supper, a name derived from the fact that the wine was being withheld from the laity.
28. In I Tim. 3:16 Christ himself is called the *sacramentum* (Vulgate). Cf. *PE* 2, 177 n. 5; Julius Köstlin, *The Theology of Luther,* trans. Charles E. Hay (Philadelphia, 1897), I, 403; and below, pp. 221-22.
29. Luther inserted this sentence instead of a subtitle as in the case of the other sacraments to follow.
30. *A Treatise Concerning the Blessed Sacrament* (1519). *PE* 2, 9-31.

to the sacrament in a single syllable. Not only because the sacrament was not yet instituted, but even more because the passage itself and the sentences following plainly show, as I have already stated,[31] that Christ is speaking of faith in the incarnate Word. For he says: "My words are spirit and life" [John 6:63], which shows that he was speaking of a spiritual eating, by which he who eats has life; whereas the Jews understood him to mean a bodily eating and therefore disputed with him. But no eating can give life except that which is by faith, for that is truly a spiritual and living eating. As Augustine[32] also says: "Why do you make ready your teeth and your stomach? Believe, and you have eaten."[33] For the sacramental eating does not give life, since many eat unworthily. Hence Christ cannot be understood in this passage to be speaking about the sacrament.

Some persons, to be sure, have misapplied these words in their teaching concerning the sacrament, as in the decretal *Dudum*[34] and many others. But it is one thing to misapply the Scriptures and another to understand them in their proper sense. Otherwise, if in this passage Christ were enjoining a sacramental eating, when he says: "Unless you eat my flesh and drink my blood, you have no life in you" [John 6:53], he would be condemning all infants, all the sick, and all those absent or in any way hindered from the sacramental eating, however strong their faith might be. Thus Augustine in his *Contra Julianum,*[35] Book II, proves from Innocent[36] that even infants eat the flesh and

---

31. Cf. p. 128.
32. St. Augustine (354-430), bishop of Hippo in North Africa.
33. *Sermo* 112, cap. 5. Migne 38, 645.
34. Luther's reference to the Decretals is correct. His citation of *Dudum* is wrong. It should have been *Quum Marthae, Decretalium Gregorii IX,* lib. iii, tit. XLI: *de celebratione missarum, et sacramento eucharistiae et divinis officiis,* cap. 6. Cf. the text in *Corpus Iuris Canonici,* ed. Aemilius Friedberg (Graz, 1955), II, col. 638.
35. *Contra Julianum* ii, cap. 36. Migne 44, 699-700.
36. Innocent I, bishop of Rome 402-417. energetic opponent of Pelagius and other heretics.

drink the blood of Christ without the sacrament; that is, they partake of them through the faith of the church. Let this then be accepted as proved: John 6 does not belong here. For this reason I have written elsewhere[37] that the Bohemians[38] cannot properly rely on this passage in support of the sacrament in both kinds.

Now there are two passages that do bear very clearly upon this matter: the Gospel narratives of the Lord's Supper and Paul in I Cor. 11. Let us examine these. Matthew [26], Mark [14], and Luke [22] agree that Christ gave the whole sacrament to all his disciples. That Paul delivered both kinds is so certain that no one has ever had the temerity to say otherwise. Add to this that Matt. [26:27] reports that Christ did not say of the bread, "eat of it, all of you," but of the cup, "drink of it, all of you." Mark [14:23] likewise does not say, "they all ate of it," but "they all drank of it." Both attach the note of universality to the cup, not to the bread, as though the Spirit foresaw this schism, by which some would be forbidden to partake of the cup, which Christ desired should be common to all. How furiously do you suppose, would they rave against us, if they had found the word "all" attached to the bread instead of to the cup? They would certainly leave us no loophole to escape. They would cry out and brand us as heretics and damn us as schismatics. But now, when the Scripture is on our side and against them, they will not allow themselves to be bound by any force of logic. Men of the most free will[39] they are, even in the things that are God's; they change and change again, and throw everything into confusion.

37. *Verklärung etlicher Artikel in einem Sermon vom heiligen Sakrament* (1520). *WA 6, 80.*
38. Followers of the martyred John Huss (1369-1415); permitted by compromise agreements with Rome to administer Communion in both kinds.
39. For Luther's denial of his opponents' doctrine of the complete freedom of the will, cf. his *De servo arbitrio* (1525), *WA* 18, 600-787, *St.L.* 18, 1668-1969; *The Bondage of the Will,* trans. J. I. Packer and O. R. Johnston (Westwood, New Jersey, 1957).

But imagine me standing over against them and interrogating my lords, the papists. In the Lord's Supper, the whole sacrament, or communion in both kinds, is given either to the priests alone or else it is at the same time given to the laity. If it is given only to the priests (as they would have it), then it is not right to give it to the laity in either kind. For it must not be given rashly to any to whom Christ did not give it when he instituted the sacrament. Otherwise, if we permit one institution of Christ to be changed, we make all of his laws invalid, and any man may make bold to say that he is not bound by any other law or institution of Christ. For a single exception, especially in the Scriptures, invalidates the whole. But if it is given also to the laity, it inevitably follows that it ought not to be withheld from them in either form. And if any do withhold it from them when they ask for it they are acting impiously and contrary to the act, example, and institution of Christ.

of given to laity, should not be with-held from them in any form.

I acknowledge that I am conquered by this argument which to me is irrefutable. I have neither read nor heard nor found anything to say against it. For here the word and example of Christ stand unshaken when he says, not by way of permission, but of command: "Drink of it, all of you" [Matt. 26:27]. For if all are to drink of it, and the words cannot be understood as addressed to the priests alone, then it is certainly an impious act to withhold the cup from the laymen when they desire it, even though an angel from heaven [Gal. 1:8] were to do it. For when they say that the distribution of both kinds is left to the decision of the church, they make this assertion without reason and put it forth without authority. It can be ignored just as readily as it can be proved. It is of no avail against an opponent who confronts us with the word and work of Christ; he must be refuted with the word of Christ, but this we[40] do not possess.

40. Here Luther identifies himself with the erring priesthood.

135

If, however, either kind may be withheld from the laity, then with equal right and reason a part of baptism or penance might also be taken away from them by this same authority of the church. Therefore, just as baptism and absolution must be administered in their entirety, so the sacrament of the bread must be given in its entirety to all laymen, if they desire it. I am much amazed, however, by their assertion that the priests may never receive only one kind in the mass under pain of mortal sin; and that for no other reason except (as they unanimously say) that the two kinds constitute one complete sacrament, which may not be divided. I ask them, therefore, to tell me why it is lawful to divide it in the case of the laity, and why they are the only ones to whom the entire sacrament is not given? Do they not acknowledge, by their own testimony, either that both kinds are to be given to the laity or that the sacrament is not valid when only one kind is given to them? How can it be that the sacrament in one kind is not complete in the case of the priests, yet in the case of the laity it is complete? Why do they flaunt the authority of the church and the power of the pope in my face? These do not annul the words of God and the testimony of the truth.

It follows, further, that if the church can withhold from the laity one kind, the wine, it can also withhold from them the other, the bread. It could therefore withhold the entire Sacrament of the Altar from the laity and completely annul Christ's institution as far as they are concerned. By what authority, I ask. If the church cannot withhold the bread, or both kinds, neither can it withhold the wine. This cannot possibly be gainsaid; for the church's power must be the same over either kind as it is over both kinds, and if it has no power over both kinds, it has none over either kind. I am curious to hear what the flatterers of Rome will have to say to this.

But what carries most weight with me, however, and is quite decisive for me is that Christ says: "This is my blood, which is poured out for you and for many for the forgiveness of sins."[41] Here you see very clearly that the blood is given to all those for whose sins it was poured out. But who will dare to say that it was not poured out for the laity? And do you not see whom he addresses when he gives the cup? Does he not give it to all? Does he not say that it is poured out for all? "For you" [Luke 22:20], he says—let this refer to the priests. "And for many" [Matt. 26:28], however, cannot possibly refer to the priests. Yet he says: "Drink of it, all of you" [Matt. 26:27]. I too could easily trifle here and with my words make a mockery of Christ's words, as my dear trifler[42] does. But those who rely on the Scriptures in opposing us must be refuted by the Scriptures.

This is what has prevented me from condemning the Bohemians,[43] who, whether they are wicked men or good, certainly have the word and act of Christ on their side, while we[44] have neither, but only that inane remark of men: "The church has so ordained." It was not the church which ordained these things, but the tyrants of the churches, without the consent of the church, which is the people of God.

But now I ask, where is the necessity, where is the religious duty, where is the practical use of denying both kinds, that is, the visible sign, to the laity, when everyone concedes to them the grace of the sacrament[45] without the sign? If they concede the grace, which is the greater, why not the sign, which is the lesser? For in every sacrament the sign as such is incomparably less than the thing

---

41. A harmony of Matt. 26:28 and Luke 22:20 in the Vulgate, whereby "for you" and "for many" are conjoined in the traditional manner of the canon of the mass. Cf. p. 154 n. 84.
42. Alveld, cf. p. 125 n. 7.
43. Cf. p. 134 n. 38.
44. Cf. n. 41 above.
45. The *res sacramenti*. The sacrament consisted of two parts—the *sacramentum*, or external sign, and the *res sacramenti*, or the thing signified, the sacramental grace.

signified. What then, I ask, is to prevent them from conceding the lesser, when they concede the greater? Unless indeed, as it seems to me, it has come about by the permission of an angry God in order to give occasion for a schism in the church, to bring home to us how, having long ago lost the grace of the sacrament, we contend for the sign, which is the lesser, against that which is the most important and the chief thing; just as some men for the sake of ceremonies contend against love. This monstrous perversion seems to date from the time when we began to rage against Christian love for the sake of the riches of this world. Thus God would show us, by this terrible sign, how we esteem signs more than the things they signify. How preposterous it would be to admit that the faith of baptism is granted to the candidate for baptism, and yet to deny him the sign of this very faith, namely, the water!

Finally, Paul stands invincible and stops the mouth of everyone when he says in I Cor. 11 [:23]: "For I received from the Lord what I also delivered to you." He does not say: "I permitted to you," as this friar of ours lyingly asserts out of his own head.[46] Nor is it true that Paul delivered both kinds on account of the contention among the Corinthians. In the first place, the text shows that their contention was not about the reception of both kinds, but about the contempt and envy between rich and poor. The text clearly states: "One is hungry and another is drunk, and you humiliate those who have nothing" [I Cor. 11:21-22]. Moreover, Paul is not speaking of the time when he first delivered the sacrament to them, for he does not say "I receive from the Lord" and "I give to you," but "I received" and "I delivered"—namely, when he first began to preach among them, a long while before this contention. This shows that he delivered both kinds to them, for "delivered" means the same as "commanded," for elsewhere he uses the

46. The passage from Alveld is quoted in WA 6, 505 n. 1.

word in this sense. Consequently there is nothing in the friar's fuming about permission; he has raked it together without Scripture, without reason, without sense. His opponents do not ask what he has dreamed, but what the Scriptures decree in the matter, and out of the Scriptures he cannot adduce one jot or tittle in support of his dreams, while they can produce mighty thunderbolts in support of their faith.

Rise up then, you popish flatterers, one and all! Get busy and defend yourselves against the charges of impiety, tyranny, and lèse-majesté against the gospel, and of the crime of slandering your brethren. You decry as heretics those who refuse to contravene such plain and powerful words of Scripture in order to acknowledge the mere dreams of your brains! If any are to be called heretics and schismatics, it is not the Bohemians or the Greeks,[47] for they take their stand upon the Gospels. It is you Romans who are the heretics and godless schismatics, for you presume upon your figments alone against the clear Scriptures of God. Wash yourself of that, men!

But what could be more ridiculous and more worthy of this friar's brains than his saying that the Apostle wrote these words and gave this permission, not to the church universal, but to a particular church, that is, the Corinthian? Where does he get his proof? Out of one storehouse, his own impious head. If the church universal receives, reads, and follows this epistle as written for itself in all other respects, why should it not do the same with this portion also? If we admit that any epistle, or any part of any epistle, of Paul does not apply to the church universal, then the whole authority of Paul falls to the ground. Then the Corinthians will say that what he teaches about faith in the

47. Greek Church is a common designation for that entire branch of Christendom known as Eastern Orthodoxy, which was split from Western or Latin Christianity in the year 1054. Its theologies and liturgies are written mostly in the Greek language.

Epistle to the Romans does not apply to them. What greater blasphemy and madness can be imagined than this! God forbid that there should be one jot or tittle in all of Paul which the whole church universal is not bound to follow and keep! The Fathers never held an opinion like this, not even down to these perilous times of which Paul was speaking [II Tim. 3:1-9] when he foretold that there would be blasphemers and blind, insensate men. This friar is one of them, perhaps even the chief.

However, suppose we grant the truth of this intolerable madness. If Paul gave his permission to a particular church, then, even from your own point of view, the Greeks and Bohemians are in the right, for they are particular churches. Hence it is sufficient that they do not act contrary to Paul, who at least gave permission. Moreover, Paul could not permit anything contrary to Christ's institution. Therefore, O Rome, I cast in your teeth, and in the teeth of all your flatterers, these sayings of Christ and Paul, on behalf of the Greeks and the Bohemians. I defy you to prove that you have been given any authority to change these things by as much as one hair, much less to accuse others of heresy because they disregard your arrogance. It is rather you who deserve to be charged with the crime of godlessness and despotism.

Concerning this point we may read Cyprian,[48] who alone is strong enough to refute all the Romanists. In the fifth book of his treatise, *On the Lapsed*, he testifies that it was the widespread custom in that church [at Carthage] to administer both kinds to the laity, even to children, indeed, to give the body of the Lord into their hands. And of this he gives many examples. Among other things, he reproves some of the people as follows: "The sacrilegious man is angered at the priests because he does not immediately

---

48. Bishop of Carthage, (249-258), who was beheaded as a martyr for the faith. The treatise was written about 251-252.

receive the body of the Lord with unclean hands, or drink the blood of the Lord with unclean lips."[49] He is speaking here, you see, of irreverent laymen who desired to receive the body and the blood from the priests. Do you find anything to snarl at here, wretched flatterer? Will you say that this holy martyr, a doctor of the church endowed with the apostolic spirit, was a heretic, and that he used this permission in a particular church?

In the same place Cyprian narrates an incident that came under his own observation. He describes at length how a deacon was administering the cup to a little[50] girl, and when she drew away from him he poured the blood of the Lord into her mouth.[51] We read the same of St. Donatus, and how trivially does this wretched flatterer dispose of his broken chalice![52] "I read of a broken chalice," he says, "but I do not read that the blood was administered."[53] No wonder! He that finds what he pleases in the Holy Scriptures will also read what he pleases in the histories. But can the authority of the church be established, or the heretics be refuted, in this way?

But enough on this subject! I did not undertake this work

---

49. St. Cyprian, "The Lapsed," trans. Maurice Bévenot, S. J. (Westminster, Maryland, 1957), p. 31. (Vol. 25 of *Ancient Christian Writers*.)

50. *infanti*, a child under the age of seven years. *St.L.* 19, 21 n. 2.

51. St. Cyprian, *op. cit.*, pp. 32-33.

52. Donatus, bishop of Arezzo, whither he had fled during the persecution of Diocletian (303-305); martyred under Julian the Apostate, August 7, 362. In a collection of legendary lives of the saints, compiled by Jacobus de Voragine (*circa* 1230-1298), it is related: "And one day, as Gregory relates in his *Dialogue*, the people were receiving the holy Communion in the Mass, and the deacon was distributing the Blood of Christ, when the pagans pushed him so rudely that he fell, and the holy chalice was shattered. As he and the people were sorely grieved thereat, Donatus gathered the fragments of the chalice, and having prayed, restored it to its former shape." *The Golden Legend of Jacobus de Voragine*, trans. Granger Ryan and Helmut Ripperger (New York, 1941), Part Two, 433-34.

53. Alveld quotes the story of the broken cup in order to refute the practice in administration of the sacrament which it implies. He says: "I read of the repairing of the chalice in Gregory, but do not find there the administration of the blood." Cf. *WA* 6, 506 n. 2.

tor the purpose of answering one who is not worthy of a reply, but to bring the truth of the matter to light.

I conclude, then, that it is wicked and despotic to deny both kinds to the laity, and that this is not within the power of any angel, much less of any pope or council. Nor does the Council of Constance[54] give me pause, for if its authority is valid, why not that of the Council of Basel as well, which decreed to the contrary that the Bohemians should be permitted to receive the sacrament in both kinds? That decision was reached only after considerable discussion, as the extant records and documents of the Council show. And to this Council the ignorant flatterer refers[55] in support of his dream; with such wisdom does he handle the whole matter.

The first captivity of this sacrament, therefore, concerns its substance or completeness, which the tyranny of Rome has wrested from us. Not that those who use only one kind sin against Christ, for Christ did not command the use of either kind, but left it to the choice of each individual, when he said: "As often as you do this, do it in remembrance of me" [I Cor. 11:25]. But they are the sinners, who forbid the giving of both kinds to those who wish to exercise this choice. The fault lies not with the laity, but with the priests. The sacrament does not belong to the priests, but to all men. The priests are not lords, but servants in duty bound to administer both kinds to those who desire them, as often as they desire them. If they wrest this right from the laity and deny it to them by force, they are tyrants; but the laity

---

54. Alveld had cited the *Decretum Constantiense*, which approved the withholding of the cup from the laity. Cf. *WA* 6, 507 n. 1.

55. The Council of Constance did sanction withholding of the cup from the laity, and burned John Huss at the stake for disputing it (July 6, 1415). Alveld, however, was wrong, as Luther says, in citing also the Council of Basel. That Council concluded the *Compactata* of Prague (November 30, 1433), granting to the followers of Huss (the "Bohemians") the privilege of administering the sacrament in both kinds.

are without fault, whether they lack one kind or both kinds. In the meantime they must be preserved by their faith and by their desire for the complete sacrament. These same servants are likewise bound to administer baptism and absolution to everyone who seeks them, because he has a right to them; but if they do not administer them, the seeker has the full merit of his faith, while they will be accused before Christ as wicked servants. Thus the holy fathers of old in the desert did not receive the sacrament in any form for many years at a time.[56] *man should take sacrament*

Therefore I do not urge that both kinds be seized upon by force, as if we were bound to this form by a rigorous command, but I instruct men's consciences so that they may endure the Roman tyranny, knowing well that they have been forcibly deprived of their rightful share in the sacrament because of their own sin. This only do I desire—that no one should justify the tyranny of Rome, as if it were doing right in forbidding one kind to the laity. We ought rather to abhor it, without our consent, and endure it just as we should do if we were held captive by the Turk and not permitted to use either kind. This is what I meant by saying that it would be a good thing, in my opinion, if this captivity were ended by the decree of a general council,[57] our Christian liberty restored to us out of the hands of the Roman tyrant, and every one left free to seek and receive this sacrament, just as he is free to receive baptism and penance. But now we are compelled by the same tyranny to receive the one kind year after year, so utterly lost is the liberty which Christ has given us. This is the due reward of our godless ingratitude.

according to conscience.

The second captivity of this sacrament is less grievous as far as the conscience is concerned, yet the gravest of dan-

56. Cf. *A Treatise Concerning the Ban*, PE 2, 40.
57. Cf. p. 126 n. 13.

gers threatens the man who would attack it, to say nothing of condemning it. Here I shall be called a Wycliffite[58] and a heretic by six hundred names. But what of it? Since the Roman bishop has ceased to be a bishop and has become a tyrant, I fear none of his decrees; for I know that it is not within his power, nor that of any general council, to make new articles of faith

Some time ago, when I was drinking in scholastic theology, the learned Cardinal of Cambrai[59] gave me food for thought in his comments on the fourth book of the *Sentences*.[60] He argues with great acumen that to hold that real bread and real wine, and not merely their accidents,[61] are present on the altar, would be much more probable and require fewer superfluous miracles—if only the church had not decreed otherwise. When I learned later what church it was that had decreed this, namely the Thomistic[62]—that is, the Aristotelian church—I grew bolder, and after floating in a sea of doubt,[63] I at last found rest for my conscience in the above view, namely, that it is real bread and real wine,

Keen insight

---

58. John Wycliffe (d. 1384), the most prominent English reformer before the Reformation and keenest of medieval critics of the doctrine of transubstantiation, was posthumously condemned as a heretic by the Council of Constance on May 4, 1415.

59. Pierre d'Ailly (1350-1420), a pupil of Ockham, influenced Luther greatly. He was chairman of that session of the Council of Constance which examined and condemned John Huss in 1415. Luther is referring to d' Ailly's *Questiones quarti libri sententiarum,* quest. 6, E; folio cclxiv a.

60. Famous medieval textbook of theology, compiled *circa* 1150 by Peter Lombard (d. 1160), and containing brief statements or "sentences" of the main arguments pro and con with respect to the principal themes in Christian doctrine. The fourth book treats of the sacraments in general.

61. The qualities which, in medieval thought, were held to adhere to the invisible "substance," and together with it, form the object. In transubstantiation the "substance" of the bread and wine was changed into the "substance" of Christ's body and blood, while only the "accidents" or "form" of the bread and wine (such as shape, color, and taste) remained.

62. The name refers to Thomas Aquinas (1225-1274), a Dominican, greatest of the scholastic theologians, still regarded as the foremost doctrinal authority in the Roman Catholic church.

63. *inter sacrum et saxum.* In his *Adagia,* Erasmus says the phrase is used of those who in their perplexity are carried to the point of grave danger. *CL* 1, 438 n. 29.

in which Christ's real flesh and real blood are present in no other way and to no less a degree than the others assert them to be under their accidents. I reached this conclusion because I saw that the opinions of the Thomists, whether approved by pope or by council, remain only opinions, and would not become articles of faith even if an angel from heaven were to decree otherwise [Gal. 1:8]. For what is asserted without the Scriptures or proven revelation may be held as an opinion, but need not be believed. But this opinion of Thomas hangs so completely in the air without support of Scripture or reason that it seems to me he knows neither his philosophy nor his logic. For Aristotle speaks of subject and accidents so very differently[64] from St. Thomas that it seems to me this great man is to be pitied not only for attempting to draw his opinions in matters of faith from Aristotle, but also for attempting to base them upon a man whom he did not understand, thus building an unfortunate superstructure upon an unfortunate foundation.

Therefore I permit every man to hold either of these opinions, as he chooses. My one concern at present is to remove all scruples of conscience, so that no one may fear being called a heretic if he believes that real bread and real wine are present on the altar, and that every one may feel at liberty to ponder, hold, and believe either one view or the other without endangering his salvation. However, I shall now set forth my own view.

In the first place, I do not intend to listen or attach the least importance to those who will cry out that this teaching of mine is Wycliffite, Hussite, heretical, and contrary to the decree of the church. No one will do this except those very persons whom I have convicted of manifold heresies in the matter of indulgences, freedom of the will and the grace of God, good works and sins, etc. If Wycliffe was once a

---

64. Aristotle held that a subject and its accidents are inseparable; neither can exist apart from the other. Cf *MA*[s] 2, 406.

heretic, they are heretics ten times over; and it is a pleasure to be blamed and accused by heretics and perverse sophists, since to please them would be the height of impiety. Besides, the only way in which they can prove their opinions and disprove contrary ones is by saying: "That is Wycliffite, Hussite, heretical!" They carry this feeble argument always on the tip of their tongues, and they have nothing else. If you ask for scriptural proof, they say: "This is our opinion, and the church (that is, we ourselves) has decided thus." To such an extent these men, who are reprobate concerning the faith [II Tim. 3:8] and untrustworthy, have the effrontery to set their own fancies before us in the name of the church as articles of faith.

But there are good grounds for my view, and this above all—no violence is to be done to the words of God, whether by man or angel. They are to be retained in their simplest meaning as far as possible. Unless the context manifestly compels it, they are not to be understood apart from their grammatical and proper sense, lest we give our adversaries occasion to make a mockery of all the Scriptures. Thus Origen[65] was rightly repudiated long ago because, ignoring the grammatical sense, he turned the trees and everything else written concerning Paradise into allegories, from which one could have inferred that trees were not created by God. *does not believe in transubstantiation.* Even so here, when the Evangelists plainly write that Christ took bread [Matt. 26:26; Mark 14:22; Luke 22:19] and blessed it, and when the Book of Acts and the Apostle in turn call it bread [Acts 2:46; I Cor. 10:16; 11:23, 26-28], we have to think of real bread and real wine, just as we do of a real cup (for even they do not say that the cup was transubstantiated). Since it is not necessary, therefore, to assume a transubstantiation effected by divine power, it

---

65. Origen of Alexandria (*circa* 184-253) whose principles of allegorical exegesis were the source of many lengthy controversies, beginning as early as the fourth century.

must be regarded as a figment of the human mind, for it rests neither on the Scriptures nor on reason, as we shall see.

Therefore it is an absurd and unheard-of juggling with words to understand "bread" to mean "the form or accidents[66] of bread," and "wine" to mean "the form or accidents of wine." Why do they not also understand all other things to mean their "forms or accidents"? And even if this might be done with all other things, it would still not be right to enfeeble the words of God in this way, and by depriving them of their meaning to cause so much harm.

Moreover, the church kept the true faith for more than twelve hundred years, during which time the holy fathers never, at any time or place, mentioned this transubstantiation (a monstrous word and a monstrous idea), until the pseudo philosophy of Aristotle began to make its inroads into the church in these last three hundred years.[67] During this time many things have been wrongfully defined, as for example, that the divine essence is neither begotten nor begets; that the soul is the substantial form of the human body. These and like assertions are made without any reason or cause, as the Cardinal of Cambrai[68] himself admits.

Perhaps they will say that the danger of idolatry demands that the bread and wine should not be really present. How ridiculous! The laymen have never become familiar with their fine-spun philosophy of substance and accidents, and could not grasp it if it were taught to them. Besides, there is the same danger in the accidents which remain and which they see, as in the case of the substance which they

---

66. Cf. p. 144 n. 61.

67. Luther is referring to the official establishment of transubstantiation as a fixed dogma by the Fourth Lateran Council of 1215 under Innocent III. The concept was perhaps several centuries in developing prior to that time, though the earliest documentable use of the term in its technical sense was probably in a treatise by Stephen of Autun (d. 1139). *The New Schaff-Herzog Encyclopedia of Religious Knowledge* (12 volumes) [hereinafter cited as Schaff-Herzog], XI, 494.

68. Cf. p. 144 n. 59.

do not see. If they do not worship the accidents, but the Christ hidden under them, why should they worship the [substance of the] bread, which they do not see?

And why could not Christ include his body in the sub stance of the bread just as well as in the accidents? In red-hot iron, for instance, the two substances, fire and iron are so mingled that every part is both iron and fire. Why is it not even more possible that the body of Christ be contained in every part of the substance of the bread?

What will they reply? Christ is believed to have been born from the inviolate womb of his mother. Let them say here too that the flesh of the Virgin was meanwhile annihilated, or as they would more aptly say, transubstantiated, so that Christ, after being enfolded in its accidents, finally came forth through the accidents! The same thing will have to be said of the shut door [John 20:19, 26] and of the closed mouth of the sepulchre,[69] through which he went in and out without disturbing them.

Out of this has arisen that Babel of philosophy of a constant quantity distinct from the substance,[70] until it has come to such a pass that they themselves no longer know what are accidents and what is substance. For who has ever proved beyond the shadow of a doubt that heat, color, cold, light, weight, or shape are mere accidents? Finally, they have been driven to pretend that a new substance is created by God for those accidents on the altar, all on account of Aristotle, who says: "It is the nature of an accident to be in something," and endless other monstrosities. They would be rid of all these if they simply permitted real bread to be present. I rejoice greatly that the simple faith of this sacrament is still to be found, at least among the common people. For as they do not understand, neither do they dispute

---

69. Matt. 28:2; Mark 16:4; Luke 24:2; John 20:1.
70. According to scholastic teaching the substance of the bread ceases to exist. Its quantity, however, together with the other accidents, remains the same. Cf. p. 144 n. 61.

whether accidents are present without substance, but believe with a simple faith that Christ's body and blood are truly contained there, and leave to those who have nothing else to do the argument about what contains them.

But perhaps they will say: "Aristotle teaches that in an affirmative proposition subject and predicate must be identical," or (to quote the monster's own words in the sixth book of his *Metaphysics*)[71]: "An affirmative proposition requires the agreement of the subject and the predicate." They interpret agreement to mean identity. Hence, when I say: "This is my body," the subject cannot be identical with the bread, but must be identical with the body of Christ.

What shall we say when Aristotle and the doctrines of men are made to be the arbiters of such lofty and divine matters? Why do we not put aside such curiosity and cling simply to the words of Christ, willing to remain in ignorance of what takes place here and content that the real body of Christ is present by virtue of the words?[72] Or is it necessary to comprehend the manner of the divine working in every detail?

But what do they say when Aristotle admits that all of the categories[73] of accidents are themselves a subject—although he grants that substance is the chief subject? Hence for him "this is white," "this large," "this something," are all subjects, of which something is predicated. If that is correct, I ask: If a "transubstantiation" must be assumed in order that Christ's body may not be identified with the bread, why not also a "transaccidentation," in order that

71. Luther should have referred not to the *Metaphysics* but to the *Organon*, where in chapter 6 of *De Interpretatione*, Aristotle indicates that for affirmative and negative propositions having the same subject and predicate to be truly contradictory, subject and predicate must be unequivocally (univocally) identical. In chapter 10 he holds that "the subject and predicate in an affirmation must each denote a single thing." Richard McKeon (ed.), *The Basic Works of Aristotle* (New York, 1941), pp. 43, 49.
72. Cf. *A Treatise Concerning the Blessed Sacrament* (1519). *PE*, 2. 20.
73. Namely: substance, quantity, quality, relation, place, time, position, state, action, and affection.

the body of Christ may not be identified with the accidents? For the same danger remains if one understands the subject to be "this white or this round[74] is my body." And for the same reason that a "transubstantiation" must be assumed, a "transaccidentation" must also be assumed, because of this identity of subject and predicate.

If however, merely by an act of intellect, you can do away with the accident, so that it will not be regarded as the subject when you say, "this is my body," why not with equal ease transcend the substance of the bread, if you do not want it to be regarded either as the subject, so that "this my body" is no less in the substance than in the accident? After all, this is a divine work performed by God's almighty power, which can operate just as much and just as well in the accident as it can in the substance.

Let us not dabble too much in philosophy, however. Does not Christ appear to have anticipated this curiosity admirably by saying of the wine, not *Hoc est sanguis meus,* but *Hic est sanguis meus?* [Mark 14:24]. He speaks even more clearly when he brings in the word "cup" and says: "This cup [*Hic calix*] is the new testament in my blood" [Luke 22:20; I Cor. 11:25]. Does it not seem as though he desired to keep us in a simple faith, sufficient for us to believe that his blood was in the cup? For my part, if I cannot fathom how the bread is the body of Christ, yet I will take my reason captive to the obedience of Christ [II Cor. 10:5], and clinging simply to his words, firmly believe not only that the body of Christ is in the bread, but that the bread is the body of Christ. My warrant for this is the words which say: "He took bread, and when he had given thanks, he broke it and said, 'Take, eat, this (that is, this bread, which he had taken and broken) is my body'" [I Cor. 11:23-24]. And Paul says: "The bread which we break, is

74. i.e., the host, or wafer.

it not a participation in the body of Christ?" [I Cor. 10:16]. He does not say "in the bread there is," but "the bread itself is[75] the participation in the body of Christ." What does it matter if philosophy cannot fathom this? The Holy Spirit is greater than Aristotle. Does philosophy fathom their transubstantiation? Why, they themselves admit that here all philosophy breaks down. That the pronoun "this," in both Greek and Latin, is referred to "body," is due to the fact that in both of these languages the two words are of the same gender. In Hebrew, however, which has no neuter gender, "this" is referred to "bread," so that it would be proper to say *Hic* [bread] *est corpus meum*. Actually, the idiom of the language[76] and common sense both prove that the subject ["this"] obviously points to the bread and not to the body, when he says: *Hoc est corpus meum, das ist meyn leyp,* that is, "This very bread here [*iste panis*] is my body."

Thus, what is true in regard to Christ is also true in regard to the sacrament. In order for the divine nature to dwell in him bodily [Col. 2:9], it is not necessary for the human nature to be transbustantiated and the divine nature contained under the accidents of the human nature. Both natures are simply there in their entirety, and it is truly said: "This man is God; this God is man." Even though philosophy cannot grasp this, faith grasps it nonetheless. And the authority of God's Word is greater than the capacity of our intellect to grasp it. In like manner, it is not necessary in the sacrament that the bread and wine be transubstantiated and that Christ be contained under their accidents in order that the real body and real blood may be present. But both remain there at the same time, and it is truly said: "This bread is my body; this wine is my

---

75. Not *in pane est* but *ipse panis est*.
76. Luther assumes that the language Jesus spoke on that occasion was certainly not Greek, but probably Hebrew.

blood," and vice versa. Thus I will understand it for the time being to the honor of the holy words of God, to which I will allow no violence to be done by petty human arguments, nor will I allow them to be twisted into meanings which are foreign to them. At the same time, I permit other men to follow the other opinion, which is laid down in the decree, *Firmiter*,[77] only let them not press us to accept their opinions as articles of faith (as I have said above).[78]

The third captivity of this sacrament is by far the most wicked of all, in consequence of which there is no opinion more generally held or more firmly believed in the church today than this, that the mass is a good work and a sacrifice. And this abuse has brought an endless host of other abuses in its train, so that the faith of this sacrament has become utterly extinct and the holy sacrament has been turned into mere merchandise, a market, and a profit-making business. Hence participations,[79] brotherhoods,[80] intercessions, merits, anniversaries,[81] memorial days[82] and the like wares are bought and sold, traded and bartered, in the church. On these the priests and monks depend for their entire livelihood.

I am attacking a difficult matter, an abuse perhaps impossible to uproot, since through century-long custom and the common consent of men it has become so firmly entrenched that it would be necessary to abolish most of the

---

77. *Firmiter, Decretalium Gregorii IX,* lib. i, tit I: *de summa trinitate et fide catholica,* cap. 1, sec. 3, *Corpus Iuris Canonici, op. cit.,* II col. 5.

78. Cf. p. 143.

79. Though not actually present, one could obtain spiritual "participation" in masses which, for example, were read in a monastery.

80. These confraternities and sodalities paid to have masses said for them, and engaged in devotional exercises for gaining merit. Membership in such an association provided each person the benefits accruing from the "good works" (prayers and attendance at masses) of all the other members.

81. Masses said on behalf of the soul of a deceased person daily for a year or annually on the anniversary of his death.

82. Masses for the dead were read on memorial days.

books now in vogue, and to alter almost the entire external form of the churches and introduce, or rather reintroduce, a totally different kind of ceremonies. But my Christ lives, and we must be careful to give more heed to the Word of God than to all the thoughts of men and of angels. I will perform the duties of my office and bring to light the facts in the case. As I have received the truth freely [Matt. 10:8], I will impart it without malice. For the rest let every man look to his own salvation; I will do my part faithfully so that no one may be able to cast on me the blame for his lack of faith and his ignorance of the truth when we appear before the judgment seat of Christ.

In the first place, in order that we might safely and happily attain to a true and free knowledge of this sacrament, we must be particularly careful to put aside whatever has been added to its original simple institution by the zeal and devotion of men: such things as vestments, ornaments, chants, prayers, organs, candles, and the whole pageantry of outward things.[83] We must turn our eyes and hearts simply to the institution of Christ and this alone, and set nothing before us but the very word of Christ by which he instituted the sacrament, made it perfect, and committed it to us. For in that word, and in that word alone, reside the power, the nature, and the whole substance of the mass. All the rest is the work of man, added to the word of Christ, and the mass can be held and remain a mass just as well without them. Now the words of Christ, in which he instituted this sacrament, are these:

"Now as they were eating, Jesus took bread, and blessed, and broke it, and gave it to his disciples and said, 'Take, eat; this is my body, which is given for you.' And he took a cup, and when he had given thanks he gave it to them, saying, 'Drink of it, all of you; for this cup is the new testament in my blood, which is poured out for you and for

83. Cf. *A Treatise on the New Testament that is the Holy Mass.* PE 1, 296-97.

many for the forgiveness of sins. Do this in remembrance of me.' "[84]

These words the Apostle also delivers and more fully expounds in I Cor. 11 [:23-26]. On them we must rest; on them we must build as on a firm rock, if we would not be carried about with every wind of doctrine [Eph. 4:14], as we have till now been carried about by the wicked doctrines of men who reject the truth [Titus 1:14]. For in these words nothing is omitted that pertains to the completeness, the use, and the blessing of this sacrament; and nothing is included that is superfluous and not necessary for us to know. Whoever sets aside these words and meditates or teaches concerning the mass will teach monstrous and wicked doctrines, as they have done who have made of the sacrament an *opus operatum*[85] and a sacrifice.

Let this stand, therefore, as our first and infallible proposition—the mass or Sacrament of the Altar is Christ's testament, which he left behind him at his death to be distributed among his believers. For that is the meaning of his words, "This cup is the new testament in my blood" [Luke 22:20; I Cor. 11:25]. Let this truth stand, I say, as the immovable foundation on which we shall base all that we have to say. For, as you will see, we are going to overthrow all the godless opinions of men which have been imported into this most precious sacrament. Christ, who is the truth, truly says that this is the new testament in his blood, poured out for us [Luke 22:20]. Not without reason

---

84. Luther's rendering of the Words of Institution is similar to that of the canon of the mass in that it represents a harmony of the several scriptural accounts, incorporating features from all of them—Matt. 26:26-28; Mark 14:22-24; Luke 22:19-20; I Cor. 11:23-25. It differs from the canon of the mass in that it excludes all phrases not explicitly found in the scriptural accounts themselves, Vulgate version. Cf. *PE* 6, 74, 107-08, 126, 160.

85. A work accomplished or finished, which is supposed to impart grace simply by virtue of its having been properly performed, without reference to any faith or lack of faith on the part of the person for whom it is performed. Cf. *A Treatise Concerning the Blessed Sacrament* (1519), *PE* 2, 22-23, where Luther discusses this term.

do I dwell on this sentence; the matter is of no small moment, and must be most deeply impressed on our minds.

Thus, if we enquire what a testament is, we shall learn at the same time what the mass is, what its right use and blessing, and what its wrong use.

A testament, as everyone knows, is a promise made by one about to die, in which he designates his bequest and appoints his heirs. A testament, therefore, involves first, the death of the testator, and second, the promise of an inheritance and the naming of the heir. Thus Paul discusses at length the nature of a testament in Rom. 4, Gal. 3 and 4, and Heb. 9. We see the same thing clearly also in these words of Christ. Christ testifies concerning his death when he says: "This is my body, which is given, this is my blood, which is poured out" [Luke 22:19-20]. He names and designates the bequest when he says "for the forgiveness of sins" [Matt. 26:28]. But he appoints the heirs when he says "For you [Luke 22:19-20; I Cor. 11:24] and for many" [Matt. 26:28; Mark 14:24], that is, for those who accept and believe the promise of the testator. For here it is faith that makes men heirs, as we shall see. *true definition of mass*

You see, therefore, that what we call the mass is a promise of the forgiveness of sins made to us by God, and such a promise as has been confirmed by the death of the Son of God. For the only difference between a promise and a testament is that the testament involves the death of the one who makes it. A testator is a promiser who is about to die, while a promiser (if I may put it thus) is a testator who is not about to die. This testament of Christ is foreshadowed in all the promises of God from the beginning of the world; indeed, whatever value those ancient promises possessed was altogether derived from this new promise that was to come in Christ. Hence the words "compact," "convenant," and "testament of the Lord" occur so frequently in the Scriptures. These words signified that God would one day die. "For where there is a testament, the death of the testator must of necessity occur" (Heb. 9 [:16]). Now God made a testament; therefore, it was necessary that he should die. But God could not die unless he became man. Thus the incarnation and the death of Christ are both comprehended most concisely in this one word, "testament."

From the above it will at once be seen what is the right and what is the wrong use of the mass, and what is the worthy and what the unworthy preparation for it. If the mass is a promise, as has been said, then access to it is to be gained, not with any works, or powers, or merits of one's own, but by faith alone. For where there is the Word of the promising God, there must necessarily be the faith of the accepting man. It is plain therefore, that the beginning of our salvation is a faith which clings to the Word of the promising God, who, without any effort on our part, in free and unmerited mercy takes the initiative and offers us the word of his promise. "He sent forth his word, and thus [*sic*] healed them,"[86] not: "He accepted our work, and thus healed us." First of all there is God's Word. After it follows faith; after faith, love; then love does every good work, for it does no wrong, indeed, it is the fulfilling of the law [Rom. 13:10]. In no other way can man come to God or deal with him than through faith. That is to say, that the author of salvation is not man, by any works of his own, but God, through his promise; and that all things depend on, and are upheld and preserved by, the word of his power [Heb. 1:3], through which he brought us forth, to be a kind of first fruits of his creatures [Jas. 1:18].

Thus, in order to raise up Adam after the fall, God gave him this promise when he said to the serpent: "I will put enmity between you and the woman, and between your seed and her seed; he shall bruise your head, and you shall bruise his heel" [Gen. 3:15]. In this word of promise Adam, together with his descendants, was carried as it were in

---

86. Ps. 107:20. *Sic* is Luther's own interpolation into the Vulgate text.

God's bosom, and by faith in it he was preserved, waiting patiently for the woman who should bruise the serpent's head, as God had promised. And in that faith and expectation he died, not knowing when or who she would be, yet never doubting that she would come. For such a promise, being the truth of God, preserves even in hell those who believe it and wait for it. After this came another promise, made to Noah—to last until the time of Abraham—when a bow was set in the clouds as a sign of the covenant [Gen. 9:12-17], by faith in which Noah and his descendants found God gracious. After that, he promised Abraham that all the nations should be blessed in his seed [Gen. 22:18]. And this is Abraham's bosom [Luke 16:22], into which his descendants have been received. Then to Moses and the children of Israel [Deut. 18:18], especially to David [II Sam. 7:12-16], he gave the plainest promise of Christ, and thereby at last made clear what the promise to the men of old really was.

And so it finally came to the most perfect promise of all, that of the new testament, in which, with plain words, life and salvation are freely promised, and actually granted to those who believe the promise. And he distinguishes this testament from the old one by a particular mark when he calls it the "new testament" [Luke 22:20; I Cor. 11:25]. For the old testament given through Moses was not a promise of forgiveness of sins or of eternal things, but of temporal things, namely, of the land of Canaan, by which no man was renewed in spirit to lay hold on the heavenly inheritance. Wherefore also it was necessary that, as a figure of Christ, a dumb beast should be slain, in whose blood the same testament might be confirmed, as the blood corresponded to the testament and the sacrifice corresponded to the promise. But here Christ says "the new testament in my blood" [Luke 22:20; I Cor. 11:25], not somebody else's, but his own, by which grace is promised through the Spirit for the forgiveness of sins, that we may obtain the inheritance.

According to its substance, therefore, the mass is nothing but the aforesaid words of Christ: "Take and eat, etc." [Matt. 26:26], as if he were saying: "Behold, O sinful and condemned man, out of the pure and unmerited love with which I love you, and by the will of the Father of mercies [II Cor. 1:3], apart from any merit or desire of yours, I promise you in these words the forgiveness of all your sins and life everlasting. And that you may be absolutely certain of this irrevocable promise of mine, I shall give my body and pour out my blood, confirming this promise by my very death, and leaving you my body and blood as a sign and memorial of this same promise. As often as you partake of them, remember me, proclaim and praise my love and bounty toward you, and give thanks."

From this you will see that nothing else is needed for a worthy holding of mass than a faith that relies confidently on this promise, believes Christ to be true in these words of his, and does not doubt that these infinite blessings have been bestowed upon it. Hard on this faith there follows, of itself, a most sweet stirring of the heart, whereby the spirit of man is enlarged and enriched (that is love, given by the Holy Spirit through faith in Christ), so that he is drawn to Christ, that gracious and bounteous testator, and made a thoroughly new and different man. Who would not shed tears of gladness, indeed, almost faint for joy in Christ, if he believed with unshaken faith that this inestimable promise of Christ belonged to him? How could he help loving so great a benefactor, who of his own accord offers, promises, and grants such great riches and this eternal inheritance to one who is unworthy and deserving of something far different?

Therefore it is our one and only misfortune that we have many masses in the world, and yet none, or very few of us, recognize, consider, and receive these promises and riches that are offered to us. Actually, during the mass, we should do nothing with greater zeal (indeed, it demands all our zeal) than to set before our eyes, meditate upon, and ponder these words, these promises of Christ—for they truly constitute the mass itself—in order to exercise, nourish, increase, and strengthen our faith in them by this daily remembrance. For this is what he commands, when he says: "Do this in remembrance of me" [Luke 22:19; I Cor. 11:24]. This should be done by the preachers of the gospel in order to impress this promise faithfully upon the people, to commend it to them, and to awaken their faith in it.

But how many are there today who know that the mass is the promise of Christ? I will say nothing of those godless preachers of fables, who teach human ordinances instead of this great promise. And even if they teach these words of Christ, they do not teach them as a promise or testament, neither therefore as a means of obtaining faith.

What we deplore in this captivity is that nowadays they take every precaution that no layman should hear these words of Christ, as if they were too sacred to be delivered to the common people. So mad are we priests[87] that we arrogate to ourselves alone the so-called words of consecration, to be said secretly,[88] yet in such a way that they do not profit even us, for we too fail to regard them as promises or as a testament for the strengthening of the faith. Instead of believing them, we reverence them with I know not what superstitious and godless fancies. What else is Satan trying to do to us through this misfortune of ours but to remove every trace of the [true] mass out of the church, though he is meanwhile at work filling every corner of the globe with [false] masses, that is, with abuses and mockeries of God's testament—burdening the world more and more heavily with most grievous sins of idolatry, to its deeper condemnation? For what more sinful idolatry can there be than to

87. Cf. p. 135 n. 40.
88. The words of consecration, indeed of the whole canon of the mass, were spoken very softly. Cf. *The Abomination of the Secret Mass* (1525) in LW 36, 310 and 314.

abuse God's promises with perverse opinions and to neglect or extinguish faith in them?

For God does not deal, nor has he ever dealt, with man otherwise than through a word of promise, as I have said. We in turn cannot deal with God otherwise than through faith in the Word of his promise. He does not desire works, nor has he need of them; rather we deal with men and with ourselves on the basis of works. But God has need of this: that we consider him faithful in his promises [Heb. 10:23], and patiently persist in this belief, and thus worship him with faith, hope, and love. It is in this way that he obtains his glory among us, since it is not of ourselves who run, but of him who shows mercy [Rom. 9:16], promises, and gives, that we have and hold all good things. Behold, this is that true worship and service of God which we ought to perform in the mass. But if the words of promise are not delivered, what exercise of faith can there be? And without faith, who can have hope or love? Without faith, hope, and love, what services of God can there be? There is no doubt, therefore, that in our day all priests and monks, together with their bishops and all their superiors, are idolators, living in a most perilous state by reason of this ignorance, abuse, and mockery of the mass, or sacrament, or promise of God.

For anyone can easily see that these two, promise and faith, must necessarily go together. For without the promise there is nothing to be believed; while without faith the promise is useless, since it is established and fulfilled through faith. From this everyone will readily gather that the mass, since it is nothing but promise, can be approached and observed only in faith. Without this faith, whatever else is brought to it by way of prayers, preparations, works, signs, or gestures are incitements to impiety rather than exercises of piety. It usually happens that those who are thus prepared imagine themselves legitimately entitled to approach the altar, when in reality they are less prepared than at any other time or by any other work, by reason of the unbelief which they bring with them. How many celebrants you can see everywhere, every day, who imagine they—wretched men—have committed criminal offenses when they make some petty mistake, such as wearing the wrong vestment, or forgetting to wash their hands, or stumbling over their prayers! But the fact that they have no regard for or faith in the mass itself, namely, the divine promise, causes them not the slightest qualms of conscience. O worthless religion of this age of ours, the most godless and thankless of all ages!

Hence the only worthy preparation and proper observance is faith, the faith by which we believe in the mass, that is, in the divine promise. Whoever, therefore, desires to approach the altar or receive the sacrament, let him beware lest he appear empty-handed [Exod. 23:15; 34:20; Deut. 16:16] before the face of the Lord God. But he will be empty-handed unless he has faith in the mass, or this new testament. By what godless work could he sin more grievously against the truth of God, than by this unbelief of his? By it, as much as in him lies, he convicts God of being a liar and a maker of empty promises. The safest course, therefore, will be to go to the mass in the same spirit in which you would go to hear any other promise of God, that is, prepared not to do or contribute much yourself, but to believe and accept all that is promised you there, or proclaimed as promises through the ministry of the priest. If you do not come in this spirit, beware of attending at all, for you will surely be going to your condemnation [I Cor. 11:29].

I was right then in saying that the whole power of the mass consists in the words of Christ, in which he testifies that forgiveness of sins is bestowed on all those who believe that his body is given and his blood poured out for them. This is why nothing is more important for those who go to hear mass than to ponder these words diligently and in full faith. Unless they do this, all else that they do is in vain. This is surely true, that to every promise of his, God usually adds some sign as a memorial or remembrance of the promise, so that thereby we may serve him the more diligently and he may admonish us the more effectually. Thus, when he promised Noah that he would not again destroy the world by a flood, he added his bow in the clouds, to show that he would be mindful of his covenant [Gen. 9:8-17]. And after promising Abraham the inheritance in his seed, he gave him circumcision as a mark of his justification by faith [Gen. 17:3-11]. Thus he granted to Gideon the dry and the wet fleece to confirm his promise of victory over the Midianites [Judg. 6:36-40]. And through Isaiah he offered to Ahaz a sign that he would conquer the king of Syria and Samaria, to confirm in him his faith in the promise [Isa. 7:10-17]. And we read of many such signs of the promises of God in the Scriptures.

So in the mass also, the foremost promise of all, he adds as a memorial sign of such a great promise his own body and his own blood in the bread and wine, when he says: "Do this in remembrance of me" [Luke 22:19; I Cor. 11:24-25]. And so in baptism, to the words of promise he adds the sign of immersion in water. We may learn from this that in every promise of God two things are presented to us, the word and the sign, so that we are to understand the word to be the testament, but the sign to be the sacrament. Thus, in the mass, the word of Christ is the testament, and the bread and wine are the sacrament. And as there is greater power in the word than in the sign, so there is greater power in the testament than in the sacrament; for a man can have and use the word or testament apart from the sign or sacrament. "Believe," says Augustine, "and you have eaten."[89] But what does one believe, other than the word of the one who promises? Therefore I can hold mass every

89. Cf. p. 133 n. 33.

day, indeed, every hour, for I can set the words of Christ before me and with them feed and strengthen my faith as often as I choose. This is a truly spiritual eating and drinking.

Here you may see what great things our theologians of the *Sentences*[90] have produced in this matter. In the first place, not one of them treats of that which is first and foremost, namely, the testament and the word of promise. And thus they make us forget faith and the whole power of the mass. In addition, they discuss exclusively the second part of the mass, namely, the sign or sacrament; yet in such a way that here too they do not teach faith, but their preparations and *opera operata*,[91] participations[92] and fruits of the mass. They come then to the profundities, babble of transubstantiation and endless other metaphysical trivialities, destroy the proper understanding and use of both sacrament and testament together with faith as such, and cause Christ's people to forget their God—as the prophet says, days without number [Jer. 2:32]. Let the others tabulate the various benefits of hearing mass; you just apply your mind to this, that you may say and believe with the prophet that God has here prepared a table before you in the presence of your enemies [Ps. 23:5], at which your faith may feed and grow fat. But your faith is fed only with the word of divine promise, for "Man shall not live by bread alone, but by every word that proceeds from the mouth of God" [Deut. 8:3; Matt. 4:4]. Hence, in the mass you must pay closest heed above all to the word of promise, as to a most lavish banquet—your utterly green pastures and sacred still waters [Ps. 23:2], in order that you might esteem this word above everything else, trust in it supremely, and cling to it most firmly, even through death and all sins. If you do this, you will obtain not merely those

90. Commentators on Peter Lombard's textbook. Cf. p. 144 n. 60.
91. Cf. p. 154 n. 85.
92. Cf. p. 152 n. 79.

tiny drops and crumbs of "fruits of the mass" which some have superstitiously invented, but the very fountainhead of life, namely, that faith in the Word out of which every good thing flows, as is said in John 4:[93] "He who believes in me, 'Out of his heart shall flow rivers of living water.'" And again, "Whoever drinks of the water that I shall give him, it will become in him a spring of water welling up to eternal life" [John 4:14].

Now there are two things that are constantly assailing us, so that we fail to gather the fruits of the mass. The first is that we are sinners, and unworthy of such great things because of our utter worthlessness. The second is that, even if we were worthy, these things are so high that our faint-hearted nature does not dare to aspire to them or hope for them. For who would not simply stand awe-struck before the forgiveness of sins and life everlasting rather than seeking after them, once he had weighed properly the magnitude of the blessings which come through them, namely, to have God as father, to be his son and heir of all his goods! Against this twofold faintness of ours we must lay hold on the word of Christ, and fix our gaze much more steadfastly on it than on these thoughts of our own weakness. For "great are the works of the Lord, studied by all who have pleasure in them" [Ps. 111:2], who is able to give "more abundantly than all that we ask or think" [Eph. 3:20]. If they did not surpass our worthiness, our grasp, and all our thoughts, they would not be divine. Thus Christ also encourages us when he says: "Fear not, little flock, for it is your Father's good pleasure to give you the kingdom" [Luke 12:32]. For it is just this incomprehensible overflowing of God's goodness, showered upon us through Christ, that moves us above all to love him most ardently in return, to be drawn to him with fullest confidence, and,

---

93. John 7:38. Luther apparently had his next quotation in mind when he cited John 4.

despising all else, be ready to suffer all things for him. Wherefore this sacrament is rightly called "a fountain of love."

Let us take an illustration of this from human experience.[94] If a very rich lord were to bequeath a thousand gulden to a beggar or to an unworthy and wicked servant, it is certain that he would boldly claim and accept them without regard to his unworthiness and the greatness of the bequest. And if anyone should seek to oppose him on the grounds of his unworthiness and the large amount of the legacy, what do you suppose the man would say? He would likely say: "What is that to you? What I accept, I accept not on my merits or by any right that I may personally have to it. I know that I am receiving more than a worthless one like me deserves; indeed, I have deserved the very opposite. But I claim what I claim by the right of a bequest and of another's goodness. If to him it was not an unworthy thing to bequeath so great a sum to an unworthy person, why should I refuse to accept it because of my unworthiness? Indeed, it is for this very reason that I cherish all the more his unmerited gift—because I am unworthy!" With that same thought every man ought to fortify his conscience against all qualms and scruples, so that he may lay hold on the promise of Christ with unwavering faith, and take the greatest care to approach the sacrament not trusting in confession, prayer, and preparation, but rather, despairing of all these, with firm confidence in Christ who gives the promise. For, as we have said often enough, the word of promise must reign alone here in pure faith; such faith is the one and only sufficient preparation.

Hence we see how great is God's wrath with us, in that he has permitted godless teachers to conceal the words of this testament from us, and thereby to extinguish this same

---

94. Repeated in a similar context in *A Treatise on the New Testament that is the Holy Mass* (1520). PE 1, 304-305.

faith, as far as they could. It is already easy to see what is the inevitable result of this extinguishing of the faith, namely, the most godless superstition of works. For where faith dies and the word of faith is silent, there works and the prescribing of works immediately crowd into their place. By them we have been carried away out of our own land, as into a Babylonian captivity, and despoiled of all our precious possessions. This has been the fate of the mass; it has been converted by the teaching of godless men into a good work. They themselves call it an *opus operatum*,[95] and by it they presume themselves to be all-powerful with God. Next they proceed to the very height of madness, and after inventing the lie that the mass is effective simply by virtue of the act having been performed, they add another one to the effect that the mass is none the less profitable to others even if it is harmful to some wicked priest who may be celebrating it. On such a foundation of sand they base their applications, participations,[96] brotherhoods,[97] anniversaries,[98] and numberless other lucrative and profitable schemes of that kind.

These fraudulent disguises are so powerful, so numerous, and so firmly entrenched that you can scarcely prevail against them unless you exercise unremitting care and bear well in mind what the mass is and what has been said above. You have seen that the mass is nothing else than the divine promise or testament of Christ, sealed with the sacrament of his body and blood. If that is true, you will understand that it cannot possibly be in any way a work; nobody can possibly do any thing in it, neither can it be dealt with in any other way than by faith alone. However, faith is not a work, but the lord and life of all works.[99]

95. Cf. p. 154 n. 85.
96. Cf. p. 152 n. 79.
97. Cf. p. 152 n. 80.
98. Cf. p. 152 n. 81.
99. On the relation between faith and works compare *A Treatise on Good Works* (1520), where Luther says faith is the first and highest of all good works. *PE* 1, 187. Cf. also p. 184 below.

Who in the world is so foolish as to regard a promise received by him, or a testament given to him as a good work, which he renders to the testator by his acceptance of it? What heir will imagine that he is doing his departed father a kindness by accepting the terms of the will and the inheritance it bequeaths to him? What godless audacity is it, therefore, when we who are to receive the testament of God come as those who would perform a good work for him! This ignorance of the testament, this captivity of so great a sacrament—are they not too sad for tears? When we ought to be grateful for benefits received, we come arrogantly to give that which we ought to take. With unheard-of perversity we mock the mercy of the giver by giving as a work the thing we receive as a gift, so that the testator, instead of being a dispenser of his own goods, becomes the recipient of ours. Woe to such sacrilege!

Who has ever been so mad as to regard baptism as a good work, or what candidate for baptism has believed that he was performing a work which he might offer to God on behalf of himself and communicate to others? If, then, there is no good work that can be communicated to others in this one sacrament and testament, neither will there be any in the mass, since it too is nothing else than a testament and sacrament. Hence it is a manifest and wicked error to offer or apply the mass for sins, for satisfactions, for the dead, or for any needs whatsoever of one's own or of others. You will readily see the obvious truth of this if you firmly hold that the mass is a divine promise, which can benefit no one, be applied to no one, intercede for no one, and be communicated to no one, except only to him who believes with a faith of his own. Who can receive or apply, in behalf of another, the promise of God, which demands the personal faith of each one individually? Can I give to another the promise of God, even if he does not believe? Can I believe for another, or cause another to believe? But this is what must happen if I am able to

wicked-ness in mass

167

apply and communicate the mass to others; for there are but two things in the mass, the divine promise and the human faith, the latter accepting what the former promises. But if it is true that I can do this, then I can also hear and believe the gospel for another, I can be baptized for another, I can be absolved from sins for another, I can also partake of the Sacrament of the Altar for another, and —to go through the list of their sacraments also—I can marry a wife for another, get ordained for another, be confirmed for another, and receive extreme unction for another!

In short, why did not Abraham believe for all the Jews? Why was faith in the promise made to Abraham demanded of every individual Jew?

Therefore, let this irrefutable truth stand fast: Where there is a divine promise, there every one must stand on his own feet; his own personal faith is demanded, he will give an account for himself and bear his own load [Gal. 6:5]; as it is said in the last chapter of Mark [16:16]: "He who believes and is baptized will be saved; but he who does not believe will be condemned." Even so each one can derive personal benefit from the mass only by his own personal faith. It is absolutely impossible to commune on behalf of anyone else. Just as the priest is unable to administer the sacrament to anyone on behalf of another, but administers the same sacrament to each one individually by himself. For in consecrating and administering, the priests are our servants. Through them we are not offering a good work or communicating something in an active sense. Rather, we are receiving through them the promises and the sign; we are being communicated unto in the passive sense. This is the view that has persisted with respect to the laity right up to the present day, for of them it is said not that they do something good but that they receive it. But the priests have strayed into godless ways; out of the sacrament and testament of God, which ought to be a good gift received, they have made for themselves a good

168

deed performed, which they then give to others and offer up to God.

But you will say: What is this? Will you not overturn the practice and teaching of all the churches and monasteries, by virtue of which they have flourished all these centuries? For the mass is the foundation of their anniversaries, intercessions, applications, communications, etc., that is to say, of their fat income. I answer: This is the very thing that has constrained me to write of the captivity of the church. For it is in this manner that the sacred testament of God has been forced into the service of a most impious traffic. It has come through the opinions and ordinances of wicked men, who, passing over the Word of God, have dished up to us the thoughts of their own hearts and led the whole world astray. What do I care about the number and influence of those who are in this error? The truth is mightier than all of them. If you are able to refute Christ, who teaches that the mass is a testament and a sacrament, then I will admit that they are in the right. Or, if you can bring yourself to say that that man is doing a good work who receives the benefit of the testament, or to that end uses this sacrament of promise, then I will gladly condemn my teachings. But since you can do neither, why do you hesitate to turn your back on the multitude who go after evil? Why do you hesitate to give God the glory and to confess his truth—that all priests today are perversely mistaken who regard the mass as a work by which they may relieve their own needs and those of others, whether dead or alive? I am uttering unheard of and startling things, but if you will consider what the mass is, you will realize that I have spoken the truth. The fault lies with our false sense of security, which blinds us to the wrath of God that is raging against us.

I am ready to admit, however, that the prayers which we pour out before God when we are gathered together to partake of the mass are good works or benefits, which we impart, apply and communicate to one another, and which we offer for one another. Thus James [5:16] teaches us to pray for one another that we may be healed, and Paul in I Tim. 2[:1-2] commands "that supplications, prayers, and intercessions be made for all men, for kings and all who are in high positions." Now these are not the mass, but works of the mass—if the prayers of heart and lips may be called works—for they flow from the faith that is kindled or increased in the sacrament. For the mass, or the promise of God, is not fulfilled by praying, but only by believing. However, as believers we pray and perform every good work. But what priest offers up the sacrifice in this sense, that he believes he is offering up only the prayers? They all imagine that they are offering up Christ himself to God the Father as an all-sufficient sacrifice, and performing a good work for all those whom they intend to benefit, for they put their trust in the work which the mass accomplishes, and they do not ascribe this work to prayer. In this way the error has gradually grown, until they have come to ascribe to the sacrament what belongs to the prayers, and to offer to God what should be received as a benefit.

We must therefore sharply distinguish the testament and sacrament itself from the prayers which we offer at the same time. Not only this, but we must also bear in mind that the prayers avail utterly nothing, either to him who offers them or to those for whom they are offered, unless the testament is first received in faith, so that it will be faith that offers the prayers; for faith alone is heard, as James teaches in his first chapter [Jas. 1:6]. There is therefore a great difference between prayer and the mass. Prayer may be extended to as many persons as one desires, while the mass is received only by the person who believes for himself, and only to the extent that he believes. It cannot be given either to God or to men. Rather it is God alone who through the ministration of the priest gives it to men, and men receive it by faith alone without any works or merits. Nor would anyone dare to be so foolish as to assert that a ragged beggar does a good work when he comes to receive a gift from a rich man. But the mass (as I have said)[100] is the gift of the divine promise, proffered to all men by the hand of the priest.

It is certain, therefore, that the mass is not a work which may be communicated to others, but the object of faith (as has been said),[101] for the strengthening and nourishing of each one's own faith. *object of faith, rather than communicated to others.*

Now there is yet a second stumbling block that must be removed, and this is much greater and the most dangerous of all. It is the common belief that the mass is a sacrifice, which is offered to God. Even the words of the canon[102] seem to imply this, when they speak of "these gifts, these presents, these holy sacrifices," and further on "this offering." Prayer is also made, in so many words, "that the sacrifice may be accepted even as the sacrifice of Abel," etc. Hence Christ is termed "the sacrifice of the altar." Added to these are the sayings of the holy fathers, the great number of examples, and the widespread practice uniformly observed throughout the world.

Over against all these things, firmly entrenched as they are, we must resolutely set the words and example of Christ. For unless we firmly hold that the mass is the promise or testament of Christ, as the words clearly say, we shall lose the whole gospel and all its comfort. Let us permit nothing to prevail against these words—even though an angel from heaven should teach otherwise [Gal. 1:8]—for they contain nothing about a work or a sacrifice. Moreover, we also have the example of Christ on our side. When he instituted this

---

100. Cf. pp. 154-63.

101. *Ibid.*

102. The canon of the mass is the invariable part of the liturgy of the mass in which the consecration of the bread and wine is effected. Its text was translated by Luther from the Latin in his treatise on *The Abomination of the Secret Mass* (1525), and appears in *LW* 314-27.

sacrament and established this testament at the Last Supper, Christ did not offer himself to God the Father, nor did he perform a good work on behalf of others, but, sitting at the table, he set this same testament before each one and proffered to him the sign. Now, the more closely our mass resembles that first mass of all, which Christ performed at the Last Supper, the more Christian it will be. But Christ's mass was most simple, without any display or vestments, gestures, chants, or other ceremonies, so that if it had been necessary to offer the mass as a sacrifice, then Christ's institution of it was not complete.

Not that any one should revile the church universal for embellishing and amplifying the mass with many additional rites and ceremonies. But what we contend for is this: No one should be deceived by the glamor of the ceremonies and entangled in the multitude of pompous forms, and thus lose the simplicity of the mass itself, and indeed practice a sort of transubstantiation by losing sight of the simple "substance" of the mass and clinging to the manifold "accidents" of outward pomp. For whatever has been added to the word and example of Christ is an "accident" of the mass, and ought to be regarded just as we regard the so-called monstrances and corporal cloths in which the host itself is contained. Therefore, just as disturbing a testament or accepting a promise differs diametrically from offering a sacrifice, so it is a contradiction in terms to call the mass a sacrifice, for the former is something that we receive and the latter is something that we give. The same thing cannot be received and offered at the same time, nor can it be both given and accepted by the same person, any more than our prayer can be the same thing as that which our prayer obtains, or the act of praying be the same thing as the act of receiving that for which we pray.

What shall we say then of the canon of the mass and the patristic authorities? First of all, I would answer: If there were nothing at all to be said against them, it would be safer to reject them all than admit that the mass is a work or a sacrifice, lest we deny the word of Christ and destroy faith together with the mass. Nevertheless, in order to retain them, we shall say that we are instructed by the Apostle in I Cor. 11 [:21,33] that it was customary for Christ's believers, when they came together for mass, to bring with them food and drink. These they called "collections," and they distributed them among all who were in want, after the example of the apostles in Acts 4 [:34-35]. From this store was taken the portion of bread and wine that was consecrated in the sacrament.[103] And since all this store was consecrated by the word and prayer [I Tim. 4:5], by being "lifted up" according to the Hebrew rite of which we read in Moses [Lev. 8:27], the words and the rite of this lifting up or offering have come down to us, although the custom of bringing along and collecting that which was offered or lifted up has long since fallen into disuse. Thus, in Isa. 37 [:4] Hezekiah commanded Isaiah to lift up his prayer in the sight of God for the remnant. In the Psalms we read: "Lift up your hands to the holy place" [Ps. 134:2]. And again: "To thee I will lift up my hands" [Ps. 63:4]. And in I Tim. 2 [:8] "In every place lifting holy hands." For this reason the words "sacrifice" and "offering" must be taken to refer not to the sacrament and testament, but to the collections themselves. From this source also the word "collect" has come down to us for prayers said in the mass.

The same thing happens when the priest elevates the bread and the cup immediately after consecrating them. By this he does not show that he is offering anything to God, for he does not say a single word here about a victim or an offering. But this elevation is either a survival of that Hebrew rite of lifting up what was received with thanksgiving and returned to God, or else it is an admonition to us to provoke us to faith in this testament which the priest

---

103. Cf. *A Treatise Concerning the Blessed Sacrament* (1519). PE 2, 16.

has set forth and exhibited in the words of Christ, so that now he also shows us the sign of the testament. Thus the oblation of the bread properly accompanies the demonstrative "this" in the words, "this is my body," and by the sign the priest addresses us gathered about him; and in like manner the oblation of the cup properly accompanies the demonstrative "this" in the words, "this cup is the new testament, etc." For it is faith that the priest ought to awaken in us by this act of elevation. And would to God that as he elevates the sign, or sacrament, openly before our eyes, he might also sound in our ears the word, or testament, in a loud, clear voice, and in the language of the people, whatever it may be, in order that faith may be the more effectively awakened. For why may mass be said in Greek and Latin and Hebrew, but not in German or any other language?

Therefore, let the priests who offer the sacrifice of the mass in these corrupt and most perilous times take heed, first, that they do not refer to the sacrament the words of the greater and lesser canon,[104] together with the collects, because they smack too strongly of sacrifice. They should refer them instead to the bread and the wine to be consecrated, or to their own prayers. For the bread and wine are offered beforehand for blessing in order that they may be sanctified by the word and by prayer [I Tim. 4:5], but after they have been blessed and consecrated they are no longer offered, but received as a gift from God. And in this rite let the priest bear in mind that the gospel is to be set above all canons and collects devised by men, and that the gospel does not sanction the idea that the mass is a sacrifice, as has been shown.

---

104. In printed missals prior to the Council of Trent, *canon minor* was the term used to designate collectively those offertory prayers within the canon itself which immediately preceded the consecration of the elements. These collects were of comparatively late origin, coming only gradually into use during the late middle ages. Valentin Thalhofer, *Handbuch der katholischen Liturgik* (Freiburg im Breisgau, 1890), II, 159.

Further, when a priest celebrates public mass, he should determine to do nothing else than to commune himself and others by means of the mass. At the same time, however, he may offer prayers for himself and others, but he must beware lest he presume to offer the mass. But let him that holds private masses[105] determine to commune himself. The private mass does not differ in the least from the ordinary communion which any layman receives at the hand of the priest, and has no greater effect. The difference is in the prayers, and in the fact that the priest consecrates the elements for himself and administers them to himself. As far as the blessing[106] of the mass and sacrament is concerned we are all equals, whether we are priests or laymen.

If a priest is requested by others to celebrate so-called "votive" masses,[107] let him beware of accepting a fee for the mass, or of presuming to offer any votive sacrifice. Rather, he should take pains to refer all this to the prayers which he offers for the dead or the living, saying to himself: "Lo, I will go and receive the sacrament for myself alone, and while doing so I will pray for this one and that one." Thus he will receive his fee for the prayers, not for the mass, and can buy food and clothing with it. Let him not be disturbed because all the world holds and practices the contrary. You have the utmost certainty of the gospel, and by relying on it, you may well disregard the belief and opinions of men. But if you disregard me and insist upon offering the mass and not the prayers alone, remember that I have faithfully warned you, and that I will be without blame on the day of judgment; you will have to bear your sin alone. I have said what I was bound to say to you as

---

105. The private mass does not require the presence of a congregation. Besides the celebrant there need be present only a ministrant. There is no music; the mass is only read.

106. The *res sacramenti*. Cf. p. 137 n. 45.

107. Masses celebrated on the request of congregations or individuals in connection with specific purposes or occasions, or in honor of certain mysteries (e.g., of the Holy Trinity, of the Holy Spirit, or of angels).

brother to brother for your salvation; yours will be the gain if you observe it, yours the loss if you neglect it. And if some should even condemn what I have said, I will reply in the words of Paul: "But evil men and impostors will go on from bad to worse, deceiving and being deceived" [II Tim. 3:13].

From the above every one will readily understand the often quoted saying of Gregory[108]: "A mass celebrated by a wicked priest is not to be considered of less effect than one celebrated by a good priest. Neither would a mass of St. Peter have been better than that of Judas the traitor, if they had offered the sacrifice of the mass." This saying has served many as a cloak to cover their godless doings, and because of it they have invented the distinction between the *opus operatum* and the *opus operantis*,[109] so as to be free to lead wicked lives themselves and yet benefit other men. Gregory speaks the truth, only they misunderstand his words. For it is true beyond a question that the testament or sacrament is given and received through the ministration of wicked priests no less completely than through the ministration of the most saintly. For who has any doubt that the gospel is preached by the ungodly? Now the mass is part of the gospel; indeed, it is the sum and substance of it. For what is the whole gospel but the good tidings of the forgiveness of sins? Whatever can be said about forgiveness of sins and the mercy of God in the broadest and richest sense is all briefly comprehended in the word of this testament. For this reason popular sermons ought to be nothing else than expositions of the mass, or explanations of the divine promise of this testament; this would be to teach the faith and truly to edify the church. But in our day

---

108. Pope Gregory I (590-604).
109. The former is the properly executed performance of the ritual of the mass —"the work wrought" (cf. p. 154 n. 85). The latter is the inner disposition, the faith, either of the recipient or of the celebrant—"the work of the doer."

the expounders of the mass make mockery and jest with allegorical explanations of human ceremonies.

Therefore, just as a wicked priest may baptize, that is, apply the word of promise and the sign of water to the candidate for baptism, so he may also set forth the promise of this sacrament and administer it to those who partake, and even partake himself, as did Judas the traitor at the supper of the Lord [Matt. 26:23-25]. It still remains the same sacrament and testament, which works its own work in the believer but an "alien work"[110] in the unbeliever. But when it comes to offering a sacrifice the case is quite different. For not the mass but the prayers are offered to God, and therefore it is as plain as day that the offerings of a wicked priest avail nothing, but, as Gregory says again: When an unworthy person is sent as the intercessor, the heart of the judge is only turned to greater disfavor. Therefore these two things—mass and prayer, sacrament and work, testament and sacrifice—must not be confused; for the one comes from God to us through the ministration of the priest and demands our faith, the other proceeds from our faith to God through the priest and demands his hearing. The former descends, the latter ascends. The former, therefore, does not necessarily require a worthy and godly minister, but the latter does indeed require such a one, for "God does not listen to sinners" [John 9:31]. He knows how to do good through evil men, but he does not accept the work of any evil man; as he showed in the case of Cain [Gen. 4:5], and as is said in Prov. 15 [:8]: "The sacrifice of the wicked is an abomination to the Lord," and in Rom. 14 [:23]: "Whatever does not proceed from faith is sin."

But let us bring this first part to an end, though I am ready to go on with the argument if an opponent should arise. From all that has been said we conclude that the mass was provided only for those who have a sad, afflicted,

---

110. Its own work is salvation. The "alien work" is condemnation. The expression derives from Isa. 28:21.

disturbed, perplexed and erring conscience, and that they alone commune worthily. For, since the word of divine promise in this sacrament sets forth the forgiveness of sins, let every one draw near fearlessly, whoever he may be, who is troubled by his sins, whether by remorse or by temptation. For this treatment of Christ is the one remedy against sins, past, present and future, if you but cling to it with unwavering faith and believe that what the words of the testament declare is freely granted to you. But if you do not believe this, you will never, anywhere, by any works or efforts of your own, be able to find peace of conscience. For faith alone means peace of conscience, while unbelief means only distress of conscience.

THE SACRAMENT OF BAPTISM

Blessed be God and the Father of our Lord Jesus Christ, who according to the riches of his mercy [Eph. 1:3, 7] has preserved in his church this sacrament at least, untouched and untainted by the ordinances of men, and has made it free to all nations and classes of mankind, and has not permitted it to be oppressed by the filthy and godless monsters of greed and superstition. For he desired that by it little children, who were incapable of greed and superstition, might be initiated and sanctified in the simple faith of his Word; even today baptism has its chief blessing for them. But if the intention had been to give this sacrament to adults and older people, I do not believe that it could possibly have retained its power and its glory against the tyranny of greed and superstition which has overthrown all things divine among us. Here too the wisdom of the flesh would doubtless have devised its preparations and dignities, its reservations, restrictions, and other like snares for catching money, until water brought as high a price as parchment[111] does now.

---

111. Leters of indulgence.

But Satan, though he could not quench the power of baptism in little children, nevertheless succeeded in quenching it in all adults, so that now there are scarcely any who call to mind their own baptism, and still fewer who glory in it; so many other ways have been discovered for remitting sins and getting to heaven. The source of these false opinions is that dangerous saying of St. Jerome[112] (either unhappily phrased or wrongly interpreted) in which he terms penance "the second plank after shipwreck," as if baptism were not penance. Hence, when men have fallen into sin, they despair of the "first plank," which is the ship, as if it had gone under, and begin to put all their trust and faith in the second plank, which is penance. This has given rise to those endless burdens of vows, religious orders, works, satisfactions, pilgrimages, indulgences, and monastic sects, and from them in turn has arisen that flood of books, questions, opinions, and man-made ordinances which the whole world cannot contain. Thus the church of God is incomparably worse off under this tyranny than the synagogue or any other nation under heaven ever was.

It was the duty of the pontiffs to remove all these evils, and to put forth every effort to recall Christians to the true understanding of baptism, so that they might know what manner of men they were and how Christians ought to live. But instead of this, their only work today is to lead the people as far astray as possible from their baptism, to immerse all men in the flood of their tyranny, and to cause the people of Christ (as the prophet says) to forget him days without number [Jer. 2:32]. How unhappy, are all who bear the name of pontiff today! For they neither know nor do what is becoming to pontiffs, but they are ignorant of what they ought to know and do. They fulfill what Isa.

---

112. St. Jerome (d. 420), ascetic, zealous exponent of the monastic life, prolific writer against the heretics, translator of an important Latin version of the Bible, was also the author of many letters—to one of which Luther is referring. *Epistola* 130, par. 9. Migne 22, 1115.

56 [:10, 11] says: "His watchmen are blind, they are all without knowledge the shepherds also have no understanding; they have all turned to their own way, each to his own gain, etc."

Now, the *first* thing to be considered about baptism is the divine promise, which says: "He who believes and is baptized will be saved" [Mark 16:16]. This promise must be set far above all the glitter of works, vows, religious orders, and whatever else man has introduced, for on it all our salvation depends. But we must so consider it as to exercise our faith in it, and have no doubt whatever that, once we have been baptized, we are saved. For unless faith is present or is conferred in baptism, baptism will profit us nothing; indeed, it will become a hindrance to us, not only at the moment when it is received, but throughout the rest of our lives. That kind of unbelief accuses God's promise of being a lie, and this is the greatest of all sins. If we set ourselves to this exercise of faith, we shall at once perceive how difficult it is to believe this promise of God. For our human weakness, conscious of its sins, finds nothing more difficult to believe than that it is saved; and yet, unless it does believe this, it cannot be saved, because it does not believe the truth of God that promises salvation.

This message should have been impressed upon the people untiringly, and this promise should have been dinned into their ears without ceasing. Their baptism should have been called to their minds again and again, and their faith constantly awakened and nourished. For just as the truth of this divine promise, once pronounced over us, continues until death, so our faith in it ought never to cease, but to be nourished and strengthened until death by the continual remembrance of this promise made to us in baptism. Therefore, when we rise from our sins or repent, we are merely returning to the power and the faith of baptism from which we fell, and finding our way back to the promise then made to us, which we deserted when we sinned. For the truth of the promise once made remains steadfast, always ready to receive us back with open arms when we return. And this, if I mistake not, is what they mean when they say, though obscurely, that baptism is the first sacrament and the foundation of all the others, without which none of the others can be received.

It will therefore be no small gain to a penitent to remember above all his baptism, and, confidently calling to mind the divine promise which he has forsaken, acknowledge that promise before his Lord, rejoicing that he is still within the fortress of salvation because he has been baptized, and abhorring his wicked ingratitude in falling away from its faith and truth. His heart will find wonderful comfort and will be encouraged to hope for mercy when he considers that the promise which God made to him, which cannot possibly lie, is still unbroken and unchanged, and indeed, cannot be changed by sins, as Paul says (II Tim. 2 [:13]): "If we are faithless, he remains faithful—for he cannot deny himself." This truth of God, I say, will sustain him, so that if all else should fail, this truth, if he believes in it, will not fail him. In it the penitent has a shield against all assaults of the scornful enemy, an answer to the sins that disturb his conscience, an antidote for the dread of death and judgment, and a comfort in every temptation—namely, this one truth—when he says: "God is faithful in his promises [Heb. 10:23; 11:11], and I received his sign in baptism. If God is for me, who is against me?" [Rom. 8:31].

The children of Israel, whenever they turned to repentance, remembered above all their exodus from Egypt, and remembering turned back to God who had brought them out. Moses impressed this memory and this protection upon them many times, and David afterwards did the same. How much more ought we to remember our exodus from Egypt, and by this remembrance turn back to him who led us through the washing of regeneration [Titus 3:5], remembrance of which is commended to us for this very reason!

This can be done most fittingly in the sacrament of bread and wine. Indeed, in former times these three sacraments—penance, baptism, and the bread—were all celebrated at the same service, and each one supplemented the other. We also read of a certain holy virgin[113] who in every time of temptation made baptism her sole defense, saying simply, "I am a Christian"; and immediately the enemy recognized the power of baptism and of her faith, which clung to the truth of a promising God, and fled from her.

Thus you see how rich a Christian is, that is, one who has been baptized! Even if he would, he could not lose his salvation, however much he sinned, unless he refused to believe. For no sin can condemn him save unbelief alone. All other sins, so long as the faith in God's promise made in baptism returns or remains, are immediately blotted out through that same faith, or rather through the truth of God, because he cannot deny himself if you confess him and faithfully cling to him in his promise. But as for contrition, confession of sins, and satisfaction,[114] along with all those carefully devised exercises of men: if you rely on them and neglect this truth of God, they will suddenly fail you and leave you more wretched than before. For whatever is done without faith in God's truth is vanity of vanities and vexation of spirit [Eccles. 1:2, 14].

You will likewise see how perilous, indeed, how false it is to suppose that penance is "the second plank after shipwreck,"[115] and how pernicious an error it is to believe that the power of baptism is broken, and the ship dashed to pieces, because of sin. The ship remains one, solid, and invincible; it will never be broken up into separate "planks." In it are all those who are brought to the harbor of salvation,

---

113. This may be a reference to Blandina, a young slave and Christian martyr, whose courage during the persecution under the Roman emperor, Marcus Aurelius (161-180), was extolled by Eusebius. *CL* 1, 462.

114. The three parts of the sacrament of penance.

115. Cf. p. 179 n. 112.

for it is the truth of God giving us its promise in the sacraments. Of course, it often happens that many rashly leap overboard into the sea and perish; these are those who abandon faith in the promise and plunge into sin. But the ship itself remains intact and holds its course unimpaired. If any one is able somehow by grace to return to the ship, it is not on any plank, but in the solid ship itself that he is borne to life. Such a person is the one who returns through faith to the abiding and enduring promise of God. Therefore Peter, in II Pet. 1 [:9], rebukes those who sin, because they have forgotten that they were cleansed from their old sins, and he clearly rebukes their wicked unbelief and their ingratitude for the baptism they had received. *people are rebuked for sinning because they have forgotten their baptism*

What is the good, then, of writing so much about baptism and yet not teaching this faith in the promise? All the sacraments were instituted to nourish faith. Yet these Godless men pass over it so completely as even to assert that a man dare not be certain of the forgiveness of sins or the grace of the sacraments. With such wicked teaching they delude the world, and not only take captive, but altogether destroy, the sacrament of baptism, in which the chief glory of our conscience consists. Meanwhile they madly rage against the miserable souls of men with their contritions, anxious confessions, circumstances,[116] satisfactions, works, and endless other such absurdities. Therefore read with great caution the "Master of the *Sentences*"[117] in his fourth book; better yet, despise him with all his commentators, who at their best write only of the "matter" and "form"[118] of the sacraments; that is, they treat of the dead and death-dealing letter [II

---

116. The penitent had to relate the conditions attendant upon his transgression to help the priest determine his state of heart and degree of guilt. Cf. Buchwald, *op. cit.*, II, 433 n. 1.

117. Cf. p. 144 n. 60.

118. These terms, derived from the philosophy of Aristotle, were introduced by scholastic theologians of the thirteenth century into their explanations of the sacraments. Matter was the sign, e.g., water in baptism. Form was the word, e.g., the Words of Institution.

Cor. 3:6] of the sacraments, but leave untouched the spirit, life, and use, that is, the truth of the divine promise and our faith.

Beware, therefore, that the external pomp of works and the deceits of man-made ordinances do not deceive you, lest you wrong the divine truth and your faith. If you would be saved, you must begin with the faith of the sacraments, without any works whatever. The works will follow faith, but do not think too lightly of faith, for it is the most excellent and difficult of all works.[119] Through it alone you will be saved, even if you should be compelled to do without any other works. For faith is a work of God, not of man, as Paul teaches [Eph. 2:8]. The other works he works through us and with our help, but this one alone he works in us and without our help.

From this we can clearly see the difference in baptism between man who administers the sacrament and God who is its author. For man baptizes, and yet does not baptize. He baptizes in that he performs the work of immersing the person to be baptized; he does not baptize, because in so doing he acts not on his own authority but in God's stead. Hence we ought to receive baptism at human hands just as if Christ himself, indeed, God himself, were baptizing us with his own hands. For it is not man's baptism, but Christ's and God's baptism, which we receive by the hand of a man, just as everything else that we have through the hand of somebody else is God's alone. Therefore beware of making any distinction in baptism by ascribing the outward part to man and the inward part to God. Ascribe both to God alone, and look upon the person administering it as simply the vicarious instrument of God, by which the Lord sitting in heaven thrusts you under the water with his own hands, and promises you forgiveness of your sins, speaking to you upon earth with a human voice by the mouth of his minister.

---

119. Cf. p. 166 n. 99.

184

This the words themselves indicate, when the priest says: "I baptize you in the name of the Father, and of the Son, and of the Holy Ghost. Amen," and not: "I baptize you in my own name." It is as though he said: "What I do, I do not by my own authority, but in the name and stead of God, so that you should regard it just as if our Lord himself had done it in a visible manner. The Doer and the minister are different persons, but the work of both is the same work, or rather, it is the work of the Doer alone, through my ministry." For I hold that "in the name of" refers to the person of the Doer, so that the name of the Lord is not only to be uttered and invoked while the work is being done; but the work itself is to be done as something not one's own—in the name and stead of Another. In this sense Christ says in Matt. 24 [:5], "Many will come in my name," and Rom. 1 [:5] says, "Through whom we have received grace and apostleship to bring about obedience for the sake of his name among all the nations."

This view I heartily endorse, for there is great comfort and a mighty aid to faith in the knowledge that one has been baptized, not by man, but by the Triune God himself, through a man acting among us in His name. This will put an end to that idle dispute about the "form" of baptism, as they term the words which are used. The Greeks say: "May the servant of Christ be baptized," while the Latins say: "I baptize."[120] Others again, adhering rigidly to their pedantry, condemn the use of the words, "I baptize you in the name of Jesus Christ,"[121] although it is certain the apostles used this formula in baptizing, as we read in the Acts of the Apostles [2:38; 10:48; 19:5]; they would allow no other form to be valid than this: "I baptize you in the name of the Father, and of the Son, and of the Holy Ghost. Amen." But their con-

---

120. Cf. p. 139 n. 47. The dispute had already been decided by the fifteenth-century popes: Eugene IV, Sixtus IV, and Alexander VI, who accepted the validity of the imperative or deprecatory formula of the Eastern church.
121. Alexander of Hales (d. 1245) denied the validity of baptism "in the name of Jesus"; Peter Lombard defended it.

who receives it.

*power of baptism faith of the one
depends upon the the one*

tention is in vain, for they bring no proof, but merely assert their own dreams. Baptism truly saves in whatever way it is administered, if only it is administered not in the name of man, but in the name of the Lord. Indeed, I have no doubt that if anyone receives baptism in the name of the Lord, even if the wicked minister should not give it in the name of the Lord, he would yet be truly baptized in the name of the Lord. For the power of baptism depends not so much on the faith or use of the one who confers it as on the faith or use of the one who receives it. We have an example of this in the story of a certain actor who was baptized in jest.[122] These and similar perplexing disputes and questions are raised for us by those who ascribe nothing to faith and everything to works and rituals, whereas we owe everything to faith alone and nothing to rituals. Faith makes us free in spirit from all those scruples and fancies.

*2nd part of baptism
sign of immersion*

The *second* part of baptism is the sign, or sacrament, which is that immersion in water from which it derives its name, for the Greek *baptizo* means "I immerse," and *baptisma* means, "immersion." For, as has been said, along with the divine promises signs have also been given to picture that which the words signify, or as they now say, that which the sacrament "effectively signifies." We shall see how much truth there is in this.

A great majority have supposed that there is some hidden spiritual power in the word and water, which works the grace of God in the soul of the recipient. Others deny this and hold that there is no power in the sacraments, but that grace is given by God alone, who according to his covenant

---

122. Mentioned also in Luther's *Explanations of the Ninety-five Theses*, LW 31, 105, the incident is more fully described in a sermon on Matthew 18, WA 47, 302-03. The court jester of a certain Roman emperor, in mockery of the Christian sacrament, had himself liberally drenched in public. But while the spectators guffawed, the fool was converted through the appearance of an angel showing him a book in which were written the words of Eph. 4:5-6. He acknowledged the mock baptism to be valid, confessed Christ, and was martyred.

is present in the sacraments which he has instituted.[123] Yet all are agreed that the sacraments are "effective signs" of grace, and they reach this conclusion by this one argument: if the sacraments of the New Law were mere signs, there would be no apparent reason why they should surpass those of the Old Law. Hence they have been driven to attribute such great powers to the sacraments of the New Law that they think the sacraments benefit even those who are in mortal sin; neither faith nor grace are required—it is sufficient that no obstacle be set in the way, that is, no actual intention to sin again.

Such views, however, must be carefully avoided and shunned, because they are godless and infidel, contrary to faith and inconsistent with the nature of the sacraments. For it is an error to hold that the sacraments of the New Law differ from those of the Old Law in the effectiveness of their signs. For in this respect they are the same. The same God who now saves us by baptism and the bread, saved Abel by his sacrifice, Noah by the rainbow, Abraham by circumcision, and all the others by their respective signs. So far as the signs are concerned, there is no difference between a sacrament of the Old Law and one of the New, provided that by the Old Law you mean that which God did among the patriarchs and other fathers in the days of the Law. But those signs which were given to the patriarchs and fathers must be clearly distinguished from the legal symbols [figurae] which Moses instituted in his law, such as the priestly usages concerning vestments, vessels, foods, houses, and the like. For these are vastly different, not only from the sacraments of the New Law, but also from those signs which God occasionally gave to the fathers living under the law, such

---

123. A point at issue among the scholastics of the Middle Ages. Some held that the grace of the sacrament was contained in the sacramental sign and directly imparted through it; thus Hugo of St. Victor. Others contended that the sign was merely a symbol, but that God, according to a *pactio*, or agreement, imparted the grace of the sacrament when the sign was being used; thus Bonaventura, and especially Duns Scotus.

as the sign of Gideon's fleece [Judg. 6:36-40], Manoah's sacrifice [Judg. 13:16-23], or that which Isaiah offered to Ahaz in Isa. 7: [:10-14]. In each of these alike some promise was given which required faith in God.

The difference, then, between the legal symbols and the new and old signs is that the legal symbols do not have attached to them any word of promise requiring faith. Hence they are not signs of justification, for they are not sacraments of the faith that alone justifies, but only sacraments of works. Their whole power and nature consisted in works, not in faith. Whoever performed them fulfilled them, even if he did it without faith. But our signs or sacraments, as well as those of the fathers, have attached to them a word of promise which requires faith, and they cannot be fulfilled by any other work. Hence they are signs or sacraments of justification, for they are sacraments of justifying faith and not of works. Their whole efficacy, therefore, consists in faith itself, not in the doing of a work. Whoever believes them, fulfils them, even if he should not do a single work. This is the origin of the saying: "Not the sacrament, but the faith of the sacrament, justifies." Thus circumcision did not justify Abraham and his seed, and yet the Apostle calls it the seal of the righteousness by faith [Rom. 4:11], because faith in the promise, to which circumcision was added, justified him and fulfilled what the circumcision signified. For faith was the spiritual circumcision of the foreskin of the heart [Deut. 10:16; Jer. 4:4], which was symbolized by the literal circumcision of the flesh. In the same way it was obviously not Abel's sacrifice that justified him, but it was his faith [Heb. 11:4] by which he offered himself wholly to God, and this was symbolized by the outward sacrifice.

Thus it is not baptism that justifies or benefits anyone, but it is faith in that word of promise to which baptism is added. This faith justifies, and fulfils that which baptism signifies. For faith is the submersion of the old man and the emerging of the new [Eph. 4:22-24; Col. 3:9-10]. Therefore the new

188

sacraments cannot differ from the old sacraments, for both alike have the divine promises and the same spirit of faith, although they do differ vastly from the old symbols—on account of the word of promise, which is the sole effective means of distinguishing them. Even so, today, the outward show of vestments, holy places, foods, and all the endless ceremonies doubtless symbolize excellent things to be fulfilled in the spirit, yet because there is now word of divine promise attached to these things, they can in no way be compared with the signs of baptism and the bread. Neither do they justify, nor benefit one in any way, since they are fulfilled in their very observance, even in their observance apart from faith. For while they are taking place, or being performed, they are being fulfilled, as the Apostle says of them in Col. 2 [:22]: "Which all perish as they are used, according to human precepts and doctrines." The sacraments, on the contrary, are not fulfilled when they are taking place, but when they are being believed.

It cannot be true, therefore, that there is contained in the sacraments a power efficacious for justification, or that they are "effective signs" of grace. All such things are said to the detriment of faith, and out of ignorance of the divine promise. Unless you should call them "effective" in the sense that they certainly and effectively impart grace where faith is unmistakably present. But it is not in this sense that efficacy is now ascribed to them; as witness the fact that they are said to benefit all men, even the wicked and unbelieving, provided they do not set an obstacle in the way—as if such unbelief were not in itself the most obstinate and hostile of all obstacles to grace. To such an extent have they exerted themselves to turn the sacrament into a command and faith into a work. For if the sacrament confers grace on me because I receive it, then indeed I receive grace by virtue of my work, and not by faith; and I gain not the promise in the sacrament but only the sign instituted and commanded by God. Thus you see clearly how completely the sacraments have been misunderstood by the theologians of the *Sentences*. In their discussions of the sacraments they have taken no account either of faith or of promise. They cling only to the sign and the use of the sign, and draw us away from faith to work, away from the word to the sign. Thus, as I have said,[124] they have not only taken the sacraments captive, but have completely destroyed them, as far as they were able.

Therefore let us open our eyes and learn to pay heed more to the word than to the sign, more to faith than to the work or use of the sign. We know that wherever there is a divine promise, there faith is required, and that these two are so necessary to each other that neither can be effective apart from the other. For it is not possible to believe unless there is a promise, and the promise is not established unless it is believed. But where these two meet, they give a real and most certain efficacy to the sacraments. Hence, to seek the efficacy of the sacrament apart from the promise and apart from the faith is to labor in vain and to find condemnation. Thus Christ says: "He who believes and is baptized will be saved; but he who does not believe will be condemned" [Mark 16:16]. He shows us in this word that faith is such a necessary part of the sacrament that it can save even without the sacrament, and for this reason he did not add: "He who does not believe, and is not baptized."

Baptism, then, signifies two things—death and resurrection, that is, full and complete justification. When the minister immerses the child in the water it signifies death, and when he draws it forth again it signifies life. Thus Paul expounds it in Rom. 6 [:4]: "We were buried therefore with Christ by baptism into death, so that as Christ was raised from the dead by the glory of the Father, we too might walk in newness of life." This death and resurrection we call the new creation, regeneration, and spiritual birth. This should not be understood only allegorically as the death of sin and the

---

124. Cf. p. 183.

life of grace, as many understand it, but as actual death and resurrection. For baptism is not a false sign. Neither does sin completely die, nor grace completely rise, until the sinful body that we carry about in this life is destroyed, as the Apostle says in the same passage [Rom. 6:6-7]. For as long as we are in the flesh, the desires of the flesh stir and are stirred. For this reason, as soon as we begin to believe, we also begin to die to this world and live to God in the life to come; so that faith is truly a death and a resurrection, that is, it is that spiritual baptism into which we are submerged and from which we rise.

It is therefore indeed correct to say that baptism is a washing away of sins, but the expression is too mild and weak to bring out the full significance of baptism, which is rather a symbol of death and resurrection. For this reason I would have those who are to be baptized completely immersed in the water, as the word says[125] and as the mystery indicates. Not because I deem this necessary, but because it would be well to give to a thing[126] so perfect and complete a sign that is also complete and perfect. And this is doubtless the way in which it was instituted by Christ. The sinner does not so much need to be washed as he needs to die, in order to be wholly renewed and made another creature, and to be conformed to the death and resurrection of Christ, with whom he dies and rises again through baptism. Although you may say that when Christ died and rose again he was washed clean of mortality, that is a less forceful way of putting it than if you said that he was completely changed and renewed. Similarly it is far more forceful to say that baptism signifies that we die in every way and rise to eternal life, than to say that it signifies merely that we are washed clean of sins.

Here again you see that the sacrament of baptism, even

---

125. Cf. p. 186 above, and *PE* 1, 56.
126. *res*; cf. p. 137 n. 45 above.

with respect to its sign, is not a matter of the moment, but something permanent. Although the ceremony itself is soon over, the thing it signifies continues until we die, yes, even until we rise on the last day. For as long as we live we are continually doing that which baptism signifies, that is, we die and rise again. We die, not only mentally and spiritually by renouncing the sins and vanities of this world, but in very truth we begin to leave this bodily life and to lay hold on the life to come, so that there is, as they say, a "real" and bodily passing out of this world unto the Father.

We must therefore beware of those who have reduced the power of baptism to such small and slender dimensions that, while they say grace is indeed inpoured by it, they maintain that afterwards it is poured out again through sin, and that then one must reach heaven by another way, as if baptism had now become entirely useless. Do not hold such a view, but understand that this is the significance of baptism, that through it you die and live again. Therefore, whether by penance or by any other way, you can only return to the power of your baptism, and do again that which you were baptized to do and which your baptism signified. Baptism never becomes useless, unless you despair and refuse to return to its salvation. You may indeed wander away from the sign for a time, but the sign is not therefore useless. Thus, you have been once baptized in the sacrament, but you need continually to be baptized by faith, continually to die and continually to live. Baptism swallowed up your whole body and gave it forth again; in the same way that which baptism signifies should swallow up your whole life, body and soul, and give it forth again at the last day, clad in the robe of glory and immortality. We are therefore never without the sign of baptism nor without the thing it signifies. Indeed, we need continually to be baptized more and more, until we fulfill the sign perfectly at the last day.

You will understand, therefore, that whatever we do in this life which mortifies the flesh or quickens the spirit has to do with our baptism. The sooner we depart this life, the *detriment of the flesh.* more speedily we fulfil our baptism; and the more cruelly we suffer, the more successfully do we conform to our baptism. Hence the church was at its best at the time when martyrs were being put to death every day and accounted as sheep for the slaughter [Ps. 44:22; Rom. 8:36], for then the power of baptism reigned supreme in the church, whereas today we have lost sight of this power amid the multitude of works and doctrines of men. For our whole life should be baptism, and the fulfilling of the sign or sacrament of baptism, since we have been set free from all else and given over to baptism alone, that is, to death and resurrection.

This glorious liberty of ours and this understanding of baptism have been taken captive in our day, and to whom can we give the blame except the Roman pontiff with his despotism? More than all others, as chief shepherd it was his first duty to proclaim this doctrine and defend this liberty, as Paul says in I Cor. 4 [:1]: "This is how one should regard us, as servants of Christ and stewards of the mysteries, or sacraments,[127] of God." Instead he seeks only to oppress us with his decrees and laws, and to ensnare us as captives to his tyrannical power. By what right, I ask you, does the pope impose his laws upon us (to say nothing of his wicked and damnable neglect to teach us these mysteries)? Who gave him power to deprive us of this liberty of ours, granted to us in baptism? One thing only, as I have said, has been enjoined upon us to do all the days of our lives—to be baptized, that is, to be put to death and to live again through faith in Christ. This, and this alone, should have been taught, especially by the chief shepherd. But now faith is passed over in silence, and the church is smothered with endless laws concerning works and ceremonies; the power and understanding of baptism are set aside, and faith in Christ is obstructed.

Therefore I say: Neither pope nor bishop nor any other

---

127. Cf. pp. 221-24.

man has the right to impose a single syllable of law upon a Christian man without his consent; if he does, it is done in the spirit of tyranny. Therefore the prayers, fasts, donations and whatever else the pope ordains and demands in all of his decrees, as numerous as they are iniquitous, he demands and ordains without any right whatever; and he sins against the liberty of the church whenever he attempts any such thing. Hence it has come to pass that the churchmen of our day are such vigorous guardians of "ecclesiastical liberty"—that is, of wood and stone, of lands and rents (for to such an extent has "ecclesiastical" today come to mean the same as "spiritual"!). Yet with such verbal fictions they not only take captive the true liberty of the church; they utterly destroy it, even worse than the Turk, and in opposition to the word of the Apostle: "Do not become slaves of men" [I Cor. 7:23]. For to be subjected to their statutes and tyrannical laws is indeed to become slaves of men.

This impious and desperate tyranny is fostered by the pope's disciples, who here twist and pervert that saying of Christ: "He who hears you hears me" [Luke 10:16]. With puffed cheeks they inflate this saying to a great size in support of their own ordinances. Though Christ spoke this word to the apostles when they went forth to preach the gospel, and though it should apply only to the gospel, they pass over the gospel and apply it only to their fables. For he says in John 10 [:27, 5]: "My sheep hear my voice, but the voice of a stranger they do not hear." He left us the gospel so that the pontiffs might sound the voice of Christ. Instead they sound their own voices, and yet hope to be heard. Moreover, the Apostle says that he was not sent to baptize, but to preach the gospel [I Cor. 1:17]. Therefore, no one is obliged to obey the ordinances of the pope, or required to listen to him, except when he teaches the gospel and Christ. And the pope should teach nothing but faith without any restrictions. But since Christ says, "He who hears you [plural] hears me" [Luke 10:16], why does not the pope also hear others? Christ does not say to Peter alone, "He who hears you" [singular]. In short, where there is true faith, there the word of faith must of necessity be also. Why then does not an unbelieving pope now and then hear a believing servant of his who has the word of faith? Blindness, sheer blindness, reigns among the pontiffs.

Others, even more shameless, arrogantly ascribe to the pope the power to make laws, on the basis of Matt. 16 [:19], "Whatever you bind, etc.," although Christ in this passage treats of binding and loosing sins, not of taking the whole church captive and oppressing it with laws. So this tyranny treats everything with its own lying words and violently twists and perverts the words of God. I admit indeed that Christians ought to bear this accursed tyranny just as they would bear any other violence of the world, according to Christ's word: "If any one strikes you on the right cheek, turn to him the other also" [Matt. 5:39]. But this is my complaint: that the godless pontiffs boastfully claim to do this by right, that they pretend to be seeking the church's welfare with this Babylon of theirs, and that they foist this fiction upon all mankind. For if they did these things and we suffered their violence, both sides being well aware that it was godlessness and tyranny, then we might easily number it among those things that contribute to the mortifying of this life and the fulfilling of our baptism, and might with a good conscience glory in the inflicted injury. But now they seek to deprive us of this consciousness of our liberty, and would have us believe that what they do is well done, and must not be censured or complained of as wrongdoing. Being wolves, they masquerade as shepherds, and being Antichrists, they wish to be honored as Christ.

I lift my voice simply on behalf of liberty and conscience, and I confidently cry: No law, whether of men or of angels, may rightfully be imposed upon Christians without their consent, for we are free of all laws. And if any laws are imposed upon us, we must bear them in such a way as to preserve

no law can be imposed on Christians w/o their consent

195

that sense of freedom which knows and affirms with certainty that an injustice is being done to it, even though it glories in bearing this injustice—so taking care neither to justify the tyrant nor to murmur against his tyranny. "Now who is there to harm you," says Peter, "if you are zealous for what is right?" [I Pet. 3:13]. "All things work together for good to them that are the elect" [Rom. 8:28].

Nevertheless, since but few know this glory of baptism and the blessedness of Christian liberty, and cannot know them because of the tyranny of the pope, I for one will disengage myself, and keep my conscience free by bringing this charge against the pope and all his papists: Unless they will abolish their laws and ordinances, and restore to Christ's churches their liberty and have it taught among them, they are guilty of all the souls that perish under this miserable captivity, and the papacy is truly the kingdom of Babylon and of the very Antichrist. For who is "the man of sin" and "the son of perdition" [II Thess. 2:3] but he who with his doctrines and his laws increases the sins and perdition of souls in the church, while sitting in the church as if he were God? [II Thess. 2:4]. All this the papal tyranny has fulfilled, and more than fulfilled, these many centuries. It has extinguished faith, obscured the sacraments and oppressed the gospel; but its own laws, which are not only impious and sacrilegious, but even barbarous and foolish, it has decreed and multiplied without end.

Behold, then, our miserable captivity. "How lonely sits the city that was full of people! How like a widow has she become, she that was great among the nations! She that was a princess among the cities has become a vassal. She has none to comfort her; all her friends have dealt treacherously with her, etc." [Lam. 1:1-2]. There are so many ordinances, so many rites, so many sects,[128] so many vows, so many exertions

---

128. Luther means the divergences, rivalries, and jealousies between the various monastic orders and theological factions. E.g., cf. p. 202 n. 138.

and so many works, in which Christians are engaged today, that they lose sight of their baptism. Because of this swarm of locusts, palmerworms, and cankerworms [Joel 1:4], no one is able to remember that he is baptized, or what blessings baptism has brought him. We should be even as little children, when they are newly baptized, who engage in no efforts or works, but are free in every way, secure and saved solely through the glory of their baptism. For we are indeed little children. continually baptized anew in Christ.

In contradiction to what has been said, some might cite the *baptism of infants* who do not comprehend the promise of God and cannot have the faith of baptism; so that therefore either faith is not necessary or else infant baptism is without effect. Here I say what all[129] say: Infants are aided by the faith of others, namely, those who bring them for baptism. For the Word of God is powerful enough, when uttered, to change even a godless heart, which is no less unresponsive and helpless than any infant. So through the prayer of the believing church which presents it, a prayer to which all things are possible [Mark 9:23], the infant is changed, cleansed, and renewed by inpoured faith. Nor should I doubt that even a godless adult could be changed, in any of the sacraments, if the same church prayed for and presented him, as we read of the paralytic in the Gospel, who was healed through the faith of others [Mark 2:3-12]. I should be ready to admit that in this sense the sacraments of the New Law are efficacious in conferring grace, not only to those who do not, but even to those who do most obstinately present an obstacle.[130] What obstacle cannot be removed by the faith of the church and the prayer of faith? Do we not believe that Stephen converted Paul the Apostle by this power? [Acts 7:58—8:1]. But then the sacraments

---

129. This was the position of Thomas Aquinas, going back to Augustine; it was ratified by Clement V at the Council of Vienna, 1311-12. *PE* 2, 236 n. 1.
130. Cf. p. 187.

do what they do not by their own power, but by the power of faith, without which they do nothing at all, as I have said.[131]

The question remains whether an unborn infant, with only a hand or a foot projecting from the womb, can be baptized. Here I will confess my ignorance and make no hasty decision. I am not sure whether the reason they give is sufficient—that in any part of the body whatsoever the entire soul resides. For it is not the soul but the body that is externally baptized with water. But neither do I share the view of those who insist that he who is not yet born cannot be born again (even though it has considerable force). I leave these things to the teaching of the Spirit, and meanwhile allow everyone to enjoy his own opinion [Rom. 14:5].

Opinions on Vows

One thing I will add—and I wish I could persuade everyone to do it—namely, that *all vows should be completely abolished and avoided,* whether of religious orders, or about pilgrimages or about any works whatsoever, that we may remain in that which is supremely religious and most rich in works—the freedom of baptism. It is impossible to say how much that most widespread delusion of vows detracts from baptism and obscures the knowledge of Christian liberty, to say nothing now of the unspeakable and infinite peril of souls which that mania for making vows and that ill-advised rashness daily increase. O most godless pontiffs and unregenerate pastors, who slumber on unheeding and indulge in your evil lusts, without pity for this most dreadful and perilous "ruin of Joseph"! [Amos 6:4-6].

Vows should either be abolished by a general edict, especially those taken for life, and all men recalled to the vows of baptism, or else everyone should be diligently warned not to take a vow rashly. No one should be encouraged to do so; indeed, permission should be given only with difficulty and

131. Cf. pp. 188-89.

reluctance. For we have vowed enough in baptism, more than we can ever fulfill; if we give ourselves to the keeping of this one vow, we shall have all we can do. But now we traverse sea and land to make many proselytes [Matt. 23:15]; *converts* we fill the world with priests, monks, and nuns, and imprison them all in lifelong vows. You will find those who argue and decree that a work done in fulfilment of a vow ranks higher than one done without a vow, and in heaven is to be rewarded above others with I know not what great rewards. Blind and godless Pharisees, who measure rightousness and holiness by the greatness, number, or other quality of the works! But God measures them by faith alone, and with him there is no difference among works, except insofar as there is a difference in faith.

With such bombast wicked men by their inventions puff up human opinion and human works in order to lure on the unthinking masses who are almost always led by the glitter of works to make shipwreck of their faith, to forget their baptism and to injure their Christian liberty. For a vow is a kind of law or requirement. When vows are multiplied, laws and works are necessarily multiplied, and when these are multiplied, faith is extinguished and the liberty of baptism is taken captive. Others, not content with these wicked allurements, assert in addition that entrance into a religious order is like a new baptism, which may afterward be repeated as often as the purpose to live the monastic life is renewed. Thus these votaries have appropriated to themselves all righteousness, salvation, and glory, and left to those who are merely baptized nothing to compare with them. Now the Roman pontiff, that fountain and source of all superstitions, confirms, approves, and adorns this mode of life with high-sounding bulls[132] and dispensations, while no one deems

---

132. *bulla*. An official mandate of the pope, which takes its name from the leaden seal with which the document was authenticated in the Middle Ages—a circular plate in form resembling an air bubble floating upon water.

baptism worthy of even a thought. And with such glittering pomp, as I have said, they drive the pliable people of Christ into a false sense of security,[133] so that in their ingratitude toward baptism they presume to achieve greater things by their works than others achieve by their faith.

Therefore, God again shows himself "perverse with the crooked" [Ps. 18:26], and to punish the makers of vows for their ingratitude and pride, he brings it about that they break their vows, or keep them only with prodigious labor, and remain sunk in them, never knowing the grace of faith and of baptism; that they continue in their hypocrisy to the end, since their spirit is not approved of God; and that at last they become a laughingstock to the whole world, ever pursuing righteousness and never attaining Righteousness, so that they fulfill the word of Isa. 2 [:8]: "Their land is filled with idols."

I am indeed far from forbidding or discouraging anyone who may desire to vow something privately and of his own free choice; for I would not altogether despise and condemn vows. But I would most strongly advise against setting up and sanctioning the making of vows as a public mode of life. It is enough that every one should have the private right to take a vow at his own peril; but to commend the vowing of vows as a public mode of life—this I hold to be most pernicious to the church and to simple souls. First, because it runs directly counter to the Christian life, for a vow is a kind of ceremonial law and a human ordinance or presumption, from which the church has been set free through baptism; for a Christian is subject to no law but the law of God. Second, because there is no instance in Scripture of such a vow, espe-

---

133. *in quascunque volent symplegadas.* Luther is alluding to the Symplegades rocks at the entrance to the Black Sea, through which, according to Greek legend, Jason had to lead his Argonauts in quest of the Golden Fleece. While they seemed to afford secure passage, the two cliffs actually moved on their bases and crushed whatever sought to pass.

cially of lifelong chastity, obedience, or poverty.[134] But whatever is without warrant of Scripture is most hazardous and should by no means be urged upon any one, much less established as a common and public mode of life, even if it be permitted to somebody who wishes to make the venture at his own peril. For certain works are wrought by the Spirit in a few men, but they must not be made an example or a mode of life for all.

Moreover, I greatly fear that these votive modes of life of the religious orders belong to those things which the Apostle foretold: "They will be teaching lies in hypocrisy, forbidding marriage and enjoining abstinence from foods which God created to be received with thanksgiving" [I Tim. 4:2-3]. Let no one retort by pointing to SS. Bernard, Francis, Dominic,[135] and others, who founded or fostered monastic orders. Terrible and marvelous is God in his counsels toward the sons of men. He could keep Daniel, Hananiah, Azariah, and Mishael [Dan. 1:6-21] holy at the court of the king of Babylon (that is, in the midst of godlessness); why could he not sanctify those men also in their perilous mode of living or guide them by the special operation of his Spirit, yet without desiring it to be an example to others? Besides, it is certain that none of them was saved through his vows and his "religious"[136] life; they were saved through faith alone, by which all men are saved, and to which that showy subservience to vows is more diametrically opposed than anything else.

But every one may hold his own view on this. I will return to my argument. Speaking now in behalf of the church's

134. The threefold vow of the monastic orders involved a pledge of poverty, chastity, and obedience.
135. Bernard of Clairvaux (1090-1153) founded 163 Cistercian monasteries in different parts of Europe, which by his death had increased in number to 343. Francis of Assisi (1182-1226) founded the Franciscan Order. Dominic (*circa* 1170-1221) founded the Order of Preachers, commonly known as the Dominican Order.
136. *religio.* In medieval Latin this was a special designation for the particular piety of the monastic orders.

liberty and the glory of baptism, I feel myself in duty bound
to set forth publicly the counsel I have learned under the
Spirit's guidance. I therefore counsel those in high places in
the churches, first of all, to abolish all those vows and religious orders, or at least not to approve and extol them. If
they will not do this, then I counsel all men who would be
assured of their salvation to abstain from all vows, above all
from the major and lifelong vows. I give this counsel especially to teen-agers and young people. This I do, first because
this manner of life has no witness or warrant in the Scriptures, as I have said, but is puffed up solely by the bulls (and
they truly are "bulls")[137] of human popes. Second, because
it greatly tends to hypocrisy, by reason of its outward show
and unusual character, which engender conceit and a contempt of the common Christian life. And if there were no
other reason for abolishing these vows, this one would be
reason enough, namely, that through them faith and baptism
are slighted and works are exalted, which cannot be done
without harmful results. For in the religious orders there is
scarcely one in many thousands who is not more concerned
about his works than about faith, and on the basis of this
madness, they claim superiority over each other, as being
"stricter" or "laxer," as they call it.[138]

Therefore I advise no one to enter any religious order
or the priesthood, indeed, I advise everyone against it—
unless he is forearmed with this knowledge and understands that the works of monks and priests, however holy
and arduous they may be, do not differ one whit in the
sight of God from the works of the rustic laborer in the
field or the woman going about her household tasks, but

[handwritten margin note: people should not enter monastery w/o being absolutely sure.]

---

137. *bulla* also means "bubble." Cf. p. 199 n. 132.

138. Divisions resulting from disputes over the interpretation of their "rules" were
common among and within the religious orders. In the case of the Franciscans, for example, there were the factions known as the *zelanti* and *relaxti*
in earlier times, and later on the division between the "Strict Observance"
and the "Conventuals." Cf. p. 126 n. 12.

202

that all works are measured before God by faith alone, as Jer. 5 [:3] says: "O Lord, do not thy eyes look for faith?"[139] and Ecclus. 32 [:23]: "In all thy works believe with faith in thy heart, for this is to keep the commandments of God." Indeed, the menial housework of a manservant or maidservant is often more acceptable to God than all the fastings and other works of a monk or priest, because the monk or priest lacks faith. Since, therefore, vows nowadays seem to tend only to the glorification of works and to pride, it is to be feared that there is nowhere less of faith and of the church than among the priets, monks, and bishops. These men are in truth heathen or hypocrites. They imagine themselves to be the church, or the heart of the church, the "spiritual" estate and the leaders of the church, when they are everything else but that. This is indeed "the people of the captivity," among whom all things freely given to us in baptism are held captive, while the few poor "people of the earth[140] who are left behind, such as the married folk,[141] appear vile in their eyes.

From what has been said we recognize two glaring errors of the Roman pontiff.

In the first place, he grants dispensation from vows, and does it as if he alone of all Christians possessed this authority; so great is the temerity and audacity of wicked men. If it is possible to grant a dispensation from a vow, then any brother may grant one to his neighbor, or even to himself.[142] But if one's neighbor cannot grant a dispensation, neither has the pope any right to do so. For where

---

139. Vulgate version.

140. The reference is to the Babylonian captivity of the Jews. "The people of the captivity" is an expression taken from the Latin title to Psalm 64 (65) in the Vulgate. Nebuchadnezzar carried into captivity in Babylon only the better classes of the population. The "people of the earth," *am haarez,* the common people, were left behind (II Kings 24:14-16) and became the nucleus of the hybrid Samaritan nation.

141. Persons under the vow of chastity held the estate of marriage to be beneath their own in terms of holiness.

142. Cf. *An Open Letter to the Christian Nobility. PE 2, 123.*

does he get this authority? From the power of the keys? But the keys belong to all, and avail only for sins (Matt. 18 [:15-18]).[143] Now they themselves claim that vows are "of divine right." Why then does the pope deceive and destroy the poor souls of men by granting dispensations in matters of divine right, in which no dispensations can be granted? In the section, "Of vows and their redemption,"[144] he babbles indeed of having the power to change vows, just as in the law the firstborn of an ass was changed for a sheep [Exod. 13:13; 34:20] as if the firstborn of an ass, and the vow he commands to be offered everywhere and always, were one and the same thing; or as if when the Lord decrees in his law that a sheep shall be changed for an ass, the pope, a mere man, may straightway claim the same power, not in his own law, but in God's! It was not a pope, but an ass changed for a pope, that made this decretal; it is so egregiously senseless and godless.

The second error is this: The pope decrees, on the other hand, that a marriage is dissolved if one party enters a monastery without the consent of the other, provided that the marriage has not yet been consummated. Now I ask you, what devil puts such monstrous things into the pope's mind? God commands men to keep faith and not break their word to one another, and again, to do good with that which is their own, for he hates "robbery with a burnt offering," as he says by the mouth of Isaiah [61:8]. But one spouse is bound by the marriage contract to keep faith with the other, and he is not his own. He cannot break his faith by any right, and whatever he does with himself is robbery, if it is done without the other's consent. Why does not one who is burdened with debt follow this same rule and obtain admission into a religious order, so as to be released from

143. Ibid., 75.
144. Magnae devotionis, Decretalium Gregorii IX, lib iii, tit. XXXIV: de voto et voti redemptione, cap. 7. Corpus Iuris Canonici, op. cit., II, col. 593.

his debts and be free to break his word? O blind, blind men! Which is greater, the fidelity commanded by God or a vow devised and chosen by men? Are you a shepherd of souls, O pope? And you who teach these things, are you doctors of sacred theology? Why then do you teach them? No doubt because you have decked out your vow as a better work than marriage; you do not exalt faith, which alone exalts all things, but works, which are nothing in the sight of God, or which are all alike as far as merit is concerned.

I am sure, therefore, that neither men nor angels can grant a dispensation from vows, if they are proper vows. But I am not fully clear in my own mind whether all the things that men vow nowadays come under the head of vows. For instance, it is simply foolish and stupid for parents to dedicate their children, before birth or in infancy, to the "religious life," or to perpetual chastity; indeed, it is certain that this can by no means be termed a vow. It seems to be a kind of mockery of God for them to vow things which are not at all in their power. As to the triple vow of the monastic orders,[145] the longer I consider it, the less I comprehend it, and I wonder where the custom of exacting this vow arose. Still less do I understand at what age vows may be taken in order to be legal and valid. I am pleased to find unanimous agreement that vows taken before the age of puberty are not valid. Nevertheless, they deceive many young children who are ignorant both of their age and of what they are vowing. They do not observe the age of puberty in receiving such children; but the children, after making their profession, are held captive and consumed by a troubled conscience as though they had afterward given their consent. As if a vow which was invalid could finally become valid with the passing of the years!

It seems absurd to me that the effective date of a legiti-

---

145. Cf. p. 201 n. 134.

mate vow should be predetermined for others by people who cannot predetermine it for themselves. Nor do I see why a vow taken at eighteen years of age should be valid, but not one taken at ten or twelve years. It will not do to say that at eighteen a man feels his carnal desires. What if he scarcely feels them at twenty or thirty, or feels them more keenly at thirty than at twenty? Why not also set a certain age limit for the vows of poverty and obedience? But what age will you set, by which a man should feel his greed and pride, when even the most spiritual persons hardly become aware of these emotions? Therefore, no vow will ever become binding and valid until we have become spiritual, and no longer have any need of vows. You see that these are uncertain and most perilous matters, and it would therefore be a wholesome counsel to keep such lofty modes of living free of vows, and leave them to the Spirit alone as they were of old, and never in any way to change them into a mode of life which is perpetually binding.

However, let this be sufficient for the present concerning baptism and its liberty. In due time I shall perhaps discuss vows at greater length,[146] and truly there is an urgent need for this.

THE SACRAMENT OF PENANCE

In the third place, we are to discuss the sacrament of penance. On this subject I have already given no little offense to many people by the treatises and disputations[147] already published, in which I have amply set forth my

---

146 This Luther did in November, 1521, during his sojourn at the Wartburg, in *De votis monasticis Martini Lutheri iudicium*. WA 8, 573-669.

147. These include, among others, the *Ninety-five Theses* (1517), LW 31, 25-33, WA 1, 233-38; *A Sermon on Indulgence and Grace* (1517), Woolf, *op. cit.*, I, 50-55, WA 1, 239-246; *Sermo de poenitentia* (1518), WA 1, 319-24; *Eine Freiheit des Sermons päpstlichen Ablass und Gnade Belangend* (1518), WA 1, 383-93; *Explanations of the Ninety-five Theses* (1518), LW 31, 83-252, WA 1, 525-628; and *A Discussion of Confession* (1520), PE 1, 81-101, WA 6, 157-69.

views. These I must now briefly repeat in order to unmask the tyranny that is rampant here no less than in the sacrament of the bread. For, because these two sacraments furnish opportunity for gain and profit, the greed of the shepherds has raged in them with incredible zeal against the flock of Christ, although, as we have just seen in our discussion of vows, baptism too has sadly declined among adults and become the servant of greed.

The first and chief abuse of this sacrament is that they have completely abolished it. Not a vestige of the sacrament remains. For this sacrament, like the other two, consists in the word of divine promise and our faith, and they have undermined both of them. For they have adapted to their own tyranny the word of promise which Christ speaks in Matt. 16 [:19] and 18 [:18]: "Whatever you bind, etc.," and in the last chapter of John [20:23]: "If you forgive the sins of any, they are forgiven, etc." By these words the faith of penitents is aroused for obtaining the forgiveness of sins. But in all their writing, teaching, and preaching, their sole concern has been, not to teach what is promised to Christians in these words, or what they ought to believe, and what great consolation they might find in them, but only through force and violence to extend their own tyranny far, wide, and deep. It has finally come to such a pass that some of them have begun to command the very angels in heaven,[148] and to boast in incredible, mad wickedness that

---

148. In the jubilee year of 1500, as thousands of pilgrims died of the plague on their way through war-ravaged Lombardy toward Rome, a spurious bull of Pope Clement VI from the year 1350 was widely promulgated, in which were the words: "We command the angels of paradise that their souls (the souls of pilgrims who died en route) be taken directly to the bliss of paradise, as being fully redeemed from purgatory." *WA* 30^{II}, 282; Buchwald, *op. cit.*, II, 457 n. 1. In *Defense and Explanation of All the Articles* (1521), Luther writes: "This is what happened in the days of John Huss. In those days the pope commanded the angels in heaven to lead to heaven the souls of those pilgrims who died on the way to Rome. John Huss objected to this horrible blasphemy and more than diabolic presumption. This protest cost him his life, but he at least caused the pope to change his tune and, embarrassed by this sacrilege, to refrain from such proclamation." *LW* 32, 74-75.

in these words they have obtained the right to rule in heaven and earth, and possess the power to bind even in heaven. Thus they say nothing of faith which is the salvation of the people, but babble only of the despotic power of the pontiffs, whereas Christ says nothing at all of power, but speaks only of faith.

For Christ has not ordained authorities or powers or lordships in his church, but ministries, as we learn from the Apostle, who says: "This is how one should regard us, as ministers of Christ and stewards of the mysteries of God" [I Cor. 4:1]. Just as, when he said: "He who believes and is baptized will be saved" [Mark 16:16], he was calling forth the faith of those who were to be baptized, so that by this word of promise a man might be certain of his salvation if he was baptized in faith. There was no conferring of any power there, but only the instituting of the ministry of those who baptize. Similarly, here where he says, "Whatever you bind, etc." [Matt. 16:19; 18:18], he is calling forth the faith of the penitent, so that by this word of promise he might be certain that if he is absolved in faith, he is truly absolved in heaven. Here there is no mention at all of power, but only of the ministry of the one who absolves. One cannot but wonder what happened to these blind and overbearing men that they did not arrogate to themselves a despotic power from the promise of baptism; or, if they did not do it there, why they presumed to do it from the promise of penance? For in both there is a like ministry, a similar promise, and the same kind of sacrament. It cannot be denied: if baptism does not belong to Peter alone, then it is a wicked usurpation of power to claim the power of the keys for the pope alone.

Again, when Christ says: "Take, this is my body, which is given for you. This is the cup in my blood, etc." [I Cor. 11:24-25], he is calling forth the faith of those who eat, so that when their conscience has been strengthened by these words they might be certain through faith that they receive the forgiveness of sins when they have eaten. Here too, nothing is said of power, but only of the ministry.

So the promise of baptism remains to some extent, at least for infants; but the promise of the bread and the cup has been destroyed and made subservient to greed, faith has become a work and the testament has become a sacrifice. The promise of penance, however, has been transformed into the most oppressive despotism, being used to establish a sovereignty which is more than merely temporal.

under the authority of the Pope.

Not content with these things, *this Babylon of ours has so completely extinguished faith* that it insolently *denies its necessity in this sacrament.* Indeed, with the wickedness of Antichrist it brands it as heresy for anyone to assert that faith is necessary. What more could this tyranny do than it has done? Truly, "by the waters of Babylon we sit down and weep, when we remember thee, O Zion. On the willows there we hang up our lyres" [Ps. 137:1-2]. May the Lord curse the barren willows of those streams! Amen.

Now that promise and faith have been thus blotted out and overthrown, let us see what they have put in their place. *They have divided penance into three parts—contrition, confession, and satisfaction;* but in such a way that they have removed whatever was good in each of them, and have established in each of them their caprice and their tyranny.

3 parts of penance

In the first place, they teach that contrition takes precedence over, and is far superior to, faith in the promise, as if contrition were not a work of faith, but a merit; indeed, they do not mention faith at all. They stick so closely to works and to those passages of Scripture where we read of many who obtained pardon by reason of their contrition and humility of heart; but they take no account of the faith which effected this contrition and sorrow of heart, as is written of the men of Nineveh in Jon. 3 [:5]: "And the people of Nineveh believed God; they proclaimed a fast, etc." Others again, more bold and wicked, have invented a so-called "attrition,"[149] which is converted into contrition by the power of the keys, of which they know nothing. This attrition they grant to the wicked and unbelieving, and thus abolish contrition altogether. O the intolerable wrath of God, that such things should be taught in the church of Christ! Thus, with both faith and its work destroyed, we go on secure in the doctrines and opinions of men, or rather we perish in them. A contrite heart is a precious thing, but it is found only where there is an ardent faith in the promises and threats of God. Such faith, intent on the immutable truth of God, makes the conscience tremble, terrifies it and bruises it; and afterwards, when it is contrite, raises it up, consoles it, and preserves it. Thus the truth of God's threat is the cause of contrition, and the truth of his promise the cause of consolation, if it is believed. By such a faith a man "merits" the forgiveness of sins. Therefore faith should be taught and aroused before all else. Once faith is obtained, contrition and consolation will follow inevitably of themselves.

Therefore, although there is some truth in their teaching that contrition is to be attained by the enumeration and contemplation (as they call it) of their sins, yet their teaching is perilous and perverse so long as they do not teach first of all the beginnings and causes of contrition—the immutable truth of God's threat and promise which calls forth faith—so that men may learn to pay more heed to the truth of God, by which they are cast down and lifted up, than to the multitude of their sins. If their sins are regarded apart from the truth of God, they will excite afresh and increase the desire for sin rather than lead to contrition. I will say nothing now of the insurmountable

---

149. Contrition involved a detestation of sin arising out of love for God and regret at having offended him. Attrition involved a hatred of sin arising out of lesser motives, such as loss of heaven, fear of hell, or the heinousness of guilt. Attrition, though imperfect, was held to be sufficient, since it predisposed the sinner to receive through the sacrament of penance that grace which transformed it into perfect contrition. Cf. *LW* 31, 21.

task which they have imposed upon us, namely, that we are to frame a contrition for every sin. That is impossible. We can know only the smaller part of our sins; and even our good works are found to be sins, according to Ps. 143 [:2][150]: "Enter not into judgment with thy servant; for no man living is righteous before thee." It is enough if we lament the sins which distress our conscience at the present moment, as well as those which we can readily call to mind. Whoever is in this frame of mind is without doubt ready to grieve and fear for all his sins, and will grieve and fear whenever they are brought to his knowledge in the future.

Beware then, of putting your trust in your own contrition and of ascribing the forgiveness of sins to your own remorse. God does not look on you with favor because of that, but because of the faith by which you have believed his threats and promises, and which has effected such sorrow within you. Thus we owe whatever good there may be in our penance, not to our scrupulous enumeration of sins, but to the truth of God and to our faith. All other things are the works and fruits which follow of their own accord. They do not make a man good, but are done by the man who is already made good through faith in the truth of God. Even so, "smoke goes up in his wrath; because he is angry he shakes the mountains and sets them on fire," as it is said in Ps. 18 [:8, 7]). First comes the terror of this threatening, which sets the wicked on fire; then faith, accepting this, sends up smoke-clouds of contrition, etc.

But the trouble is not so much that contrition has been exposed to tyranny and avarice, as that it has been given over completely to wickedness and pestilent teaching. It is confession and satisfaction that have become the chief workshops of greed and power.

---

150. Where Luther cites correctly the Vulgate version, in which Psalms 10-146 are numbered differently from the numbering used in the RSV, we have given the corresponding RSV Psalm reference.

Let us first take up *confession.*

There is no doubt that confession of sins is necessary and commanded of God, in Matt. 3 [:6]: "They were baptized by John in the river Jordan, confessing their sins," and in I John 1 [:9-10]: "If we confess our sins, he is faithful and just, and will forgive our sins. If we say we have not sinned, we make him a liar, and his word is not in us." If the saints may not deny their sin, how much more ought those who are guilty of great and public sins to make confession! But the institution of confession is proved most effectively of all by Matt. 18 [:15-17], where Christ teaches that a sinning brother should be told of his fault, brought before the church, accused, and if he will not hear, be excommunicated. He "hears" if he needs the rebuke and acknowledges and confesses his sin.

As to the current practice of private confession, I am heartily in favor of it, even though it cannot be proved from the Scriptures. It is useful, even necessary, and I would not have it abolished. Indeed, I rejoice that it exists in the church of Christ, for it is a cure without equal for distressed consciences. For when we have laid bare our conscience to our brother and privately made known to him the evil that lurked within, we receive from our brother's lips the word of comfort spoken by God himself. And, if we accept this in faith, we find peace in the mercy of God speaking to us through our brother. There is just one thing about it that I abominate, and that is the fact that this kind of confession has been subjected to the despotism and extortion of the pontiffs. They reserve[151] to themselves even the secret sins, and command that they be made known to confessors named by them, only to trouble the consciences of men. They merely play the pontiff, while they utterly despise the

---

151. In "reserved cases," *casus episcopales* or *casus papales,* only the bishop or pope, or one appointed by them, could absolve. Cf. *An Open Letter to the Christian Nobility. PE* 2, 105-06.

true duties of pontiffs, which are to preach the gospel and to care for the poor. Indeed, the godless despots leave the great sins to the common priests, and reserve to themselves only those sins which are of less consequence, such as those ridiculous and fictitious things in the bull *Coena domini*.[152] To make the wickedness of their error even more apparent, they not only fail to reserve, but actually teach and approve things which are against the service of God, against faith and the chief commandments—such as their running about on pilgrimages, the perverse worship of the saints, the lying saints' legends, the various ways of trusting in works and ceremonies and practicing them. Yet in all of these faith in God is extinguished and idolatry fostered, as we see in our day. As a result we have the same kind of priests today as Jeroboam ordained of old in Dan and Beersheba, ministers of the golden calves [I Kings 12:26-32], men who are ignorant of the law of God, of faith, and of whatever pertains to the feeding of Christ's sheep. They inculcate in the people nothing but their own inventions with fear and violence.

Although I urge that this outrage of reserved cases should be borne patiently, even as Christ bids us bear all the tyranny of men, and teaches us that we should obey these extortioners; nevertheless, I deny that they have the right to make such reservations, and I do not believe that they can bring one jot or tittle of proof that they have it. But I am going to prove the contrary. In the first place, Christ speaks in Matt. 18 [:15-17] of public sins and says that if our brother hears us, when we tell him his fault, we have

---

152. *Coena domini* was a papal bull published annually against heretics since 1364 in the Lateran Church at Rome on Holy Thursday. But to the condemnation of their heresies were added those offenses, absolvable only by the pope or by his authorization, which might conceivably endanger or impair the papal state. Luther was named in the bull for the first time on March 28, 1521, along with Wycliffe and Huss. In 1522 Luther translated this bull into German as a New Year's present for the pope. *WA* 8, 691; cf. *PE* 2, 105-06.

saved the soul of our brother, and that he is to be brought before the church only if he refuses to hear us, so that his sin can be corrected among brethren. How much more will it be true of secret sins, that they are forgiven if one brother freely makes confession to another? So it is not necessary to tell it to the church, that is, as these babblers interpret it, to the prelate or priest. On this matter we have further authority from Christ, where he says in the same chapter: "Whatever you bind on earth shall be bound in heaven, and whatever you loose on earth shall be loosed in heaven" [Matt. 18:18]. For this is said to each and every Christian. Again, he says in the same place: "Again I say to you, if two of you agree on earth about anything they ask, it will be done for them by my father in heaven" [Matt. 18:19]. Now, the brother who lays his secret sins before his brother and craves pardon, certainly agrees with his brother on earth, in the truth which is Christ. Of this Christ says even more clearly, confirming his preceding words: "For truly, I say to you, where two or three are gathered in my name, there am I in the midst of them" [Matt. 18:20].

Hence, I have no doubt but that every one is absolved from his secret sins when he has made confession, privately before any brother, either of his own accord or after being rebuked, and has sought pardon and amended his ways, no matter how much the violence of the pontiffs may rage against it. For Christ has given to every one of his believers the power to absolve even open sins. Add yet this little point: If any reservation of secret sins were valid, so that one could not be saved unless they were forgiven, then a man's salvation would be prevented most of all by those aforementioned good works and idolatries which are taught by the popes nowadays. But if these most grievous sins do not prevent one's salvation, how foolish it is to reserve those lighter sins! In truth, it is the foolishness and blindness of the shepherds that produce these monstrous things in the church. Therefore I would admonish those princes of Baby-

214

lon and bishops of Beth-aven[153] to refrain from reserving any cases whatsoever. Let them, moreover, permit all brothers and sisters most freely to hear the confession of secret sins, so that the sinner may make his sins known to whomever he will and seek pardon and comfort, that is, the word of Christ, by the mouth of his neighbor. For with these presumptions of theirs they only ensnare the consciences of the weak without necessity, establish their wicked despotism, and fatten their avarice on the sins and ruin of their brethren. Thus they stain their hands with the blood of souls; sons are devoured by their parents. Ephraim devours Judah, and Syria Israel, with an open mouth, as Isaiah [9:20-21] says.

To these evils they have added the "circumstances,"[154] and also the mothers, daughters, sisters, sisters-in-law, branches and fruits of sins; since these most astute and idle men have worked out, if you please, a kind of family tree of relationships and affinities even among sins—so prolific is wickedness coupled with ignorance. For this conception, whatever rogue may be its author, has become a public law, like many others. Thus do the shepherds keep watch over the church of Christ: whatever new work or superstition those most stupid devotees may have dreamed of, they immediately drag to the light of day, deck out with indulgences, and fortify with bulls. So far are they from suppressing such things and preserving for God's people true faith and liberty. For what has our liberty to do with the tyranny of Babylon?

My advice would be to ignore all "circumstances" whatsoever. With Christians there is only one circumstance—that a brother has sinned. For there is no person to be compared with a Christian brother. And the observance of

---

153. Hos. 4:15, 10:5. The prophet altered the name Bethel (house of God) to Beth-aven (house of nothingness or idolatry) because of the images which had been erected there.
154. Cf. p. 183 n. 116.

places, times, days, persons,[155] and all other rank superstition, only magnifies the things that are nothing, to the injury of the things which are everything; as if anything could be of greater weight or importance than the glory of Christian brotherhood! Thus they bind us to places, days, and persons, so that the name of "brother" loses its value, and we serve in bondage instead of being free—we, to whom all days, places, persons, and all external things are one and the same.

How unworthily they have dealt with *satisfaction,* I have abundantly shown in the controversies concerning indulgences.[156] They have grossly abused it, to the ruin of Christians in body and soul. To begin with, they have taught it in such a manner that the people have never had the slightest understanding what satisfaction really is, namely, the renewal of a man's life. Then, they so continually harp on it and emphasize its necessity that they leave no room for faith in Christ. With these scruples they torture poor consciences to death; and one runs to Rome, one to this place, another to that; this one to Chartreuse,[157] that one to some other place; one scourges himself with rods, another mortifies his body with fasts and vigils; and all cry with the same mad zeal: "Lo, here is Christ! Lo, there!" believing that the kingdom of Christ, which is within us, will come with observation.[158]

For these monstrous things we are indebted to you, O

---

155. Sins were assessed differently according to whether they were committed at a holy place or not, on holy days or on ordinary days. Murder of a priest was a more grievous sin than murder of a layman. Buchwald, *op cit.,* II, 465.

156. Cf. p. 206 n. 147; especially in the *Explanations of the Ninety-five Theses, LW* 31, 85, 94-96, 152-53.

157. This was the mother cloister and headquarters of the rigidly ascetic Carthusian order.

158. Luke 17:20-21. A play on *observantia,* which also means "observance," a fling at the Observants. Cf. p. 202 n. 138.

Roman See, and to your murderous laws and ceremonies, with which you have corrupted all mankind, so that they believe they can with works make satisfaction for sin to God, when he can be satisfied only by the faith of a contrite heart! Not only do you keep this faith silent with this uproar of yours, but you even oppress it, only so that your insatiable bloodsucker may have those to whom it may say, "Give, give!" [Prov. 30:15] and may traffic in sins.

Some have gone even farther and have constructed those instruments for driving souls to despair, their decrees that the penitent must rehearse all sins anew for which he neglected to make the imposed satisfaction. What would they not venture to do, these men who were born for the sole purpose of carrying all things into a tenfold captivity? Moreover, how many, I ask, are possessed with the notion that they are in a saved state and are making satisfaction for their sins, if they only mumble over, word for word, the prayers imposed by the priest, even though meanwhile they never give a thought to the amending of their way of life! They believe that their life is changed in the one moment of contrition and confession, and there remains only to make satisfaction for their past sins. How should they know better if they have not been taught otherwise? No thought is given here to the mortifying of the flesh, no value is attached to the example of Christ, who, when he absolved the woman caught in adultery, said: "Go, and do not sin again" [John 8:11], thereby laying upon her the cross, that is, the mortifying of her flesh. This perverse error is greatly encouraged by the fact that we absolve sinners before the satisfaction has been completed, so that they are more concerned about completing the satisfaction, which is a lasting thing, than they are about contrition, which they suppose to be over and done with when they have made confession. Absolution ought rather to follow on the completion of satisfaction, as it did in the early church, with the result that, after completing the work, penitents gave themselves with much greater diligence to faith and the living of a new life.

But this must suffice in repetition of what I have said more fully in connection with indulgences, and *in general this must suffice for the present concerning the three sacraments,* which have been treated, and yet not treated, in so many harmful books on the *Sentences* and on the laws. It remains to attempt some discussion of the other "sacraments" [159] also, lest I seem to have rejected them without cause.

CONFIRMATION

It is amazing that it should have entered the minds of these men to make a sacrament of confirmation out of the laying on of hands. We read that Christ touched the little children in that way [Mark 10:16], and that by it the apostles imparted the Holy Spirit [Acts 8:17; 19:6], ordained presbyters [Acts 6:6], and cured the sick [Mark 16:18]; as the Apostle writes to Timothy: "Do not be hasty in the laying on of hands" [I Tim. 5:22]. Why have they not also made a "confirmation" out of the sacrament of the bread? For it is written in Acts 9 [:19]: "And he took food and was strengthened," [160] and in Ps. 104 [:15]: "And bread to strengthen man's heart." Confirmation would thus include three sacraments—the bread, ordination, and confirmation itself. But if everything the apostles did is a sacrament, why have they not rather made preaching a sacrament?

bread
ordination
confirmation

I do not say this because I condemn the seven sacraments, but because I deny that they can be proved from the Scriptures. Would that there were in the church such a laying on of hands as there was in apostolic times, whether we chose to call it confirmation or healing! But there is nothing left of it now but what we ourselves have invented

159. Cf. pp. 132 and 240.
160. Luther correctly quotes *confortatus,* but thinks *confirmatus.*

to adorn the office of bishops, that they may not be entirely without work in the church. For after they relinquished to their inferiors those arduous sacraments together with the Word as being beneath their attention (since whatever the divine majesty has instituted must needs be despised of men!) it was no more than right that we should discover something easy and not too burdensome for such delicate and great heroes to do, and should by no means entrust it to the lower clergy as something common, for whatever human wisdom has decreed must be held in honor among men! Therefore, as the priests are, so let their ministry and duty be. For a bishop who does not preach the gospel or practice the cure of souls—what is he but an idol in the world [I Cor. 8:4], who has nothing but the name and appearance of a bishop?

But instead of this we seek sacraments that have been divinely instituted, and among these we see no reason for numbering confirmation. For to constitute a sacrament there must be above all things else a word of divine promise, by which faith may be exercised. But we read nowhere that Christ ever gave a promise concerning confirmation, although he laid hands on many and included the laying on of hands among the signs in the last chapter of Mark [16:18]: "They will lay their hands on the sick; and they will recover." Yet no one has applied this to a sacrament, for that is not possible.

For this reason it is sufficient to regard confirmation as a certain churchly rite or sacramental ceremony, similar to other ceremonies, such as the blessing of water and the like. For if every other creature is sanctified by the Word and by prayer [I Tim. 4:4-5], why should not man much rather be sanctified by the same means? Still, these things cannot be called sacraments of faith, because they have no divine promise connected with them, neither do they save; but the sacraments do save those who believe the divine promise.

Not only is marriage regarded as a sacrament without the least warrant of Scripture, but the very ordinances which extol it as a sacrament have turned it into a farce. Let us look into this a little.

We have said that in every sacrament there is a word of divine promise, to be believed by whoever receives the sign, and that the sign alone cannot be a sacrament. Nowhere do we read that the man who marries a wife receives any grace of God. There is not even a divinely instituted sign in marriage, nor do we read anywhere that marriage was instituted by God to be a sign of anything. To be sure, whatever takes place in a visible manner can be understood as a figure or allegory of something invisible. But figures or allegories are not sacraments, in the sense in which we use the term.

Furthermore, since marriage has existed from the beginning of the world and is still found among unbelievers, there is no reason why it should be called a sacrament of the New Law and of the church alone. The marriages of the ancients were no less sacred than are ours, nor are those of unbelievers less true marriages than those of believers, and yet they are not regarded as sacraments. Besides, even among believers there are married folk who are wicked and worse than any heathen; why should marriage be called a sacrament in their case and not among the heathen? Or are we going to talk the same sort of nonsense about baptism and the church and say that marriage is a sacrament only in the church, just as some make the mad claim that temporal power exists only in the church? That is childish and foolish talk, by which we expose our ignorance and foolhardiness to the ridicule of unbelievers.

But they will say, "The Apostle says in Eph. 5 [:31-32],

'The two shall become one. This is a great sacrament.' [161] Surely you are not going to contradict so plain a statement of the Apostle!" I reply: This argument like the others betrays great shallowness and a careless and thoughtless reading of Scripture. Nowhere in all of the Holy Scriptures is this word *sacramentum* employed in the sense in which we use the term; it has an entirely different meaning. For wherever it occurs it denotes not the sign of a sacred thing, but the sacred, secret, hidden thing itself. Thus Paul writes in I Cor. 4 [:1]: "This is how one should regard us, as servants of Christ and stewards of the 'mysteries' of God," that is, the sacraments. For where we have [in the Vulgate] the word *sacramentum* the Greek original has *mysterion*, which the translator sometimes translates and sometimes retains in its Greek form. Thus our verse in the Greek reads: "They two shall become one. This is a great mystery." This explains how they came to understand a sacrament of the New Law here, a thing they would never have done if they had read *mysterium*, as it is in the Greek.[162]

Thus Christ himself is called a "sacrament" in I Tim. 3 [:16]: "Great indeed, is the sacrament (that is the mystery): He was manifested in the flesh, vindicated in the Spirit, seen by angels, preached among the nations, believed on in the world, taken up in glory." Why have they not drawn out of this passage an eighth sacrament [163] of the New Law, since they have the clear authority of Paul? But if they restrained themselves here, where they had a most excellent opportunity to invent new sacraments, why are they so

161. The quotation is from the Vulgate. Luther points to its divergence from the Greek original, which the English versions have more literally rendered with the word "mystery."
162. Erasmus edited the first published Greek New Testament in March, 1516. Luther used Erasmus' work as soon as it came out, as may be seen in his lectures on Romans, 1515-16. In an interesting letter to Luther of February 14, 1519, Froben announces the second edition of Erasmus' New Testament, which Luther used in making his translation, 1521-22. *PE* 2, 258 n. 2.
163. Cf. pp. 132 and 240.

unrestrained in the other passage? Plainly, it was their ignorance of both words and things that betrayed them. They clung to the mere sound of the words, indeed, to their own fancies. For, having once arbitrarily taken the word *sacramentum* to mean a sign, they immediately, without thought or scruple, made a "sign" of it every time they came upon it in the Holy Scriptures. Such new meanings of words, human customs, and other things they have dragged into the Holy Scriptures. They have transformed the Scriptures according to their own dreams, making anything out of any passage whatsoever. Thus they continually chatter nonsense about the terms: good work, evil work, sin, grace, righteousness, virtue, and almost all the fundamental words and things. For they employ them all after their own arbitrary judgment, learned from the writings of men, to the detriment of both the truth of God and of our salvation.

Therefore, sacrament, or mystery, in Paul is that wisdom of the Spirit, hidden in a mystery, as he says in I Cor. 2 [:7], which is Christ, who for this very reason is not known to the rulers of this world, wherefore they also crucified him, and for them he remains to this day folly [I Cor. 1:23], an offense, a stumbling stone [Rom. 9:32-33], and a sign that is spoken against [Luke 2:34]. The preachers he calls stewards [I Cor. 4:1] of these mysteries because they preach Christ, the power and the wisdom of God [I Cor. 1:24], yet in such a way that, unless you believe, you *def. of* cannot understand it. Therefore, a sacrament is a mystery, *a* or secret thing, which is set forth in words, but received *sacra-* by the faith of the heart. Such a sacrament is spoken of in *ment.* the passage before us: "The two shall become one. This is a great sacrament" [Eph. 5:31-32], which they understand as spoken of marriage, whereas Paul himself wrote these words as applying to Christ and the church, and clearly explained them himself by saying: "I take it to mean Christ and the church" [Eph. 5:32]. See how well Paul and these men agree! Paul says he is proclaiming a great sacrament in Christ and the church, but they proclaim it in terms of man and a woman! If such liberty in the interpretation of the sacred Scriptures is permitted, it is small wonder that one finds here anything he pleases, even a hundred sacraments.

marriage of Christ & the church.

Christ and the church are, therefore, a mystery, that is, a great and secret thing which can and ought to be represented in terms of marriage as a kind of outward allegory. But marriage ought not for that reason to be called a sacrament. The heavens are a type of the apostles, as Ps. 19 declares; the sun is a type of Christ; the waters, of the peoples; but that does not make those things sacraments, for in every case there are lacking both the divine institution and the divine promise, which constitute a sacrament. Hence Paul, in Eph. 5 [:29-32], following his own mind, applies to Christ these words of Gen. 2 [:24] about marriage; or else, following the general view,[164] he teaches that the spiritual marriage of Christ is also contained therein, when he says: "As Christ cherishes the church, because we are members of his body, of his flesh and his bones. 'For this reason a man shall leave his father and mother and be joined to his wife, and the two shall become one.' This is a great sacrament, and I take it to mean Christ and the church." You see, he would have the whole passage apply to Christ, and is at pains to admonish the reader to understand that the sacrament is in Christ and the church, not in marriage.[165]

---

164. The precise meaning is not clear.
165. The following paragraph, because it clearly breaks into the context and belongs elsewhere, is here relegated to a footnote:

I admit, of course, that the sacrament of penance existed in the Old Law, and even from the beginning of the world. But the new promise of penance and the gift of the keys are peculiar to the New Law. Just as we now have baptism instead of circumcision, so we have the keys instead of sacrifices and other signs of penance. We said above that the same God at various times gave different promises and diverse signs for the remission of sins and the salvation of men; nevertheless, all received the same grace. Thus it is said in II Cor. 4 [:13]: "Since we have the same spirit of

Granted that marriage is a figure of Christ and the church; yet it is not a divinely instituted sacrament, but invented by men in the church who are carried away by their ignorance of both the word and the thing. This ignorance, when it does not conflict with the faith, is to be borne in charity, just as many other human practices due to weakness and ignorance are borne in the church, so long as they do not conflict with the faith and the Holy Scriptures. But we are now arguing for the certainty and purity of faith and the Scriptures. We expose our faith to ridicule if we affirm that a certain thing is contained in the sacred Scriptures and in the articles of our faith, only to be refuted and shown that it is not contained in them; being found ignorant of our own affairs, we become a stumbling block to our opponents and to the weak. But most of all we should guard against impairing the authority of the Holy Scriptures. For those things which have been delivered to us by God in the sacred Scriptures must be sharply distinguished from those that have been invented by men in the church, no matter how eminent they may be for saintliness and scholarship.

So far concerning marriage itself.

But what shall we say *concerning the wicked laws of men by which this divinely ordained way of life has been ensnared* and tossed to and fro? Good God! It is dreadful to contemplate the audacity of the Roman despots, who

---

faith, we too believe, and so we speak." And in I Cor. 10 [:1-4]: "Our fathers all ate the same supernatural food and drank the same supernatural drink. For they drank from the supernatural Rock which followed them, and the Rock was Christ." Thus also in Heb. 11 [:13, 40]: "These all died, not having received what was promised, since God had foreseen something better for us, that apart from us they should not be made perfect." For Christ himself is, yesterday and today and forever [Heb. 13:8], the head of his church, from the beginning even to the end of the world. Therefore there are diverse signs, but the faith of all is the same. Indeed, without faith it is impossible to please God, yet by it Abel did please him (Heb. 11 [:4]).

both dissolve and compel marriages as they please. I ask you, has mankind been handed over to the caprice of these men for them to mock them and in every way abuse them and make of them whatever they please, for the sake of filthy lucre?

There is circulating far and wide and enjoying a great reputation a book whose contents have been confusedly poured together out of all the dregs and filth of man-made ordinances. Its title is "The Angelic *Summa*," [166] although it ought rather to be "The More than Devilish *Summa*." Among endless other monstrosities, which are supposed to instruct the confessors, whereas they most mischievously confuse them, there are enumerated in this book eighteen impediments to marriage.[167] If you will examine these with the just and unprejudiced eye of faith, you will see that they belong to those things which the Apostle foretold: "There shall be those that give heed to the spirits of demons, speaking lies in hypocrisy, forbidding to marry" [I Tim. 4:1-3]. What is "forbidding to marry" if it is not this—to invent all those hindrances and set those snares in order to prevent people from marrying, or, if they are married, to annul their marriage? Who gave this power to men? Granted that they were holy men and impelled by godly zeal, why should another's holiness disturb my liberty? Why should another's zeal take me captive? Let whoever will be a saint and a zealot, and to his heart's content, only let him not bring harm upon another, and let him not rob me of my liberty!

---

166. The *Summa de Casibus Conscientiae*, popularly named after its author, Angelo Carletti di Chivasso (1411-1495); a favorite handbook on casuistry treating alphabetically all possible cases of conscience, for the guidance of priests hearing confession. Under the heading of "Matrimony" it listed 18 impediments to marriage. The book went through 31 editions between 1476 and 1520, and was among the papal books burned by Luther, together with the bull, December 10, 1520. (Cf. Luther's letter to Spalatin on the same day, WA Br 2, 234 and 235 n. 2.)

167. For fuller discussion of the impediments see Luther's *Vom ehelichen Leben* (1522) in WA 10^II, 280-287; also the article on "Marriage" by E. Sehling, in Schaff-Herzog, *op. cit.*, VII, 200-03.

Yet I am glad that those shameful laws have at last reached their full measure of glory, which is this: that the Romanists of our day have through them become merchants. What is it that they sell? Vulvas and genitals—merchandise indeed most worthy of such merchants, grown altogether filthy and obscene through greed and godlessness. For there is no impediment nowadays that may not be legalized through the intercession of mammon. These laws of men seem to have sprung into existence for the sole purpose of serving those greedy men and rapacious Nimrods [Gen. 10:8-9] [168] as snares for taking money and as nets for catching souls, and in order that "abomination" might stand in "the holy place" [Matt. 24:15], the church of God, and openly sell to men the _pudenda_ of both sexes, or (as the Scriptures say) "shame and nakedness" [Lev. 18:6-18], of which they had previously robbed them by means of their laws. O worthy trade for our pontiffs to ply, instead of the ministry of the gospel, which in their greed and pride they despise, being given up to a reprobate mind [Rom. 1.28] with utter shame and infamy.

external genital organs.

But what shall I say or do? If I enter into details, the treatise will grow beyond all bounds. Everything is in such dire confusion that one does not know where to begin, how far to go, and where to leave off. This I do know, that no state is governed successfully by means of laws. If the ruler is wise, he will govern better by a natural sense of justice than by laws. If he is not wise, he will foster nothing but evil through legislation, since he will not know what use to make of the laws nor how to adapt them to the case at hand. Therefore, in civil affairs more stress should be laid on putting good and wise men in office than on making laws; for such men will themselves be the very best of laws, and will judge every variety of case with a lively sense of equity. And if there is knowledge of the divine

---

168. Cf. p. 124.

law combined with natural wisdom, then written laws will be entirely superfluous and harmful. Above all, love needs no laws whatever.

Nevertheless, I will say and do what I can. I ask and urge all priests and friars[169] when they encounter any impediment to marriage from which the pope can grant dispensation but which is not stated in the Scriptures, by all means to confirm[170] all marriages that may have been contracted[171] in any way contrary to the ecclesiastical or pontifical laws. But let them arm themselves with the divine law which says: "What God has joined together, let no man put asunder" [Matt. 19:6]. For the joining together of a man and a woman is of divine law and is binding, however much it may conflict with the laws of men; the laws of men must give way before it without any hesitation. For if a man leaves father and mother and cleaves to his wife [Matt. 19:5], how much more will he tread underfoot the silly and wicked laws of men, in order to cleave to his wife! And if pope, bishop, or official[172] should annul any marriage because it was contracted contrary to the laws of men, he is Antichrist, he does violence to nature, and is guilty of treason against the Divine Majesty, because this word stands: "What God has joined together, let no man put asunder" [Matt. 19:6].

Besides this, no man had the right to frame such laws, and Christ has granted to Christians a liberty which is above all the laws of men, especially where a law of God conflicts with them. Thus it is said in Mark 2 [:28]: "The Son of man is lord even of the sabbath," and "Man was not made for the sabbath, but the sabbath for man" [Mark

---

169. It is to be borne in mind that all that follows is in the nature of advice to confessors in dealing with difficult cases of conscience, and is parallel to the closing paragraphs of the section on the Sacrament of the Bread.

170. Namely, by officiating at the marriage ceremony.

171. Namely, by betrothal.

172. Judge of the bishop's court.

2:27]. Moreover, such laws were condemned beforehand by Paul when he foretold that there would be men forbidding to marry [I Tim. 4:3]. Here, therefore, those inflexible impediments derived from affinity, by spiritual or legal relationship,[173] and from blood relationship must give way, so far as the Scriptures permit, in which the second degree of consanguinity alone is prohibited. Thus it is written in Lev. 18 [:6-18], where there are twelve persons a man is prohibited from marrying: his mother, stepmother, full sister, half-sister by either parent, granddaughter, father's or mother's sister, daughter-in-law, brother's wife, wife's sister, stepdaughter, and his uncle's wife. Here only the first degree of affinity and the second degree of consanguinity are forbidden; yet not without exception, as will appear on closer examination, for the brother's or sister's daughter—the niece—is not included in the prohibition, although she is in the second degree. Therefore, if a marriage has been contracted outside of these degrees, which are the only ones which have been prohibited by God's appointment, it should by no means be annulled on account of the laws of men. For marriage itself, being a divine institution, is incomparably superior to any laws, so that marriage should not be annulled for the sake of the law, rather the laws should be broken for the sake of marriage.

In the same way that nonsense about compaternities, commaternities, confraternities, consororities, and confilieties must be completely abolished in the contracting of marriage. What was it but the superstition of men that invented this "spiritual affinity"? If one who baptized is not permitted to marry her whom he has baptized or stood sponsor for, what right has any Christian man to marry a Christian woman? Is the relationship that grows out of the external rite or sign of the sacrament more inimate than

173. Relationship arising from sponsorship at baptism or through legal adoption. Cf. *An Open Letter to the Christian Nobility, PE* 2, 128-29.

that which grows out of the blessing of the sacrament[174] itself? Is not a Christian man the brother of a Christian woman, and is she not his sister? Is not a baptized man the spiritual brother of a baptized woman? How foolish we are! If a man instructs his wife in the gospel and in faith in Christ, does he not truly become her father in Christ? And is it not lawful for her to remain his wife? Would not Paul have had the right to marry a girl from among the Corinthians, of whom he boasts that he became their father in Christ? [I Cor. 4:15]. See then, how Christian liberty has been suppressed through the blindness of human superstition.

There is even less in the "legal affinity," and yet they have set it above the divine right of marriage. Nor would I agree to that impediment which they call "disparity of religion," which forbids one to marry an unbaptized person, either simply, or on condition that she be converted to the faith. Who made this prohibition? God or man? Who gave to men the power to prohibit such a marriage? Indeed, the spirits that speak lies in hypocrisy, as Paul says [I Tim. 4:2]. Of them it must be said: "Godless men have told me fables which do not conform to thy law" [Ps. 119:85].[175] The heathen Patricius married the Christian Monica, mother of St. Augustine; why should that not be permitted today? The same stupid, or rather, wicked severity is seen in the "impediment of crime," as when a man has married a woman with whom he previously had committed adultery, or when he plotted to bring about the death of a woman's husband in order to be able to wed the widow. I ask you, whence comes this cruelty of man toward man, which even God never demanded? Do they pretend not to know that Bathsheba, the wife of Uriah, was wed by David, a most saintly man, after the double crime of adultery and mur-

---

174. *res sacramenti,* cf. p. 137 n. 45.
175. Vulgate version.

der? [II Sam. 11:1-27]. If the divine law did this, what are these despotic men doing to their fellow servants?

They also recognize what they call "the impediment of a tie," that is, when a man is bound to another woman by betrothal. Here they conclude that, if he has had sexual relations with a second woman, his engagement to the first becomes null and void. This I do not understand at all. I hold that he who has betrothed himself to one woman no longer belongs to himself. Because of this fact, by the prohibition of the divine law, he belongs to the first with whom he has not had intercourse, even though he has had intercourse with the second. For it was not in his power to give the latter what was no longer his own; he has deceived her and actually committed adultery. But they regard the matter differently because they pay more heed to the carnal union than to the divine command, according to which the man, having plighted his troth to the first, is bound to keep it forever. For whoever would give anything must give of that which is his own. And God forbids a man to transgress and wrong his brother in any matter [I Thess. 4:6]. This must be observed over and above all the ordinances of all men. Therefore I believe that such a man cannot with a good conscience live in marriage with a second woman, and this impediment should be completely reversed. For if a monastic vow makes a man no longer his own, why does not a pledge of mutual faithfulness[176] do the same? After all, faithfulness is one of the precepts and fruits of the Spirit, in Gal. 5: [22], while a monastic vow is of human invention. And if a wife may claim her husband back, despite the fact that he has taken a monastic vow, why may not an engaged woman claim back her betrothed, even though he has intercourse with another?

---

176. *fides data et accepta.* Luther here regards the *fides* of Gal. 5:22 as *Treue* or "faithfulness." In his New Testament he later translates it as *Glaube* or "faith."

But we have said above[177] that he who has plighted his troth to a girl may not take a monastic vow, but is in duty bound to marry her because he is in duty bound to keep faith with her; and this faith he may not break for any ordinance of men, because it is commanded by God. Much more should the man here keep faith with his first betrothed, since he could not plight his troth to a second except with a lying heart; and therefore did not really plight it, but deceived her, his neighbor, against God's command. Therefore, the "impediment of error"[178] enters in here, by which his marriage to the second woman is rendered null and void.

The "impediment of ordination" is also the mere invention of men, especially since they prate that it annuls even a marriage already contracted. They constantly exalt their own ordinances above the commands of God. I do not indeed sit in judgment on the present state of the priestly order, but I observe that Paul charges a bishop to be the husband of one wife [I Tim. 3.2]. Hence, no marriage of deacon, priest, bishop or any other order can be annulled, although it is true that Paul knew nothing of this species of priests and of the orders we have today. Perish then those cursed man-made ordinances which have crept into the church only to multiply perils, sins, and evils! There exists, therefore, between a priest and his wife a true and indissoluble marriage, approved by the divine commandment. But what if wicked men in sheer despotism prohibit or annul it? So be it! Let it be wrong among men; it is nevertheless right before God, whose command must take precedence if it conflicts with the commands of men [Acts 5:29].

An equally lying invention is that "impediment of public

177. Cf. p. 204.
178. With fine sarcasm Luther here plays off one impediment against another. "Error" generally meant cases of mistaken identity or false information concerning prior marital status. Cf. WA 10ᴵᴵ, 285.

decency," by which contracted marriages are annulled. I am incensed at that barefaced wickedness which is so ready to put asunder what God has joined together that one may well recognize Antichrist in it, for it opposes all that Christ has done and taught. What earthly reason is there for holding that no relative of a deceased fiancé, even to the fourth degree of consanguinity, may marry his fiancée? That is not a judgment of public decency, but ignorance[179] of public decency. Why was not this judgment of public decency found among the people of Israel, who were endowed with the best laws, the laws of God? On the contrary, the next of kin was even compelled by the law of God to marry the widow of his relative [Deut. 25:5]. Must the people of Christian liberty be burdened with more severe laws than the people of legal bondage?

But, to make an end of these—figments rather than impediments—I will say that so far there seem to me to be no impediments that may justly annul a contracted marriage except these: sexual impotence, ignorance of a previously contracted marriage, and a vow of chastity. Still, concerning this latter vow, I am to this day so far from certain that I do not know at what age such a vow is to be regarded as binding, as I also said above in discussing the sacrament of baptism.[180] Thus you may learn, from this one question of marriage, how wretchedly and desperately all the activities of the church have been confused, hindered, ensnared and subjected to danger through the pestilent, ignorant, and wicked ordinances of men, so that there is no hope of betterment unless we abolish at one stroke all the laws of all men, and having restored the gospel of liberty we follow it in judging and regulating all things. Amen.

We must therefore speak of sexual impotence, in order

---

179. An untranslatable pun: *non iustitia sed inscitia*.
180. Cf. pp. 205-06.

that we may the more readily advise the souls that are laboring in peril.[181] But first I wish to state that what I have said about impediments is intended to apply after a marriage has been contracted. I mean to say that no marriage should be annulled by any such impediment. But as to marriages which are yet to be contracted, I would briefly repeat what I have said above.[182] If there is the stress of youthful passion or some other necessity for which the pope grants dispensation, then any brother may also grant a dispensation to another or even to himself, and following that counsel snatch his wife out of the power of tyrannical laws as best he can. For with what right am I deprived of my liberty by somebody else's superstition and ignorance? If the pope grants a dispensation for money, why should not I, for my soul's salvation, grant a dispensation to myself or to my brother? Does the pope set up laws? Let him set them up for himself, and keep hands off my liberty, or I will take it by stealth!

Now let us discuss the matter of *impotence*.

Re-read — contracted marriage & marriage of body.

Consider the following case: A woman, wed to an impotent man, is unable to prove her husband's impotence in court, or perhaps she is unwilling to do so with the mass of evidence and all the notoriety which the law demands; yet she is desirous of having children or is unable to remain continent. Now suppose I had counseled her to procure a divorce from her husband in order to marry another, satisfied that her own and her husband's conscience and their experience were ample testimony of his impotence; but the husband refused his consent to this. Then I would further counsel her, with the consent of the man (who is not really her husband, but only a dweller under the same roof with her), to have intercourse with another, say her husband's brother, but to keep this marriage secret and to ascribe the

181. Cf. p. 227 n. 169
182. Cf. pp. 224-25.

children to the so-called putative father. The question is: Is such a woman saved and in a saved state? I answer: Certainly, because in this case an error,[183] ignorance of the man's impotence, impedes the marriage; and the tyranny of the laws permits no divorce. But the woman is free through the divine law, and cannot be compelled to remain continent. Therefore the man ought to concede her right, and give up to somebody else the wife who is his only in outward appearance.

Moreover, if the man will not give his consent, or agree to this separation—rather than allow the woman to burn [I Cor. 7:9] or to commit adultery—I would counsel her to contract a marriage with another and flee to a distant unknown place. What other counsel can be given to one constantly struggling with the dangers of natural emotions? Now I know that some are troubled by the fact that the children of this secret marriage are not the rightful heirs of their putative father. But if it was done with the consent of the husband, then the children will be the rightful heirs. If, however, it was done without his knowledge or against his will, then let unbiased Christian reason, or better, charity, decide which one of the two has done the greater injury to the other. The wife alienates the inheritance, but the husband has deceived his wife and is defrauding her completely of her body and her life. Is not the sin of a man who wastes his wife's body and life a greater sin than that of the woman who merely alienates the temporal goods of her husband? Let him, therefore, agree to a divorce, or else be satisfied with heirs not his own, for by his own fault he deceived an innocent girl and defrauded her both of life and of the full use of her body, besides giving her an almost irresistible cause for committing adultery. Let both be weighed in the same scales. Certainly, by every right, fraud should recoil on the fraudulent, and

183. Cf. p. 231 n. 178.

234

whoever has done an injury must make it good. What is the difference between such a husband and the man who holds another man's wife captive together with her husband? Is not such a tyrant compelled to support wife and children and husband, or else to set them free? Why should not the same hold true here? Therefore I maintain that the man should be compelled either to submit to a divorce or to support the other man's child as his heir. Doubtless this would be the judgment of charity. In that case, the impotent man, who is not really the husband, should support the heir of his wife in the same spirit in which he would at great expense wait on his wife if she fell sick or suffered some other ill; for it is by his fault and not by his wife's that she suffers this ill. This I have set forth to the best of my ability, for the strengthening of anxious consciences, because my desire is to bring my afflicted brethren in this captivity what little comfort I can.[184]

As to divorce, it is still a question for debate whether it is allowable. For my part I so greatly detest divorce that I

---

184. Several factors ought to be considered in evaluating the two preceding paragraphs, a much criticized section which Wace and Buchheim have omitted altogether from their translation: (1) Couched in the language of the scholars only, this Latin treatise was not intended for popular consumption but rather as a guide for bewildered and confused priests, who were called upon in the confessional to give practical advice and spiritual comfort to troubled souls (cf. p. 227 n. 169). (2) The impediment of impotency was, even according to Roman church law, sufficient ground for declaring a marriage null and void. (3) But the legal process of securing an annulment demanded such an involved procedure for establishing proof that it was equally unpleasant for both parties. (4) Then, as now, divorce under any circumstances was absolutely forbidden by Roman church law. (5) As an alternate to an impossible legal solution, Luther's suggestion of a secret marriage was not without precedent; common law in parts of Westphalia and Lower Saxony, for example, prescribed that a man who could not perform his conjugal duty was required to seek satisfaction for his wife through a neighbor (Jacob Grimm, *Weisthümer* [Göttingen, 1842], III(42, 48, 70, 311). (6) That Luther's position did not involve any unconditional license for frustrated wives to engage in extra-marital liaisons, as his malicious interpreters promptly inferred, is underscored in his *Sermon vom ehelichen Leben* of 1522, where he scores the offending husband even more severely than he does now ("when I was still shy"). WA 10[II], 278-279. Cf. Buchwald, *op. cit.*, II, 482 n. 4, and Woolf, *op. cit.*, p. 303 n. 2.

should prefer bigamy to it[185]; but whether it is allowable, I do not venture to decide. Christ himself, the Chief Shepherd, says in Matt. 5 [:32]: "Every one who divorces his wife, except on the ground of unchastity, makes her an adulteress; and whoever marries a divorced woman commits adultery." Christ, then, permits divorce, but only on the ground of unchastity. The pope must, therefore, be in error whenever he grants a divorce for any other cause; and no one should feel safe who has obtained a dispensation by this temerity (not authority) of the pope. Yet it is still a greater wonder to me why they compel a man to remain unmarried after being separated from his wife by divorce, and why they will not permit him to remarry. For if Christ permits divorce on the ground of unchastity and compels no one to remain unmarried, and if Paul would rather have us marry than burn [I Cor. 7:9], then he certainly seems to permit a man to marry another woman in the place of the one who has been put away. I wish that this subject were fully discussed and made clear and decided, so that counsel might be given in the infinite perils of those who, without any fault of their own, are nowadays compelled to remain unmarried; that is, those whose wives or husbands have run away and deserted them, to come back perhaps after ten years, perhaps never! This matter troubles and distresses me, for there are daily cases, whether by the special malice of Satan or because of our neglect of the Word of God.

I, indeed, who alone against all cannot establish any rule in this matter would yet greatly desire at least the passage in I Cor. 7 [:15] to be applied here: "But if the unbelieving partner desires to separate, let it be so; in such a case the brother or sister is not bound." Here the Apostle gives permission to put away the unbeliever who departs and to

---

185. As he actually did later in the case of Henry VIII and Philip of Hesse, considering it to be the lesser of two evils insofar as it was not without divinely sanctioned precedent in the Old Testament.

set the believing spouse free to marry again. Why should not the same hold true when a believer—that is, a believer in name, but in truth as much an unbeliever as the one Paul speaks of—deserts his wife, especially if he intends never to return. I certainly can see no difference between the two. But I believe that if in the Apostle's day an unbelieving deserter had returned and had become a believer or had promised to live again with his believing wife, it would not have been permitted, but he too would have been given the right to marry again. Nevertheless, in these matters I decide nothing (as I have said), although there is nothing that I would rather see decided, since nothing at present more grievously perplexes me, and many others with me. I would have nothing decided here on the mere authority of the pope and the bishops; but if two learned and good men agreed [Matt. 18:19-20] in the name of Christ and published their opinion in the spirit of Christ, I should prefer their judgment even to such councils as are assembled nowadays, famous only for numbers and authority, not for scholarship and saintliness. Therefore I hang up my lyre[186] on this matter until a better man confers with me about it.

ORDINATION

Of this sacrament the church of Christ knows nothing; it is an invention of the church of the pope. Not only is there nowhere any promise of grace attached to it, but there is not a single word said about it in the whole New Testament. Now it is ridiculous to put forth as a sacrament of God something that cannot be proved to have been instituted by God. I do not hold that this rite, which has been observed for so many centuries, should be condemned; but in sacred things I am opposed to the invention of human fictions. And it is not right to give out as divinely instituted

---

186. This is an allusion to the fact that he is writing a "prelude." Cf. Ps. 137:2.

what was not divinely instituted, lest we become a laughingstock to our opponents. We ought to see that every article of faith of which we boast is certain, pure, and based on clear passages of Scripture. But we are utterly unable to do that in the case of the sacrament under consideration.

The church has no power to make new divine promises of grace, as some prate who hold what is decreed by the church is of no less authority than what is decreed by God, since the church is under the guidance of the Holy Spirit. For the church was born by the word of promise through faith, and by this same word is nourished and preserved. That is to say, it is the promises of God that make the church, and not the church that makes the promise of God. For the Word of God is incomparably superior to the church, and in this Word the church, being a creature, has nothing to decree, ordain, or make, but only to be decreed, ordained, and made. For who begets his own parent? Who first brings forth his own maker?

This one thing indeed the church can do: It can distinguish the Word of God from the words of men; as Augustine confesses that he believed the gospel because he was moved by the authority of the church which proclaimed that this is the gospel.[187] Not that the church is therefore above the gospel; if that were true, she would also be above God, in whom we believe because the church proclaims that he is God. But, as Augustine says elsewhere,[188] the truth itself lays hold on the soul and thus renders it able to judge most certainly of all things; however, the soul is not able to judge the truth, but is compelled to say with unerring certainty that this is the truth. For

187. "Against the Epistle of Manichaeus Called Fundamental" in *The Nicene and Post-Nicene Fathers of the Christian Church,* ed. Philip Schaff (Buffalo, 1887), Series I, IV, 131. Migne 42, 176. Luther gives a fuller interpretation of the meaning of Augustine's statement in *A Reply to the Texts Quoted in Defense of the Doctrines of Men* (1522). PE 2, 451-53.
188. "The Trinity," 9, 6, 10, ed. John Baillie, *et al., The Library of Christian Classics* (Philadelphia, 1955), VIII, 64. Migne 42, 966.

example, our mind declares with unerring certainty that three and seven are ten; and yet it cannot give a reason why this is true, although it cannot deny that it is true. It is clearly taken captive by the truth; and, rather than judging the truth, it is itself judged by it. There is such a mind also in the church, when under the enlightenment of the Spirit she judges and approves doctrines; she is unable to prove it, and yet is most certain of having it. For as among philosophers no one judges the general concepts, but all are judged by them, so it is among us with the mind of the Spirit, Who judges all things and is judged by no one, as the Apostle says [Cor. 2:16]. But of this another time.

Let this then stand fast: The church can give no promise of grace; that is the work of God alone. Therefore she cannot institute a sacrament. But even if she could, it still would not necessarily follow that ordination is a sacrament. For who knows which is the church that has the Spirit? For when such decisions are made there are usually only a few bishops or scholars present; and it is possible that these may not be really of the church. All may err, as councils have repeatedly erred, particularly the Council of Constance,[189] which erred most wickedly of all. Only that which has the approval of the church universal, and not of the Roman church alone, rests on a trustworthy foundation. I therefore admit that ordination is a certain churchly rite, on a par with many others introduced by the church fathers, such as the consecration of vessels, houses, vestments, water, salt,[190] candles,[191] herbs,[192] wine,[193] and the like. No one calls any of these a sacrament, nor is there in them any

---

189. Cf. p. 142 n. 55 and p. 144 n. 18.
190. Used in connection with baptism.
191. Used on Candlemas, Feast of the Purification of Mary, February 2.
192. Used on the Feasts of the Assumption of Mary, August 15; and of St. Peter's Chains, August 1.
193. Not the sacramental element, but the wine consecrated on the Feast of St. John, December 27, and drunk as a remembrance of John at the time of weddings, dying, and departing on a journey. Cf. Buchwald, *op. cit.*, II, 489 n. 2.

promise. In the same manner, to anoint a man's hands with oil, or to shave his head and the like is not to administer a sacrament, since no promise is attached to them; they are simply being prepared for a certain office, like a vessel or an instrument.

But you will say: "What do you do with Dionysius,[194] who in his *Ecclesiastical Hierachy* enumerates six sacraments, among which he also includes ordination?" I answer: I am well aware that this is the one writer of antiquity who is cited in support of the seven sacraments, although he omits marriage and so has only six.[195] But we read nothing at all about these "sacraments" in the rest of the fathers; nor do they ever regard them as sacraments when they speak of these things. For the invention of sacraments is of recent date.[196] Indeed, to speak more boldly, it greatly displeases me to assign such importance to this Dionysius, whoever he may have been, for he shows hardly any signs of solid learning. I would ask, by what authority and with what arguments does he prove his hodge-podge about the angels in his *Celestial Hierachy*—a book over which many curious superstitious spirits have cudgeled their brains? If one were to read and judge without prejudice, is not everything in it his own fancy and very much like a dream? But in his *Theology*, which is rightly called *Mystical,* of which certain very ignorant theologians make so much, he is downright dangerous, for he is more of a Platonist than a Chris-

---

194. Dionysius, the Areopagite, was the pseudonym of the unknown author (*circa* 500, in Syria?) of the neoplantonic writings. Of *the Celestial Hierarchy, Of the Ecclesiastical Hierachy,* and *Of Mystical Theology.* J. P. Migne (ed.), *Patrologiae, Series Graeca,* vol. 3. Luther was among the first to question the high repute and ancient origin which tradition has assigned to these writings when it identified their author with Paul's convert of Acts 17.34.

195. Omitting marriage, confirmation, and penance, Dionysius mentions six sacraments: baptism, eucharist, unction, ordination of priests, ordination of monks, and burial rites. Schaff-Herzog, *op. cit.,* X, 142.

196. The system of seven sacraments was first generally accepted on the authority of Peter Lombard, and was first made official doctrine by the Council of Florence, 1439. Buchwald, *op. cit.,* II, 490 n. 2.

tian. So if I had my way, no believing soul would give the least attention to these books. So far, indeed, from learning Christ in them, you will lose even what you already know of him. I speak from experience. Let us rather hear Paul, that we may learn Jesus Christ and him crucified [I Cor. 2:2]. He is the way, the life, and the truth; he is the ladder [Gen. 28:12] by which we come to the Father, as he says: "No one comes to the Father, but by me" [John 14:6].

Similarly, in the *Ecclesiastical Hierarchy*, what does this Dionysius do but describe certain churchly rites, and amuse himself with allegories without proving anything? Just as has been done in our time by the author of the book entitled *Rationale divinorum*.[197] Such allegorical studies are for idle men. Do you think I should find it difficult to amuse myself with allegories about anything in creation? Did not Bonaventura by allegory draw the liberal arts into theology?[198] And Gerson even converted the smaller Donatus into a mystical theologian.[199] It would not be difficult for me to compose a better hierarchy than that of Dionysius; for he knew nothing of pope, cardinals and archbishops, and put the bishop at the top. Who has so weak a mind as not to be able to launch into allegories? I would not have a theologian devote himself to allegories until he has exhausted the legitimate and simple meaning of the Scripture; other-

197. William Durandus (1237-96), bishop of Mende. His book, written in 1296, is the standard authority for the laws, ceremonies, customs, and symbolism of thirteenth-century Roman rites and vestments. *Catholic Encyclopedia, op. cit.,* V, 207.

198. In his *De reductione artium ad theologiam,* the Franciscan Bonaventura (1221-1274) sought to relate all human knowledge to theology. All the arts and sciences were found to have points of contact in Scripture; and their several activities were regarded as parables of heavenly processes. Buchwald, *op. cit.,* II, 491 n. 4.

199. Donatus (*circa* 350 A.D.), famous Latin grammarian, whose *Ars Minor* was the favorite medieval textbook. The chancellor of the University of Paris, John Gerson (1363-1429), published a *Donatus moralisatus seu per allegoriam traductus,* a mystical grammar, in which the noun was compared to man, the pronoun to man's sinful state, the verb to the divine command to love, the adverb to the fulfilment of the divine law, etc.

wise his theology will bring him into danger, as Origen[200] discovered.

Therefore a thing does not need to be a sacrament simply because Dionysius so describes it. Otherwise, why not also make a sacrament of the [funeral] processions, which he describes in his book, and which continue to this day? There will then be as many sacraments as there have been rites and ceremonies multiplied in the church. Standing on so unsteady a foundation, they have nevertheless invented "characters" [201] which they attribute to this sacrament of theirs and which are indelibly impressed on those who are ordained. Whence do such ideas come, I ask? By what authority, with what arguments, are they established? We do not object to their being free to invent, say, and assert whatever they please; but we also insist on our liberty, that they shall not arrogate to themselves the right to turn their opinions into articles of faith, as they have hitherto presumed to do. It is enough that we accommodate ourselves to their rites and ceremonies for the sake of peace; but we refuse to be bound by such things as if they were necessary to salvation, which they are not. Let them lay aside their despotic demand, and we shall yield free obedience to their wishes, in order that we may live in peace with one another.

---

200. Cf. p. 146 n. 65. Woolf regards Luther's anti-allegorical insistence on the plain sense of Scripture as his greatest single contribution to modern biblical scholarship, and sees a most excellent example of his exegetical method in *LW* 36, 117-23, where he is discussing extreme unction. Cf. Woolf, *op. cit.*, 312 n. 1.

201. The so-called *character indelibilis,* peculiar gift of ordination, meant that "once a priest, always a priest." This "indelible mark" received authoritative statement in the bull Exultate Deo (1439). Eugene IV, summing up the decrees of the Council of Florence, says: "Among these sacraments there are three—baptism, confirmation, and orders—which indelibly impress upon the soul a character, i.e., a certain spiritual mark which distinguishes them from the rest." The Council of Trent (1563) further defined the correct Roman teachings as follows: "The Holy Synod justly condemns the opinion of those who assert that the priests of the New Testament have only temporary power, and that those once rightly ordained can again be made laymen, if they do not exercise the ministry of the Word of God." *PE* 2, 68 n. 5.

It is a shameful and wicked slavery for a Christian man, who is free, to be subject to any but heavenly and divine ordinances.

We come now to their strongest argument. It is this: Christ said at the Last Supper: "Do this in remembrance of me" [Luke 22:19; I Cor. 11:24-25]. "Look," they say, "here Christ ordained the apostles to the priesthood." From this passage they also concluded, among other things, that both kinds are to be administered to the priest alone.[202] In fact, they have drawn out of this passage whatever they pleased, as men who would arrogate to themselves the liberty to prove anything whatever from any words of Christ. But is that interpreting the words of God? I ask you: is it? Christ gives us no promise here, but only commands that this be done in remembrance of him. Why do they not conclude that he also ordained priests when he laid upon them the office of the Word and baptism, and said: "Go into all the world and preach the gospel to the whole creation, baptizing them in the name, etc." [Mark 16:15; Matt. 28:19]. For it is the proper duty of priests to preach and to baptize. Or, since it is nowadays the chief, and (as they say) indispensable duty of priests to read the canonical hours,[203] why have they not discovered the sacrament of ordination in those passages in which Christ commanded them to pray, as he did in many places—particularly in the garden, that they might not enter into temptation? [Matt. 26:41]. But perhaps they will evade this argument by saying that it is not commanded to pray; it is enough to read the canonical hours. Then it follows that this priestly work can be proved nowhere in the Scriptures, and thus their praying priesthood is not of God; as, indeed, it is not.

But which of the ancient Fathers claimed that in this

202. Cf. pp. 134-42.
203. The stated daily prayers, fixed by canon, and contained in the breviary. The seven hours are respectively: matins (including nocturns and lauds), prime, tierce, sext, nones, vespers, and compline.

passage priests were ordained? Where does this new interpretation come from? I will tell you. They have sought by this means to set up a seed bed of implacable discord, by which clergy and laymen should be separated from each other farther than heaven from earth, to the incredible injury of the grace of baptism and to the confusion of our fellowship in the gospel. Here, indeed, are the roots of that detestable tyranny of the clergy over the laity. Trusting in the external anointing by which their hands are consecrated, in the tonsure and in vestments, they not only exalt themselves above the rest of the lay Christians, who are only anointed with the Holy Spirit, but regard them almost as dogs and unworthy to be included with themselves in the church. Hence they are bold to demand, to exact, to threaten, to urge, to oppress, as much as they please. In short, the sacrament of ordination has been and still is an admirable device for establishing all the horrible things that have been done hitherto in the church, and are yet to be done. Here Christian brotherhood has perished, here shepherds have been turned into wolves, servants into tyrants, churchmen into worse than worldlings.

If they were forced to grant that all of us that have been baptized are equally priests, as indeed we are, and that only the ministry was committed to them, yet with our common consent, they would then know that they have no right to rule over us except insofar as we freely concede it. For thus it is written in I Pet. 2 [:9]: "You are a chosen race, a royal priesthood, and a priestly royalty." Therefore we are all priests, as many of us as are Christians.[204] But the priests, as we call them, are ministers chosen from among us. All that they do is done in our name; the priesthood is

204. Cf. *An Open Letter to the Christian Nobility*. PE 2, 69. The fullest development of Luther's doctrine of the spiritual priesthood of believers is to be found in his writings against Emser (cf. p. 124 n. 4), especially his *Answer to the Superchristian, Superspiritual, and Superlearned Book of Goat Emser of Leipzig* (1521). PE 3, 310-401. Cf. also *The Misuse of the Mass* in LW 36, 127-230.

nothing but a ministry. This we learn from I Cor. 4 [:1]: "This is how one should regard us, as servants of Christ and stewards of the mysteries of God."

From this it follows that whoever does not preach the Word, though he was called by the church to do this very thing, is no priest at all, and that the sacrament of ordination can be nothing else than a certain rite by which the church chooses its preachers. For this is the way a priest is defined in Mal. 2 [:7]: "The lips of a priest should guard knowledge, and men should seek instruction from his mouth, for he is the messenger of the Lord of hosts." You may be certain, then, whoever is not a messenger of the Lord of hosts, or whoever is called to do anything else than such messenger service—if I may so term it—is in no sense a priest; as Hos. 4 [:6] says: "Because you have rejected knowledge, I reject you from being a priest to me." They are also called pastors because they are to pasture, that is, to teach. Therefore, those who are ordained only to read the canonical hours and to offer masses are indeed papal priests, but not Christian priests, because they not only do not preach, but they are not even called to preach. Indeed, it comes to this, that a priesthood of that sort is a different estate altogether from the office of preaching. Thus they are hour-reading and mass-saying priests—sort of living idols called priests—really such priests as Jeroboam ordained, in Beth-aven,[205] taken from the lowest dregs of the people, and not of Levi's tribe [I Kings 12:31].

See how far the glory of the church has departed! The whole earth is filled with priests, bishops, cardinals, and clergy; yet not one of them preaches so far as his official duty is concerned, unless he is called to do so by a different call over and above his sacramental ordination. Every one thinks he is doing full justice to his ordination by mumbling the vain repetitions of his prescribed prayers and by cele-

205. Cf. p. 215 n. 153.

brating masses. Moreover, he never really prays when he repeats those hours; or if he does pray, he prays them for himself. And he offers his mass as if it were a sacrifice, which is the height of perversity because the mass consists in the use made of the sacrament. It is clear, therefore, that the ordination, which, as a sacrament, makes clergymen of this sort of men, is in truth nothing but a mere fiction, devised by men who understand nothing about the church, the priesthood, the ministry of the Word, or the sacraments. Thus, as the "sacrament" is, so are the priests it makes. To such errors and such blindness has been added a still worse captivity: in order to separate themselves still farther from other Christians whom they deem profane, they have unmanned themselves, like the Galli, who were the priests of Cybele,[206] and they have taken upon themselves the burden of a spurious celibacy.

To satisfy this hypocrisy and the working of this error it was not enough that bigamy should be prohibited, that is, the having of two wives at one time, as it was forbidden in the law (and as is the accepted meaning of the term); but they have called it bigamy if a man marries two virgins, one after the other, or if he marries one widow. Indeed, so holy is the holiness of this most holy sacrament that no man can become a priest if he has married a virgin and his wife is still living. And—here we reach the very summit of sanctity—a man is even prevented from entering the priesthood if he has married a woman who was not a virgin, though he did so in ignorance or by unfortunate mischance. But if one has defiled six hundred harlots, or violated countless matrons and virgins, or even kept many Ganymedes, that would be no impediment to his becoming bishop or cardinal or pope. Moreover, the Apostle's word "husband of one wife" [I Tim. 3-2] must now be interpreted to mean

---

206. The eunuch priests of Cybele, "the Great Mother," ancient Phrygian nature goddess, were known as Galli. They ran about with dreadful cries, beating cymbals and cutting their flesh with knives.

"the prelate of one church," and this has given rise to the "incompatible benefices."[207] At the same time the pope, that munificent dispenser, may join to one man three, twenty or a hundred wives, that is, churches, if he is bribed with money or power, that is, "moved by godly charity and constrained by the care of the churches" [II Cor. 11:28].

O pontiffs worthy of this venerable sacrament of ordination! O princes, not of the catholic churches, but of the synagogues of Satan [Rev. 2:9] and of darkness itself! I would cry out with Isaiah [Isa. 28:14], "You scoffers, who rule this people in Jerusalem"; and with Amos 6 [:1], "Woe to those who are at ease in Zion, and to those who feel secure on the mountain of Samaria, the notable men of the first of the nations, that go in with state into the house of Israel, etc!" O the disgrace that these monstrous priests bring upon the church of God! Where are there any bishops or priests who even know the gospel, not to speak of preaching it? Why then do they boast of being priests? Why do they desire to be regarded as holier and better and mightier than other Christians, who are merely laymen? To read the hours—what unlearned men, or (as the Apostle says) men speaking with tongues [I Cor. 14:23] cannot do that? But to pray the hours—that belongs to monks, hermits, and men in private life, even though they are laymen. The duty of a priest is to preach, and if he does not preach he is as much a priest as a picture of a man is a man. Does ordaining such babbling priests make one a bishop? Or blessing churches and bells? Or confirming children? Certainly not. Any deacon or layman could do as much. It is the ministry of the Word that makes the priest and the bishop.

Therefore my advice is: Begone, all of you that would

---

207. The Fourth Lateran Council of 1215 had decreed that no one could simultaneously hold two offices involving pastoral care. The clever and lucrative ways in which the popes legally circumvented this statute Luther describes in *An Open Letter to the Christian Nobility*, pp. 87-42.

live in safety; flee, young men, and do not enter upon this holy estate, unless you are determined to preach the gospel, and can believe that you are made not one whit better than the laity through this "sacrament" of ordination! For to read the hours is nothing, and to offer mass is to receive the sacrament. What then is there left to you that every layman does not have? Tonsure and vestments? A sorry priest, indeed, who consists of tonsure and vestments! Or the oil poured on your fingers? But every Christian is anointed and sanctified both in body and soul with the oil of the Holy Spirit. In ancient times every Christian handled the sacrament with his hands as often as the priests do now.[208] But today our superstition counts it a great crime if the laity touch either the bare chalice or the corporal; not even a nun who is a pure virgin would be permitted to wash the palls[209] and the sacred linens of the altar. O God! See how far the sacrosanct sanctity of this "sacrament" of ordination has gone! I expect the time will come when the laity will not be permitted to touch the altar—except when they offer their money. I almost burst with indignation when I contemplate the wicked tyrannies of these brazen men, who with their farcical and childish fancies mock and overthrow the liberty and glory of the Christian religion.

Let everyone, therefore, who knows himself to be a Christian, be assured of this, that we are all equally priests, that is to say, we have the same power in respect to the Word and the sacraments. However, no one may make use of this power except by the consent of the community or by the call of a superior. (For what is the common property of all, no individual may arrogate to himself, unless he is called.) And therefore this "sacrament" of ordination, if it is anything at all, is nothing else than a certain rite whereby one is called to the ministry of the church. Furthermore, the

208. Cf. pp. 140-41.
209. Covers for the chalice.

priesthood is properly nothing but the ministry of the Word —the Word, I say; not the law, but the gospel. And the diaconate is the ministry, not of reading the Gospel or the Epistle, as is the present practice, but of distributing the church's aid to the poor, so that the priests may be relieved of the burden of temporal matters and may give themselves more freely to prayer and the Word. For this was the purpose of the institution of the diaconate, as we read in Acts 5 [6:1-6]. Whoever, therefore, does not know or preach the gospel is not only no priest or bishop, but he is a kind of pest to the church, who under the false title of priest or bishop, or dressed in sheep's clothing, actually does violence to the gospel and plays the wolf [Matt. 7:15] in the church.

Therefore, unless these priests and bishops, with whom the church abounds today, work out their salvation [Phil. 2:12] in some other way; unless they realize that they are not priests or bishops, and bemoan the fact that they bear the name of an office whose duties they either do not know or cannot fulfil, and thus with prayers and tears lament their wretched hypocritical life—unless they do this, they are truly the people of eternal perdition, and the words of Isa. 5 [:13f.] are fulfilled in them: "Therefore my people go into exile for want of knowledge; their honored men are dying of hunger, and their multitude is parched with thirst. Therefore Hell has enlarged its appetite and opened its mouth beyond measure, and the nobility of Jerusalem and her multitude go down, her throng and he who exults in her." What a dreadful word for our age, in which Christians are swallowed up in so deep an abyss!

According to what the Scriptures teach us, what we call the priesthood is a ministry. So I cannot understand at all why one who has once been made a priest cannot again become a layman; for the sole difference between him and a layman is his ministry. But to depose a man from the priesthood is by no means impossible, because even now it is the usual penalty imposed upon guilty priests. They are either suspended temporarily, or permanently deprived of their office. For that fiction of an "indelible character" [210] has long since become a laughingstock. I admit that the pope imparts this "character," but Christ knows nothing of it; and a priest who is consecrated with it becomes the lifelong servant and captive, not of Christ, but of the pope, as is the case nowadays. Moreover, unless I am greatly mistaken, if this sacrament and this fiction ever fall to the ground, the papacy with its "characters" will scarcely survive. Then our joyous liberty will be restored to us; we shall realize that we are all equal by every right. Having cast off the yoke of tyranny, we shall know that he who is a Christian has Christ; and that he who has Christ has all things that are Christ's, and can do all things [Phil. 4:13]. Of this I will write more,[211] and more vigorously, as soon as I perceive that the above has displeased my friends the papists.

THE SACRAMENT OF EXTREME UNCTION

To this rite of anointing the sick the theologians of our day have made two additions which are worthy of them: first, they call it a sacrament, and second, they make it the last sacrament. So it is now the sacrament of extreme unction, which is to be administered only to those who are at the point of death. Since they are such subtle dialecticians, perhaps they have done this in order to relate it to the first unction of baptism[212] and the two subsequent ones of confirmation and ordination. But here they are able to cast in my teeth that, in the case of this sacrament, there are on the authority of the apostle James both promise and sign, which, as I have maintained all along, do constitute

210. Cf. p. 242 n. 201.
211. These basic ideas received expanded treatment about six weeks later in *The Freedom of a Christian*, pp. 277-316.
212. In the order for baptism, just after the Creed, the child was anointed with oil on chest and shoulders. Buchwald, *op. cit.*, II 501 n. 1.

a sacrament. For the apostle says [Jas. 5:14-15]: "Is any among you sick? Let him call for the elders of the church, and let them pray over him, anointing him with oil in the name of the Lord; and the prayer of faith will save the sick man, and the Lord will raise him up; and if he has committed sins, he will be forgiven." There, they say, you have the promise of the forgiveness of sins and the sign of the oil.

But I say: If ever folly has been uttered, it has been uttered especially on this subject: I will say nothing of the fact than many[213] assert with much probability that this epistle is not by James the apostle, and that it is not worthy of an apostolic spirit; although, whoever was its author, it has come to be regarded as authoritative. But even if the apostle James did write it, I still would say, that no apostle has the right on his own authority to institute a sacrament, that is, to give a divine promise with a sign attached. For this belongs to Christ alone. Thus Paul says that he received from the Lord [I Cor. 11:23] the sacrament of the Eucharist, and that he was not sent to baptize, but to preach the gospel [I Cor. 1:17]. And nowhere do we read in the gospel of the sacrament of extreme unction. But let us also pass over this point. Let us examine the words of the apostle, or whoever was the author of the epistle, and we shall see at once how little heed these multipliers of sacraments have given to them.

In the first place, if they believe the apostle's words to be true and binding, by what right do they change and contradict them? Why do they make an extreme and a special kind of unction out of that which the apostle wished to be general? For the apostle did not desire it to be an extreme unction or administered only to the dying, but he

---

213. Eusebius (*circa* 275-340) classed it among the *antilegomena* or contested writings. Jerome (*circa* 340-420) says it was regarded as pseudonymous in the Latin church. Luther's contemporaries, the humanist Erasmus and the Catholic Cajetan, both contested its authenticity.

says expressly: "Is any one sick?" He does not say: "Is any one dying?" I do not care what learned discussions Dionysius has on this point in his *Ecclesiastical Hierarchy*.[214] The apostle's words are clear enough, on which he has well as they rely; but they do not follow them. It is evident, therefore, that they have arbitrarily and without any authority made a sacrament and an extreme unction out of the words of the apostle which they have wrongly interpreted. And this works to the detriment of all other sick persons, whom they have deprived on their own authority of the benefit of the unction which the apostle enjoined.

But this is even a finer point: The apostle's promise expressly declares: "The prayer of faith will save the sick man, and the Lord will raise him up, etc." [Jas. 5:15]. See, the apostle in this passage commands us to anoint and to pray, in order that the sick man may be healed and raised up; that is, that he may not die, and that it may not be an extreme unction. This is proved also by the prayers which are used even to this day during the anointing, because the prayers are for the recovery of the sick man. But they say, on the contrary, that the unction must be administered to none but the dying;[215] that is, that they may not be healed and raised up. If it were not so serious a matter, who could help laughing at this beautiful, apt, and sensible exposition of the apostle's words? Is not the folly of the sophists here shown in its true colors? Because here, as in so many other places, it affirms what the Scriptures deny, and denies what the Scriptures affirm. Why should we not give thanks to these excellent masters of ours?[216] Surely I spoke the truth when I said that they never uttered greater folly than on this subject.

Furthermore, if this unction is a sacrament, it must neces-

---

214. Cf. p. 240 n. 194.
215. All editions have *discessuris*, "departing," but WA 6, 568 n. 35, suggests *decessuris*, "dying."
216. Cf. pp. 123-24

sarily be (as they say) an "effective sign" [217] of that which it signifies and promises. Now it promises health and recovery to the sick, as the words plainly say: "The prayer of faith will save the sick man, and the Lord will raise him up" [Jas. 5:15]. But who does not see that this promise is seldom, if ever, fulfilled? Scarcely one in a thousand is restored to health, and when one is restored nobody believes that it came about through the sacrament, but through the working of nature or of medicine. Indeed to the sacrament they ascribe the opposite effect. What shall we say then? Either the apostle lies in making this promise or else this unction is no sacrament. For the sacramental promise is certain; but this promise fails in the majority of cases. Indeed—and here again we recognize the shrewdness and foresight of these theologians—for this very reason they would have it to be extreme unction, that the promise should not stand; in other words, that the sacrament should be no sacrament. For if it is extreme unction, it does not heal, but gives way to the disease; but if it heals, it cannot be extereme unction. Thus, by the interpretation of these masters, James is shown to have contradicted himself, and to have instituted a sacrament in order not to institute one; for they must have an extreme unction just to make untrue what the apostle intends, namely, the healing of the sick by it. If this is not madness, I ask you what is?

The word of the apostle in I Tim. 1 [:7] describes these people: "Desiring to be teachers of the law, without understanding either what they are saying or the things about which they make assertions." Thus they read and follow everything uncritically. With the same carelessness they have also found auricular confession in the apostle's words: "Confess your sins to one another" [Jas. 5:16]. But they do not observe the command of the apostle that the elders of the church be called, and prayer be made for the sick

217. Cf. pp. 186-87.

[Jas. 5:14]. Scarcely one insignificant priest is sent nowadays, although the apostle would have many present, not because of the unction, but because of the prayer. That is why he says: "The prayer of faith will save the sick man, etc." [Jas. 5:15]. I have my doubts, however, whether he would have us understand "priests" when he says "presbyters," that is, "elders." For one who is an elder is not necessarily a priest or a minister. We may suspect that the apostle desired the older, graver men in the church to visit the sick, to perform a work of mercy, and pray in faith and thus heal him. Yet, it cannot be denied that the churches were once ruled by older persons, chosen for this purpose without these ordinations and consecrations, solely on account of their age and long experience.

Therefore I take it that this unction is the same as that practiced by the apostles, of whom it is written in Mark 6 [:13]: "They anointed with oil many that were sick and healed them." It was a rite of the early church by which they worked miracles on the sick, and which has long since ceased. In the same way Christ, in the last chapter of Mark [16:18], gave to believers the power to pick up serpents, lay hands on the sick, etc. It is a wonder that they have not made sacraments of those words also, for they have the same power and promise as these words of James. Therefore this extreme—which is to say fictitious—unction is not a sacrament, but a counsel of James, which anyone who will may follow; and it is derived from Mark 6 [:13], as I have said. I do not believe that it was a counsel given to all sick persons, for the church's infirmity is her glory and death is gain [Phil. 1:21]; but it was given only to such as might bear their sickness impatiently and with little faith, those whom the Lord allowed to remain in order that miracles and the power of faith might be manifest in them.

James made careful and diligent provision in this case by attaching the promise of healing and the forgiveness of sins not to the unction, but to the prayer of faith. For he says: "And the prayer of faith will save the sick man, and the Lord will raise him up; and if he has committed sins, he will be forgiven" [Jas. 5:15]. A sacrament does not demand prayer and faith on the part of the minister, since even a wicked person may baptize and consecrate without prayer; a sacrament depends solely on the promise and institution of God, and requires faith on the part of the recipient. But where is the prayer of faith in our present use of extreme unction? Who prays over the sick one in such faith as not to doubt that he will recover? Such a prayer of faith James here describes, of which he said at the beginning of his epistle: "But let him ask in faith, with no doubting" [Jas. 1:6]. And Christ says of it: "Whatever you ask in prayer, believe that you receive it, and you will" [Mark 11:24].

There is no doubt at all that, even if today such a prayer were made over a sick man, that is, made in full faith by older, graver, and saintly men, as many as we wished would be healed. For what could not faith do? But we neglect this faith which the authority of the apostle demands above all else. Further, by "presbyters"—that is, men pre-eminent by reason of their age and faith—we understand the common herd of priests. Moreover, we turn the daily or temporally unrestricted unction into an extreme unction. And finally, we do not obtain the result promised by the apostle, namely, the healing of the sick, but we render the promise ineffective by doing the very opposite. And yet we boast that our sacrament, or rather figment, is established and proved by this saying of the apostle, which is diametrically opposed[218] to it. O what theologians!

Now I do not condemn this our "sacrament" of extreme unction, but I firmly deny that it is what the apostle James prescribes; for his unction agrees with ours neither in form.

218. *bis diapason*. In his *Adagia*, Erasmus explains the intense degree of separation and conflict connoted by this originally Greek phrase. It describes the relationship between two things that are worlds apart, unalterably opposed, and most sharply to be distinguished. *CL* 1, 509 n. 1.

use, power, nor purpose. Nevertheless, we shall number it among those "sacraments" which we have instituted, such as the blessing and sprinkling of salt[219] and water. For we cannot deny that any creature whatsoever may be consecrated by the Word and by prayer, as the apostle Paul teaches us [I Tim. 4:4-5]. We do not deny, therefore, that forgiveness and peace are granted through extreme unction; not because it is a sacrament divinely instituted, but because he who receives it believes that these blessings are granted to him. For the faith of the recipient does not err, however much the minister may err. For one who baptizes or absolves in jest,[220] that is, one who does not absolve so far as the minister is concerned, nevertheless does truly baptize and absolve if the person to be baptized or absolved believes. How much more will one who administers extreme unction confer peace, even though he does not really confer peace so far as his ministry is concerned, since there is no sacrament there! The faith of the one anointed receives even that which the minister either could not give or did not intend to give. It is sufficient for the one anointed to hear and believe the Word. For whatever we believe we shall receive, that we really do receive, no matter what the minister may or may not do, or whether he dissembles or jests. The saying of Christ holds good: "All things are possible to him who believes" [Mark 9:23], and again: "Be it done for you as you have believed" [Matt. 8:13]. But in treating the sacraments our sophists say nothing at all of this faith, but only babble with all their might about the virtues of the sacraments themselves. They will "listen to anybody and can never arrive at a knowledge of the truth" [II Tim. 3:7].

Still it was a good thing that this unction was made the extreme or "last" unction, for thanks to that, it has been abused and distorted least of all the sacraments by tyranny

219. Cf. p. 239 n. 190.
220. Cf. p. 186 n. 122

and greed. This one last mercy, to be sure, has been left to the dying—they may be anointed without charge, even without confession and communion. If it had remained a practice of daily occurrence, especially if it had cured the sick, even without taking away sins, how many worlds, do you think, would not the pontiffs have under their control today? For through the one sacrament of penance and the power of the keys, as well as through the sacrament of ordination, they have become such mighty emperors and princes. But now it is a fortunate thing that they despise the prayer of faith, and therefore do not heal any sick, and that they have made for themselves, out of an ancient ceremony, a brand-new sacrament.

Let this now suffice for these four sacraments. I know how it will displease those who believe that the number and use of the sacraments are to be learned not from the sacred Scriptures, but from the Roman See. As if the Roman See had given these "sacraments" and had not rather received them from the lecture halls of the universities, to which it is unquestionably indebted for whatever it has. The papal despotism would not have attained its present position had it not taken over so many things from the universities. For there was scarcely another of the celebrated bishoprics that had so few learned pontiffs as Rome. Only by violence, intrigue, and superstition has she till now prevailed over the rest. For the men who occupied the See a thousand years ago differed so vastly from those who have since come into power that one is compelled to refuse the name of Roman pontiff to one group or the other.

There are still a few other things which it might seem possible to regard as sacraments; namely, all those things to which a divine promise has been given, such as prayer, the Word, and the cross. For Christ has promised, in many places, that those who pray should be heard; especially in Luke 11 [:5-13], where by many parables he invites us to pray. Of the Word he says: "Blessed are those who hear the Word of God and keep it" [Luke 11:28]. And who can count all the times he promises aid and glory to those who are afflicted, suffer, and are cast down? Indeed, who can recount all the promises of God? Why, the whole Scripture is concerned with provoking us to faith; now driving us with commands and threats, now drawing us with promises and consolations. In fact, everything in Scripture is either a command or a promise. The commands humble the proud with their demands, the promises exalt the humble with their forgiveness.

Nevertheless, it has seemed proper to restrict the name of sacrament to those promises which have signs attached to them. The remainder, not being bound to signs, are bare promises. *Hence there are, strictly speaking, but two sacraments in the church of God—baptism and the bread.* For only in these two do we find both the divinely instituted sign and the promise of forgiveness of sins. The sacrament of penance, which I added to these two,[221] lacks the divinely instituted visible sign, and is, as I have said,[222] nothing but a way and a return to baptism. Nor can the scholastics say that their definition fits penance, for they too ascribe to the true sacrament a visible sign, which is to impress upon the senses the form of that which it effects invisibly. But penance or absolution has no such sign. Therefore they are compelled by their own definition either to admit that penance is not a sacrament and thus to reduce their number, or else to bring forth another definition of a sacrament.

Baptism, however, which we have applied to the whole of life, will truly be a sufficient substitute for all the sacra-

---

221. Cf. p. 132.
222. Cf. pp. 180-81.

ments which we might need as long as we live. And the
bread is truly the sacrament of the dying and departing;
for in it we commemorate the passing of Christ out of this
world, that we may imitate him. Thus we may apportion
these two sacraments as follows: baptism may be allotted
to the beginning and the entire course of life, while the
bread belongs to the end and to death. And the Christian should use them both as long as he is in this mortal
frame, until, fully baptized and strengthened, he passes out
of this world, and is born into the new eternal life, to eat
with Christ in the kingdom of his Father, as he promised
at the Last Supper, when he said: "Truly, I say to you, I
shall not drink again of this fruit of the vine until it is
fulfilled in the kingdom of God" [Matt. 26:29, Mark 14:25,
Luke 22:18]. Thus he clearly seems to have instituted the
sacrament of the bread with a view to our entrance into
the life to come. For then, when the purpose[223] of both
sacraments is fulfilled, baptism and bread will cease.

Herewith I conclude this prelude, and freely and gladly
offer it to all pious souls who desire to know the genuine
sense of the Scriptures and the proper use of the sacraments. For it is a gift of no mean importance, to know the
gifts that are given to us, as it is said in I Cor. 2 [:12], and
what use we ought to make of them. For if we are
instructed with this judgment of the spirit, we shall not
mistakenly rely on those things which are wrong. These
two things our theologians never taught us; indeed, they
seem to have taken pains to hide them from us. If I have
not taught them, I certainly managed not to conceal them,
and have given occasion to others to think out something
better. It has at least been my endeavor to set them both
forth. Nevertheless, "not all can do all things."[224] To the

---

223. *res sacramenti,* cf. p. 137 n. 45.
224. Vergil *Eclogues* viii, 63.

godless, on the other hand, and those who in obstinate tyranny force on us their own teachings instead of God's, I confidently and freely oppose these pages. I shall be completely indifferent to their senseless fury. Yet I wish even them a right understanding. And I do not despise their efforts; I only distinguish them from what is sound and truly Christian.

I hear a rumor that new bulls and papal maledictions are being prepared against me, in which I am urged to recant or be declared a heretic. If that is true, I desire this little book to be part of the recantation that I shall make; so that the arrogant despots might not complain of having acted in vain. The remainder I will publish very soon; please Christ, it will be such as the Roman See has never seen or heard before. I shall give ample proof of my obedience.[225] In the name of our Lord Jesus Christ. Amen.

> "Why doth that impious Herod fear
> When told that Christ the King is near?
> He takes not earthly realms away,
> Who gives the realms that ne'er decay."[226]

---

225. The remainder of Luther's "recantation" was *The Freedom of a Christian*. In *An Open Letter to Pope Leo X*, which accompanied it, he gave ample proof of his obedience. See pp. 266-76.

226. The eighth stanza of Coelius Sedulius' *Hymnus acrostichis totam vitam Christi continens* (beginning *A solis ortus cardine*), of the fifth century. Stanzas 8, 9, 11, and 13 were used as an Epiphany hymn, which Luther translated on December 12, 1541—"*Was fürchtst du, Feind Herodes, sehr.*" The above translation is taken from *Hymns Ancient and Modern*, No. 60. Woolf, *op. cit.*, 329, has this translation from *The English Hymnary*:

> Why, impious Herod, shouldst thou fear
> Because the Christ is come so near?
> He who doth heavenly kingdoms grant
> Thine earthly realm can never want.

THE FREEDOM
OF A CHRISTIAN

1520

Translated by W. A. Lambert
Revised by Harold J. Grimm

Introduction

After the Leipzig Debate Luther returned to Wittenberg, where he resumed his heavy responsibilities and at the same time devoted a large amount of time to study and writing. The list of his publications alone was phenomenal. In addition to writing much devotional literature, often at the request of the elector and his court, he produced sermons, lectures, and polemical tracts. Within six months, in 1520, he published three important Reformation tracts which clarified his new evangelical theology for his ever-increasing following.

In *An Open Letter to the German Nobility,* on August 18, he attacked the authority of the papacy over secular rulers, denied that the pope was the final interpreter of Scripture, assailed the corruption of the Roman Curia, enunciated his important doctrine of the universal priesthood of believers, and called for a drastic reform of the church. In *The Babylonian Captivity of the Church,* published October 6, he attacked the sacramental system of the church by means of which the ecclesiastical hierarchy had gained its control over all Christians. *The Freedom of a Christian,* published early in November, differed from the preceding two pamphlets in that it was written in a conciliatory spirit. Yet it contained a positive and unequivocal statement of Luther's evangelical theology as applied to Christian life. It owed its origin to a final attempt on the part of Miltitz* to prevent a rift in the church.

compatible — attempt to win over.

---

* Cf. *LW* 31, xvii-xix.

262

Despite the fact that Miltitz' first meeting with Luther had failed to end the indulgence controversy, and animosities had been increased by the Leipzig Debate, Miltitz had a second interview with Luther at Liebenwerda on October 9, 1519, at which time the Reformer agreed to present his case before the archbishop of Trier. This also failed. Miltitz did not, however, give up his attempt to counteract the tactics of Eck, even after the Roman Curia had issued the *Exsurge Domine* on June 15, 1520.[†] On August 28 he attended a chapter meeting of the Augustinians at Eisleben where he conferred with Johann von Staupitz, who retired from his office as vicar general at that time, and Wenceslaus Link, his successor. He persuaded these two to visit Luther and to induce him to write a friendly letter to Leo X, assuring the pope that he had never intended to attack him personally. This they did September 6, and Luther agreed to comply with their wishes. Miltitz, however, wanting to make certain that the letter would be written in the proper spirit, had another interview with Luther on October 12, 1520, this time at Lichtenberg. There Luther agreed to write a conciliatory letter and a devotional booklet to accompany it, and even to date the letter September 6 to indicate that he was not motivated by the publication in Germany of the *Exsurge Domine*.

Luther immediately began writing his open letter to Leo and *The Freedom of a Christian,* both, of course, in Latin. It is not known whether the pope received these two documents. If he did, he must have been shocked by the fact that Luther now wrote him as an equal, offered him advice as though he were the papal father confessor, and expressed his evangelical views without a sign of retraction. Although the tract breathed the spirit of late-medieval mysticism and was favorably commented upon by a number of papal

---

† Cf. Carl Mirbt, *Quellen zur Geschichte des Papsttums und des roemischen Katholizimus* (2d ed.; Tübingen and Leipzig, 1901), pp. 183-85.

supporters, it makes clear that a believing Christian is free from sin through faith in God, yet bound by love to serve his neighbor.

Soon after the completion of the open letter to Leo and *The Freedom of a Christian,* Luther made a free translation of the latter into German and sent it to Hermann Mühlphordt of Zwickau. Although this German version is the most widely read, the clearer and more complete Latin text given in *WA* 7, 49-73, and translated into English in *PE* 2, 312-348, is included in this volume with minor revisions. A recent English translation of the German text in *WA* 7, 20-38, is given in Bertram Lee Woolf, *Reformation Writings of Martin Luther,* I, 356-379. The open letter to Leo X was published separately in Wittenberg before November 4, 1520. The translation of it in *PE* 2, 301-311, revised for this volume, was based on the Latin in *WA* 7, 42-49. The most detailed English account of the three important pamphlets of 1520 is that of Mackinnon, *Luther and the Reformation,* II, 222-270.

THE FREEDOM

OF A CHRISTIAN

LETTER OF DEDICATION TO MAYOR MÜHLPHORDT

To the learned and wise gentleman, Hieronymus Mühl-phordt,[1] mayor of Zwickau, my exceptionally gracious friend and patron, I, Martin Luther, Augustinian, present my compliments and good wishes.

My learned and wise sir and gracious friend, the venerable Master Johann Egran, your praiseworthy preacher, spoke to me in terms of praise concerning your love for and pleasure in the Holy Scripture, which you also diligently confess and unceasingly praise before all men. For this reason he desired to make me acquainted with you. I yielded willingly and gladly to his persuasion, for it is a special pleasure to hear of someone who loves divine truth. Unfortunately there are many people, especially those who are proud of their titles, who oppose the truth with all their power and cunning. Admittedly it must be that Christ, set as a stumbling block and a sign that is spoken against, will be an offense and a cause for the fall and rising of many [I Cor. 1:23; Luke 2:34].

In order to make a good beginning of our acquaintance and friendship, I have wished to dedicate to you this treatise or discourse in German, which I have already dedicated to the people in Latin, in the hope that my teachings and writings concerning the papacy will not be considered objectionable by anybody. I commend myself to you and to the grace of God. Amen. Wittenberg, 1520.[2]

---

1. The given name of Mühlphordt was Hermann, not Hieronymus, as Luther has it.
2. In place of the German version of the treatise which Luther sent to Mühl-phordt, the Latin version dedicated to the pope is used as the basis of the English translation in this volume.

AN OPEN LETTER TO POPE LEO X

To Leo X, Pope at Rome, Martin Luther wishes salvation in Christ Jesus our Lord. Amen.

Living among the monsters of this age with whom I am now for the third year waging war, I am compelled occasionally to look up to you, Leo, most blessed father, and to think of you. Indeed, since you are occasionally regarded as the sole cause of my warfare, I cannot help thinking of you. To be sure, the undeserved raging of your godless flatterers against me has compelled me to appeal from your see to a future council, despite the decrees of your predecessors Pius and Julius, who with a foolish tyranny forbade such an appeal. Nevertheless, I have never alienated myself from Your Blessedness to such an extent that I should not with all my heart wish you and your see every blessing, for which I have besought God with earnest prayers to the best of my ability. It is true that I have been so bold as to despise and look down upon those who have tried to frighten me with the majesty of your name and authority. There is one thing, however, which I cannot ignore and which is the cause of my writing once more to Your Blessedness. It has come to my attention that I am accused of great indiscretion, said to be my great fault, in which, it is said, I have not spared even your person.

I freely vow that I have, to my knowledge, spoken only good and honorable words concerning you whenever I have thought of you. If I had ever done otherwise, I myself could by no means condone it, but should agree entirely with the judgment which others have formed of me; and I should do nothing more gladly than recant such indiscretion and impiety. I have called you a Daniel in Babylon; and everyone who reads what I have written knows how zealously I defended your innocence against your defamer Sylvester.[3] Indeed, your reputation and the fame of your blameless life, celebrated as they are throughout the world by the writings of many great men, are too well known and too honorable to be assailed by anyone, no matter how great he is. I am not so foolish as to attack one whom all people praise. As a matter of fact, I have always tried, and will always continue, not to attack even those whom the public dishonors, for I take no pleasure in the faults of any man, since I am conscious of the beam in my own eye. I could not, indeed, be the first one to cast a stone at the adulteress [John 8:1-11].

I have, to be sure, sharply attacked ungodly doctrines in general, and I have snapped at my opponents, not because of their bad morals, but because of their ungodliness. Rather than repent this in the least, I have determined to persist in that fervent zeal and to despise the judgment of men, following the example of Christ who in his zeal called his opponents "a brood of vipers," "blind fools," "hypocrites," "children of the devil" [Matt. 23:13, 17, 33; John 8:44]. Paul branded Magus [Elymas, the magician] as the "son of the devil, . . . full of all deceit and villainy" [Acts 13:10], and he calls others "dogs," "deceivers," and "adulterers" [Phil 3:2; II Cor. 11:13; 2:17]. If you will allow people with sensitive feelings to judge, they would consider no person more stinging and unrestrained in his denunciations than Paul. Who is more stinging than the prophets? Nowadays, it is true, we are made so sensitive by the raving crowd of flatterers that we cry out that we are stung as soon as we meet with disapproval. When we cannot ward off the truth with any other pretext, we flee from it by ascribing it to a fierce temper, impatience, and immodesty. What is the good of salt if it does not bite? Of

3. Sylvester Mazzolini (1456-1523), usually called Prierias after Prierio, the city of his birth, had published three books against Luther. In these he had exaggerated the authority of the papacy.

what use is the edge of a sword if it does not cut? "Cursed is he who does the work of the Lord deceitfully . . ." [Jer. 48:10].

Therefore, most excellent Leo, I beg you to give me a hearing after I have vindicated myself by this letter, and believe me when I say that I have never thought ill of you personally, that I am the kind of person who would wish you all good things eternally, and that I have no quarrel with any man concerning his morals but only concerning the word of truth. In all other matters I will yield to any man whatsoever; but I have neither the power nor the will to deny the Word of God. If any man has a different opinion concerning me, he does not think straight or understand what I have actually said.

I have truly despised your see, the Roman Curia, which, however, neither you nor anyone else can deny is more corrupt than any Babylon or Sodom ever was, and which, as far as I can see, is characterized by a completely depraved, hopeless, and notorious godlessness. I have been thoroughly incensed over the fact that good Christians are mocked in your name and under the cloak of the Roman church. I have resisted and will continue to resist your see as long as the spirit of faith lives in me. Not that I shall strive for the impossible or hope that by my efforts alone anything will be accomplished in that most disordered Babylon, where the fury of so many flatterers is turned against me; but I acknowledge my indebtedness to my Christian brethren, whom I am duty-bound to warn so that fewer of them may be destroyed by the plagues of Rome, at least so that their destruction may be less cruel.

As you well know, there has been flowing from Rome these many years—like a flood covering the world—nothing but a devastation of men's bodies and souls and possessions, the worst examples of the worst of all things. All this is clearer than day to all, and the Roman church, once the holiest of all, has become the most licentious den of thieves

[Matt. 21:13], the most shameless of all brothels, the kingdom of sin, death, and hell. It is so bad that even Antichrist himself, if he should come, could think of nothing to add to its wickedness.

Meanwhile you, Leo, sit as a lamb in the midst of wolves [Matt. 10:16] and like Daniel in the midst of lions [Dan. 6:16]. With Ezekiel you live among scorpions [Ezek. 2:6]. How can you alone oppose these monsters? Even if you would call to your aid three or four well learned and thoroughly reliable cardinals, what are these among so many? You would all be poisoned[4] before you could begin to issue a decree for the purpose of remedying the situation. The Roman Curia is already lost, for God's wrath has relentlessly fallen upon it. It detests church councils, it fears a reformation, it cannot allay its own corruption; and what was said of its mother Babylon also applies to it: "We would have cured Babylon, but she was not healed. Let us forsake her" [Jer. 51:9].

It was your duty and that of your cardinals to remedy these evils, but the gout of these evils makes a mockery of the healing hand, and neither chariot nor horse responds to the rein [Vergil, *Georgics* i. 514]. Moved by this affection for you, I have always been sorry, most excellent Leo, that you were made pope in these times, for you are worthy of being pope in better days. The Roman Curia does not deserve to have you or men like you, but it should have Satan himself as pope, for he now actually rules in that Babylon more than you do.

Would that you might discard that which your most profligate enemies boastfully claim to be your glory and might live on a small priestly income of your own or on your family inheritance! No persons are worthy of glorying in that honor except the Iscariots, the sons of perdition. What do you accomplish in the Roman Curia, my Leo? The

---

4. An attempt to poison Leo X had been made in the summer of 1517.

more criminal and detestable a man is, the more gladly will he use your name to destroy men's possessions and souls, to increase crime, to suppress faith and truth and God's whole church. O most unhappy Leo, you are sitting on a most dangerous throne. I am telling you the truth because I wish you well.

If Bernard felt sorry for Eugenius[5] at a time when the Roman See, which, although even then very corrupt, was ruled with better prospects for improvement, why should not we complain who for three hundred years have had such a great increase of corruption and wickedness? Is it not true that under the vast expanse of heaven there is nothing more corrupt, more pestilential, more offensive than the Roman Curia? It surpasses beyond all comparison the godlessness of the Turks so that, indeed, although it was once a gate of heaven, it is now an open mouth of hell, such a mouth that it cannot be shut because of the wrath of God. Only one thing can we try to do, as I have said:[6] we may be able to call back a few from that yawning chasm of Rome and save them.

Now you see, my Father Leo, how and why I have so violently attacked that pestilential see. So far have I been from raving against your person that I even hoped I might gain your favor and save you if I should make a strong and stinging assault upon that prison, that veritable hell of yours. For you and your salvation and the salvation of many others with you will be served by everything that men of ability can do against the confusion of this wicked Curia. They serve your office who do every harm to the Curia; they glorify Christ who in every way curse it. In short, they are Christians who are not Romans.

To enlarge upon this, I never intended to attack the

5. Bernard of Clairvaux wrote a devotional book, *On Consideration,* to Pope Eugenius III (1145-53), in which he discussed the duties of the pope and the dangers connected with his office. Migne 182, 727-808.

6. Cf. p. 268.

Roman Curia or to raise any controversy concerning it. But when I saw all efforts to save it were hopeless, I despised it, gave it a bill of divorce [Deut. 24:1], and said, "Let the evildoer still do evil, and the filthy still be filthy" [Rev. 22:11]. Then I turned to the quiet and peaceful study of the Holy Scriptures so that I might be helpful to my brothers around me. When I had made some progress in these studies, Satan opened his eyes and then filled his servant Johann Eck, a notable enemy of Christ, with an insatiable lust for glory and thus aroused him to drag me unawares to a debate, seizing me by means of one little word which I had let slip concerning the primacy of the Roman church. Then that boastful braggart,[7] frothing and gnashing his teeth, declared that he would risk everything for the glory of God and the honor of the Apostolic See. Puffed up with the prospect of abusing your authority, he looked forward with great confidence to a victory over me. He was concerned not so much with establishing the primacy of Peter as he was with demonstrating his own leadership among the theologians of our time. To that end he considered it no small advantage to triumph over Luther. When the debate ended badly for the sophist, an unbelievable madness overcame the man, for he believed that it was his fault alone which was responsible for my disclosing all the infamy of Rome.

Allow me, I pray, most excellent Leo, this once to plead my cause and to indict your real enemies. You know, I believe, what dealings your legate, cardinal of St. Sisto,[8] an unwise and unfortunate, or rather, an unreliable man, had with me. When out of reverence for your name I had placed myself and my cause in his hands, he did not try to establish peace. He could easily have done so with a single word, for at that time I promised to keep silent and to

---

7. Thraso, in the original, is the name of a braggart soldier in Terence's *Eunuch*.
8. Cardinal Cajetan, cf. *LW* 31, 264, n. 10.

end the controversy, provided my opponents were ordered to do likewise. As he was a man who sought glory, however, and was not content with such an agreement, he began to defend my opponents, to give them full freedom, and to order me to recant, even though this was not included in his instructions. When matters went fairly well, he with his churlish arbitrariness made them far worse. Therefore Luther is not to blame for what followed. All the blame is Cajetan's, who did not permit me to keep silent, as I at that time most earnestly requested him to do. What more should I have done?

There followed Karl Miltitz,[9] also a nuncio of Your Holiness, who exerted much effort and traveled back and forth, omitting nothing that might help restore the order which Cajetan had rashly and arrogantly disturbed. He finally, with the help of the most illustrious prince, the Elector Frederick, managed to arrange several private conferences with me.[10] Again I yielded out of respect for your name, was prepared to keep silent, and even accepted as arbiter either the archbishop of Trier or the bishop of Naumburg. So matters were arranged. But while this arrangement was being followed with good prospects of success, behold, that other and greater enemy of yours, Eck, broke in with the Leipzig Debate which he had undertaken against Dr. Karlstadt. When the new question of the primacy of the pope was raised, he suddenly turned his weapons against me and completely upset our arrangement for maintaining peace. Meanwhile Karl Miltitz waited. The debate was held and judges were selected. But again no decision was reached, which is not surprising, for through Eck's lies, tricks, and wiles everything was stirred up, aggravated, and confused worse than ever. Regardless of

9. Karl von Miltitz had induced Luther to be silent with respect to the indulgence controversy, provided his opponents did likewise. Cf. *LW* 31, 310 and above, pp. 262-63.

10. At Altenburg on January 5 or 6, 1519.

the decision which might have been reached, a greater conflagration would have resulted, for he sought glory, not the truth. Again I left undone nothing that I ought to have done.

I admit that on this occasion no small amount of corrupt Roman practices came to light, but whatever wrong was done was Eck's fault, who undertook a task beyond his capacities. Striving insanely for his own glory, he revealed the shame of Rome to all the world. This man is your enemy, my dear Leo, or rather the enemy of your Curia. From his example alone we can learn that no enemy is more pernicious than a flatterer. What did he accomplish with his flattery but an evil which not even a king could have accomplished? The name of the Roman Curia is today a stench throughout the world, papal authority languishes, and notorious Roman ignorance is in ill repute. We should have heard nothing of all this if Eck had not upset the peace arrangements made by Karl [von Miltitz] and myself. Eck himself now clearly sees this and, although it is too late and to no avail, he is furious that my books were published. He should have thought of this when, like a whinnying horse, he was madly seeking his own glory and preferred his own advantage through you and at the greatest peril to you. The vain man thought that I would stop and keep silent out of fear for your name, for I do not believe that he entirely trusted his cleverness and learning. Now that he sees that I have more courage than that and have not been silenced, he repents of his rashness, but too late, and perceives—if indeed he does finally understand that there is One in heaven who opposes the proud and humbles the haughty [I Pet. 5:5; Jth. 6:15].

Since we gained nothing from this debate except greater confusion to the Roman cause, Karl Miltitz, in a third attempt to bring about peace, came to the fathers of the Augustinian Order assembled in their chapter and sought their advice in settling the controversy which had now grown most disturbing and dangerous. Because, by God's favor, they had no hope of proceeding against me by violent means, some of their most famous men were sent to me. These men asked me at least to show honor to the person of Your Blessedness and in a humble letter to plead as my excuse your innocence and mine in the matter. They said that the affair was not yet in a hopeless state, provided Leo X out of his innate goodness would take a hand in it. As I have always both offered and desired peace so that I might devote myself to quieter and more useful studies, and have stormed with such great fury merely for the purpose of overwhelming my unequal opponents by the volume and violence of words no less than of intellect, I not only gladly ceased but also joyfully and thankfully considered this suggestion a very welcome kindness to me, provided our hope could be realized.

So I come, most blessed father, and, prostrate before you, pray that if possible you intervene and stop those flatterers, who are the enemies of peace while they pretend to keep peace. But let no person imagine that I will recant unless he prefer to involve the whole question in even greater turmoil. Furthermore, I acknowledge no fixed rules for the interpretation of the Word of God, since the Word of God, which teaches freedom in all other matters, must not be bound [II Tim. 2:9]. If these two points are granted, there is nothing that I could not or would not most willingly do or endure. I detest contentions. I will challenge no one. On the other hand, I do not want others to challenge me. If they do, as Christ is my teacher, I will not be speechless. When once this controversy has been cited before you and settled, Your Blessedness will be able with a brief and ready word to silence both parties and command them to keep the peace. That is what I have always wished to hear.

Therefore, my Father Leo, do not listen to those sirens who pretend that you are no mere man but a demigod so that you may command and require whatever you wish. It will not be done in that manner and you will not have such remarkable power. You are a servant of servants,[11] and more than all other men you are in a most miserable and dangerous position. Be not deceived by those who pretend that you are lord of the world, allow no one to be considered a Christian unless he accepts your authority, and prate that you have power over heaven, hell, and purgatory. These men are your enemies who seek to destroy your soul [I Kings 19:10], as Isaiah says: "O my people, they that call thee blessed, the same deceive thee" [Isa. 3:12]. They err who exalt you above a council and the church universal. They err who ascribe to you alone the right of interpreting Scripture. Under the protection of your name they seek to gain support for all their wicked deeds in the church. Alas! Through them Satan has already made much progress under your predecessors. In short, believe none who exalt you, believe those who humble you. This is the judgment of God, that ". . . he has put down the mighty from their thrones and exalted those of low degree" [Luke 1:52]. See how different Christ is from his successors, although they all would wish to be his vicars. I fear that most of them have been too literally his vicars. A man is a vicar only when his superior is absent. If the pope rules, while Christ is absent and does not dwell in his heart, what else is he but a vicar of Christ? What is the church under such a vicar but a mass of people without Christ? Indeed, what is such a vicar but an antichrist and an idol? How much more properly did the apostles call themselves servants of the present Christ and not vicars of an absent Christ.

Perhaps I am presumptuous in trying to instruct so exalted a personage from whom we all should learn and from whom the thrones of judges receive their decisions,

---

11. *Servus servorum* was the usual title of the pope.

as those pestilential fellows of yours boast. But I am following the example of St. Bernard in his book, *On Consideration*,[12] to Pope Eugenius, a book every pope should know from memory. I follow him, not because I am eager to instruct you, but out of pure and loyal concern which compels us to be interested in all the affairs of our neighbors, even when they are protected, and which does not permit us to take into consideration either their dignity or lack of dignity since it is only concerned with the dangers they face or the advantages they may gain. I know that Your Blessedness is driven and buffeted about in Rome, that is, that far out at sea you are threatened on all sides by dangers and are working very hard in the miserable situation so that you are in need of even the slightest help of the least of your brothers. Therefore I do not consider it absurd if I now forget your exalted office and do what brotherly love demands. I have no desire to flatter you in so serious and dangerous a matter. If men do not perceive that I am your friend and your most humble subject in this matter, there is One who understands and judges [John 8:50].

Finally, that I may not approach you empty-handed, blessed father, I am sending you this little treatise[13] dedicated to you as a token of peace and good hope. From this book you may judge with what studies I should prefer to be more profitably occupied, as I could be, provided your godless flatterers would permit me and had permitted me in the past. It is a small book if you regard its size. Unless I am mistaken, however, it contains the whole of Christian life in a brief form, provided you grasp its meaning. I am a poor man and have no other gift to offer, and you do not need to be enriched by any but a spiritual gift. May the Lord Jesus preserve you forever. Amen.

Wittenberg, September 6, 1520.

---

12. Cf. p. 270 n. 5.　　　　　13. *The Freedom of a Christian.*

Martin Luther's Treatise on Christian Liberty

[The Freedom of a Christian]

Many people have considered Christian faith an easy thing, and not a few have given it a place among the virtues. They do this because they have not experienced it and have never tasted the great strength there is in faith. It is impossible to write well about it or to understand what has been written about it unless one has at one time or another experienced the courage which faith gives a man when trials oppress him. But he who has had even a faint taste of it can never write, speak, meditate, or hear enough concerning it. It is a living "spring of water welling up to eternal life," as Christ calls it in John 4 [:14].

As for me, although I have no wealth of faith to boast of and know how scant my supply is, I nevertheless hope that I have attained to a little faith, even though I have been assailed by great and various temptations; and I hope that I can discuss it, if not more elegantly, certainly more to the point, than those literalists and subtile disputants have previously done, who have not even understood what they have written.

To make the way smoother for the unlearned—for only them do I serve—I shall set down the following two propositions concerning the freedom and the bondage of the spirit:

1. A Christian is a perfectly free lord of all, subject to none.
2. A Christian is a perfectly dutiful servant of all, subject to all.

These two theses seem to contradict each other. If, however, they should be found to fit together they would serve our purpose beautifully. Both are Paul's own statements, who says in I Cor. 9 [:19], "For though I am free from all men, I have made myself a slave to all," and in Rom. 13 [:8], "Owe no one anything, except to love one another." Love by its very nature is ready to serve and be subject to him who is loved. So Christ, although he was Lord of all, was "born of woman, born under the law" [Gal. 4:4], and therefore was at the same time a free man and a servant, "in the form of God" and "of a servant" [Phil. 2:6-7].

Let us start, however, with something more remote from our subject, but more obvious. Man has a twofold nature, a spiritual and a bodily one. According to the spiritual nature, which men refer to as the soul, he is called a spiritual, inner, or new man. According to the bodily nature, which men refer to as flesh, he is called a carnal, outward, or old man, of whom the Apostle writes in II Cor. 4 [:16], "Though our outer nature is wasting away, our inner nature is being renewed every day." Because of this diversity of nature the Scriptures assert contradictory things concerning the same man, since these two men in the same man contradict each other, "for the desires of the flesh are against the Spirit, and the desires of the Spirit are against the flesh," according to Gal. 5 [:17].

First, let us consider the inner man to see how a righteous, free, and pious Christian, that is, a spiritual, new, and inner man, becomes what he is. It is evident that no external thing has any influence in producing Christian righteousness or freedom, or in producing unrighteousness or servitude. A simple argument will furnish the proof of this statement. What can it profit the soul if the body is well, free, and active, and eats, drinks, and does as it pleases? For in these respects even the most godless slaves of vice may prosper. On the other hand, how will poor health or imprisonment or hunger or thirst or any other external misfortune harm the soul? Even the most godly men, and those who are free because of clear consciences, are afflicted with these things. None of these things touch either the freedom or the servitude of the soul. It does not help the soul if the body is adorned with the sacred robes of priests or dwells in sacred places or is occupied with sacred duties or prays, fasts, abstains from certain kinds of food, or does any work that can be done by the body and in the body. The righteousness and the freedom of the soul require something far different, since the things which have been mentioned could be done by any wicked person. Such works produce nothing but hypocrites. On the other hand, it will not harm the soul if the body is clothed in secular dress, dwells in unconsecrated places, eats and drinks as others do, does not pray aloud, and neglects to do all the above-mentioned things which hypocrites can do.

Furthermore, to put aside all kinds of works, even contemplation, meditation, and all that the soul can do, does not help. One thing, and only one thing, is necessary for Christian life, righteousness, and freedom. That one thing is the most holy Word of God, the gospel of Christ, as Christ says, John 11 [:25], "I am the resurrection and the life; he who believes in me, though he die, yet shall he live"; and John 8 [:36], "So if the Son makes you free, you will be free indeed"; and Matt. 4 [:4], "Man shall not live by bread alone, but by every word that proceeds from the mouth of God." Let us then consider it certain and firmly established that the soul can do without anything except the Word of God and that where the Word of God is missing there is no help at all for the soul. If it has the Word of God it is rich and lacks nothing, since it is the Word of life, truth, light, peace, righteousness, salvation, joy, liberty, wisdom, power, grace, glory, and of every incalculable blessing. This is why the prophet in the entire Psalm [119] and in many other places yearns and sighs for the Word of God and uses so many names to describe it.

On the other hand, there is no more terrible disaster with which the wrath of God can afflict men than a famine of the hearing of his Word, as he says in Amos [8:11]. Likewise there is no greater mercy than when he sends forth his Word, as we read in Psalm 107 [:20]: "He sent forth his word, and healed them, and delivered them from destruction." Nor was Christ sent into the world for any other ministry except that of the Word. Moreover, the entire spiritual estate—all the apostles, bishops, and priests —has been called and instituted only for the ministry of the Word.

You may ask, "What then is the Word of God, and how shall it be used, since there are so many words of God?" I answer: The Apostle explains this in Romans 1. The Word is the gospel of God concerning his Son, who was made flesh, suffered, rose from the dead, and was glorified through the Spirit who sanctifies. To preach Christ means to feed the soul, make it righteous, set it free, and save it, provided it believes the preaching. Faith alone is the saving and efficacious use of the Word of God, according to Rom. 10 [:9]: "If you confess with your lips that Jesus is Lord and believe in your heart that God raised him from the dead, you will be saved." Furthermore, "Christ is the end of the law, that every one who has faith may be justified" [Rom. 10:4]. Again, in Rom. 1 [:17], "He who through faith is righteous shall live." The Word of God cannot be received and cherished by any works whatever but only by faith. Therefore it is clear that, as the soul needs only the Word of God for its life and righteousness, so it is justified by faith alone and not any works; for if it could be justified by anything else, it would not need the Word, and consequently it would not need faith.

This faith cannot exist in connection with works—that is to say, if you at the same time claim to be justified by works, whatever their character—for that would be the same as "limping with two different opinions" [I Kings 18:21], as worshiping Baal and kissing one's own hand [Job 31:27-28], which, as Job says, is a very great iniquity.

280

Therefore the moment you begin to have faith you learn that all things in you are altogether blameworthy, sinful, and damnable, as the Apostle says in Rom. 3 [:23], "Since all have sinned and fall short of the glory of God," and, "None is righteous, no, not one; . . . all have turned aside, together they have gone wrong" (Rom. 3:10-12). When you have learned this you will know that you need Christ, who suffered and rose again for you so that, if you believe in him, you may through this faith become a new man in so far as your sins are forgiven and you are justified by the merits of another, namely, of Christ alone.

Since, therefore, this faith can rule only in the inner man, as Rom. 10 [:10] says, "For man believes with his heart and so is justified," and since faith alone justifies, it is clear that the inner man cannot be justified, frced, or saved by any outer work or action at all, and that these works, whatever their character, have nothing to do with this inner man. On the other hand, only ungodliness and unbelief of heart, and no outer work, make him guilty and a damnable servant of sin. Wherefore it ought to be the first concern of every Christian to lay aside all confidence in works and increasingly to strengthen faith alone and through faith to grow in the knowledge, not of works, but of Christ Jesus, who suffered and rose for him, as Peter teaches in the last chapter of his first Epistle (I Pet. 5:10). No other work makes a Christian. Thus when the Jews asked Christ, as related in John 6 [:28], what they must do "to be doing the work of God," he brushed aside the multitude of works which he saw they did in great profusion and suggested one work, saying, "This is the work of God, that you believe in him whom he has sent" [John 6:29]; "for on him has God the Father set his seal" [John 6:27].

Therefore true faith in Christ is a treasure beyond comparison which brings with it complete salvation and saves man from every evil, as Christ says in the last chapter of Mark [16:16]: "He who believes and is baptized will be saved; but he who does not believe will be condemned." Isaiah contemplated this treasure and foretold it in chapter 10: "The Lord will make a small and consuming word upon the land, and it will overflow with righteousness" [Cf. Isa. 10:22]. This is as though he said, "Faith, which is a small and perfect fulfillment of the law, will fill believers with so great a righteousness that they will need nothing more to become righteous." So Paul says, Rom. 10 [:10], "For man believes with his heart and so is justified."

Should you ask how it happens that faith alone justifies and offers us such a treasure of great benefits without works in view of the fact that so many works, ceremonies, and laws are prescribed in the Scriptures, I answer: First of all, remember what has been said, namely, that faith alone, without works, justifies, frees, and saves; we shall make this clearer later on. Here we must point out that the entire Scripture of God is divided into two parts: commandments and promises. Although the commandments teach things that are good, the things taught are not done as soon as they are taught, for the commandments show us what we ought to do but do not give us the power to do it. They are intended to teach man to know himself, that through them he may recognize his inability to do good and may despair of his own ability. That is why they are called the Old Testament and constitute the Old Testament. For example, the commandment, "You shall not covet" [Exod. 20:17], is a command which proves us all to be sinners, for no one can avoid coveting no matter how much he may struggle against it. Therefore, in order not to covet and to fulfill the commandment, a man is compelled to despair of himself, to seek the help which he does not find in himself elsewhere and from someone else, as stated in Hosea [13:9]: "Destruction is your own, O Israel: your help is only in me." As we fare with respect to one commandment, so we fare with all, for it is equally impossible for us to keep any one of them.

Now when a man has learned through the commandments to recognize his helplessness and is distressed about
how he might satisfy the law—since the law must be fulfilled so that not a jot or tittle shall be lost, otherwise man
will be condemned without hope—then, being truly
humbled and reduced to nothing in his own eyes, he finds
in himself nothing whereby he may be justified and saved.
Here the second part of Scripture comes to our aid, namely,
the promises of God which declare the glory of God, saying,
"If you wish to fulfill the law and not covet, as the law
demands, come, believe in Christ in whom grace, righteousness, peace, liberty, and all things are promised you. If you
believe, you shall have all things; if you do not believe, you
shall lack all things." That which is impossible for you to
accomplish by trying to fulfill all the works of the law—
many and useless as they all are—you will accomplish
quickly and easily through faith. God our Father has made
all things depend on faith so that whoever has faith will
have everything, and whoever does not have faith will have
nothing. "For God has consigned all men to disobedience,
that he may have mercy upon all," as it is stated in Rom.
11 [:32]. Thus the promises of God give what the commandments of God demand and fulfill what the law prescribes so that all things may be God's alone, both the commandments and the fulfilling of the commandments. He
alone commands, he alone fulfills. Therefore the promises
of God belong to the New Testament. Indeed, they are the
New Testament.

Since these promises of God are holy, true, righteous, free,
and peaceful words, full of goodness, the soul which clings
to them with a firm faith will be so closely united with
them and altogether absorbed by them that it not only will
share in all their power but will be saturated and intoxi-
cated by them. If a touch of Christ healed, how much
more will this most tender spiritual touch, this absorbing
of the Word, communicate to the soul all things that be-

long to the Word. This, then, is how through faith alone without works the soul is justified by the Word of God, sanctified, made true, peaceful, and free, filled with every blessing and truly made a child of God, as John 1 [:12] says: "But to all who . . . believed in his name, he gave power to become children of God."

From what has been said it is easy to see from what source faith derives such great power and why a good work or all good works together cannot equal it. No good work can rely upon the Word of God or live in the soul, for faith alone and the Word of God rule in the soul. Just as the heated iron glows like fire because of the union of fire with it, so the Word imparts its qualities to the soul. It is clear, then, that a Christian has all that he needs in faith and needs no work to justify him; and if he has no need of works, he has no need of the law; and if he has no need of the law, surely he is free from the law. It is true that "the law is not laid down for the just" [I Tim. 1:9]. This is that Christian liberty, our faith, which does not induce us to live in idleness or wickedness but makes the law and works unnecessary for any man's righteousness and salvation.

This is the first power of faith. Let us now examine also the second. It is a further function of faith that it honors him whom it trusts with the most reverent and highest regard since it considers him truthful and trustworthy. There is no other honor equal to the estimate of truthfulness with which we honor him whom we trust. Could we ascribe to a man anything greater than truthfulness and righteousness and perfect goodness? On the other hand, there is no way in which we can show greater contempt for a man than to regard him as false and wicked and to be suspicious of him, as we do when we do not trust him. So when the soul firmly trusts God's promises, it regards him as truthful and righteous. Nothing more excellent than this can be ascribed to God. The very highest worship of God

284

is this that we ascribe to him truthfulness, righteousness, and whatever else should be ascribed to one who is trusted. When this is done, the soul consents to his will. Then it hallows his name and allows itself to be treated according to God's good pleasure for, clinging to God's promises, it does not doubt that he who is true, just, and wise will do, dispose, and provide all things well.

Is not such a soul most obedient to God in all things by this faith? What commandment is there that such obedience has not completely fulfilled? What more complete fulfillment is there than obedience in all things? This obedience, however, is not rendered by works, but by faith alone. On the other hand, what greater rebellion against God, what greater wickedness, what greater contempt of God is there than not believing his promise? For what is this but to make God a liar or to doubt that he is truthful?—that is, to ascribe truthfulness to one's self but lying and vanity to God? Does not a man who does this deny God and set himself up as an idol in his heart? Then of what good are works done in such wickedness, even if they were the works of angels and apostles? Therefore God has rightly included all things, not under anger or lust, but under unbelief, so that they who imagine that they are fulfilling the law by doing the works of chastity and mercy required by the law (the civil and human virtues) might not be saved. They are included under the sin of unbelief and must either seek mercy or be justly condemned.

When, however, God sees that we consider him truthful and by the faith of our heart pay him the great honor which is due him, he does us that great honor of considering us truthful and righteous for the sake of our faith. Faith works truth and righteousness by giving God what belongs to him. Therefore God in turn glorifies our righteousness. It is true and just that God is truthful and just, and to consider and confess him to be so is the same as being truthful and just. Accordingly he says in I Sam. 2 [:30], "Those who honor me I will honor, and those who despise me shall be lightly esteemed." So Paul says in Rom. 4 [:3] that Abraham's faith "was reckoned to him as righteousness" because by it he gave glory most perfectly to God, and that for the same reason our faith shall be reckoned to us as righteousness if we believe.

The third incomparable benefit of faith is that it unites the soul with Christ as a bride is united with her bridegroom. By this mystery, as the Apostle teaches, Christ and the soul become one flesh [Eph. 5:31-32]. And if they are one flesh and there is between them a true marriage— indeed the most perfect of all marriages, since human marriages are but poor examples of this one true marriage— it follows that everything they have they hold in common, the good as well as the evil. Accordingly the believing soul can boast of and glory in whatever Christ has as though it were its own, and whatever the soul has Christ claims as his own. Let us compare these and we shall see inestimable benefits. Christ is full of grace, life, and salvation. The soul is full of sins, death, and damnation. Now let faith come between them and sins, death, and damnation will be Christ's, while grace, life, and salvation will be the soul's; for if Christ is a bridegroom, he must take upon himself the things which are his bride's and bestow upon her the things that are his. If he gives her his body and very self, how shall he not give her all that is his? And if he takes the body of the bride, how shall he not take all that is hers?

Here we have a most pleasing vision not only of communion but of a blessed struggle and victory and salvation and redemption. Christ is God and man in one person. He has neither sinned nor died, and is not condemned, and he cannot sin, die, or be condemned; his righteousness, life, and salvation are unconquerable, eternal, omnipotent. By the wedding ring of faith he shares in the sins, death, and pains of hell which are his bride's. As a matter of fact, he makes them his own and acts as if they were his own and as if he himself had sinned; he suffered, died, and descended into hell that he might overcome them all. Now since it was such a one who did all this, and death and hell could not swallow him up, these were necessarily swallowed up by him in a mighty duel; for his righteousness is greater than the sins of all men, his life stronger than death, his salvation more invincible than hell. Thus the believing soul by means of the pledge of his faith is free in Christ, its bridegroom, free from all sins, secure against death and hell, and is endowed with the eternal righteousness, life, and salvation of Christ its bridegroom. So he takes to himself a glorious bride, "without spot or wrinkle, cleansing her by the washing of water with the word" [Cf. Eph. 5:26-27] of life, that is, by faith in the Word of life, righteousness, and salvation. In this way he marries her in faith, steadfast love, and in mercies, righteousness, and justice, as Hos. 2 [:19-20] says.

Who then can fully appreciate what this royal marriage means? Who can understand the riches of the glory of this grace? Here this rich and divine bridegroom Christ marries this poor, wicked harlot, redeems her from all her evil, and adorns her with all his goodness. Her sins cannot now destroy her, since they are laid upon Christ and swallowed up by him. And she has that righteousness in Christ, her husband, of which she may boast as of her own and which she can confidently display alongside her sins in the face of death and hell and say, "If I have sinned, yet my Christ, in whom I believe, has not sinned, and all his is mine and all mine is his," as the bride in the Song of Solomon [2:16] says, "My beloved is mine and I am his." This is what Paul means when he says in I Cor. 15 [:57], "Thanks be to God, who gives us the victory through our Lord Jesus Christ," that is, the victory over sin and death, as he also says there, "The sting of death is sin, and the power of sin is the law" [I Cor. 15:56].

From this you once more see that much is ascribed to

faith, namely, that it alone can fulfill the law and justify without works. You see that the First Commandment, which says, "You shall worship one God," is fulfilled by faith alone. Though you were nothing but good works from the soles of your feet to the crown of your head, you would still not be righteous or worship God or fulfill the First Commandment, since God cannot be worshiped unless you ascribe to him the glory of truthfulness and all goodness which is due him. This cannot be done by works but only by the faith of the heart. Not by the doing of works but by believing do we glorify God and acknowledge that he is truthful. Therefore faith alone is the righteousness of a Christian and the fulfilling of all the commandments, for he who fulfills the First Commandment has no difficulty in fulfilling all the rest.

But works, being inanimate things, cannot glorify God, although they can, if faith is present, be done to the glory of God. Here, however, we are not inquiring what works and what kind of works are done, but who it is that does them, who glorifies God and brings forth the works. This is done by faith which dwells in the heart and is the source and substance of all our righteousness. Therefore it is a blind and dangerous doctrine which teaches that the commandments must be fufilled by works. The commandments must be fulfilled before any works can be done, and the works proceed from the fulfillment of the commandments [Rom. 13-10], as we shall hear.

That we may examine more profoundly that grace which our inner man has in Christ, we must realize that in the Old Testament God consecrated to himself all the first-born males. The birthright was highly prized for it involved a twofold honor, that of priesthood and that of kingship. The first-born brother was priest and lord over all the others and a type of Christ, the true and only first-born of God the Father and the Virgin Mary and true king and priest, but not after the fashion of the flesh and the world, for his kingdom is not of this world [John 18:36]. He reigns in heavenly and spiritual things and consecrates them—things such as righteousness, truth, wisdom, peace, salvation, etc. This does not mean that all things on earth and in hell are not also subject to him—otherwise how could he protect and save us from them?—but that his kingdom consists neither in them nor of them. Nor does his priesthood consist in the outer splendor of robes and postures like those of the human priesthood of Aaron and our present-day church; but it consists of spiritual things through which he by an invisible service intercedes for us in heaven before God, there offers himself as a sacrifice, and does all things a priest should do, as Paul describes him under the type of Melchizedek in the Epistle to the Hebrews [Heb. 6-7]. Nor does he only pray and intercede for us but he teaches us inwardly through the living instruction of his Spirit, thus performing the two real functions of a priest, of which the prayers and the preaching of human priests are visible types.

Now just as Christ by his birthright obtained these two prerogatives, so he imparts them to and shares them with everyone who believes in him according to the law of the above-mentioned marriage, according to which the wife owns whatever belongs to the husband. Hence all of us who believe in Christ are priests and kings in Christ, as I Pet. 2 [:9] says: "You are a chosen race, God's own people, a royal priesthood, a priestly kingdom, that you may declare the wonderful deeds of him who called you out of darkness into his marvelous light."

The nature of this priesthood and kingship is something like this: First, with respect to the kingship, every Christian is by faith so exalted above all things that, by virtue of a spiritual power, he is lord of all things without exception, so that nothing can do him any harm. As a matter of fact, all things are made subject to him and are compelled to serve him in obtaining salvation. Accordingly Paul says in Rom. 8 [:28], "All things work together for good for the

elect," and in I Cor. 3 [:21-23], "All things are yours
whether . . . life or death or the present or the future, all
are yours; and you are Christ's. . . ." This is not to say
that every Christian is placed over all things to have and
control them by physical power—a madness with which
some churchmen are afflicted—for such power belongs to
kings, princes, and other men on earth. Our ordinary experience in life shows us that we are subjected to all, suffer
many things, and even die. As a matter of fact, the more
Christian a man is, the more evils, sufferings, and deaths
he must endure, as we see in Christ the first-born prince
himself, and in all his brethren, the saints. The power of
which we speak is spiritual. It rules in the midst of
enemies and is powerful in the midst of oppression. This
means nothing else than that "power is made perfect in
weakness" [II Cor. 12:9] and that in all things I can find
profit toward salvation [Rom. 8:28], so that the cross and
death itself are compelled to serve me and to work together
with me for my salvation. This is a splendid privilege and
hard to attain, a truly omnipotent power, a spiritual dominion in which there is nothing so good and nothing so
evil but that it shall work together for good to me, if only
I believe. Yes, since faith alone suffices for salvation, I
need nothing except faith exercising the power and dominion of its own liberty. Lo, this is the inestimable power and
liberty of Christians.

Not only are we the freest of kings, we are also priests
forever, which is far more excellent than being kings, for
as priests we are worthy to appear before God to pray for
others and to teach one another divine things. These are
the functions of priests, and they cannot be granted to any
unbeliever. Thus Christ has made it possible for us, provided we believe in him, to be not only his brethren, co-
heirs, and fellow-kings, but also his fellow-priests. Therefore we may boldly come into the presence of God in the
spirit of faith [Heb. 10:19, 22] and cry "Abba, Father!" pray

for one another, and do all things which we see done and foreshadowed in the outer and visible works of priests.

He, however, who does not believe is not served by anything. On the contrary, nothing works for his good, but he himself is a servant of all, and all things turn out badly for him because he wickedly uses them to his own advantage and not to the glory of God. So he is no priest but a wicked man whose prayer becomes sin and who never comes into the presence of God because God does not hear sinners [John 9:31]. Who then can comprehend the lofty dignity of the Christian? By virtue of his royal power he rules over all things, death, life, and sin, and through his priestly glory is omnipotent with God because he does the things which God asks and desires, as it is written, "He will fulfill the desire of those who fear him; he also will hear their cry and save them" [Cf. Phil. 4:13]. To this glory a man attains, certainly not by any works of his, but by faith alone.

From this anyone can clearly see how a Christian is free from all things and over all things so that he needs no works to make him righteous and save him, since faith alone abundantly confers all these things. Should he grow so foolish, however, as to presume to become righteous, free, saved, and a Christian by means of some good work, he would instantly lose faith and all its benefits, a foolishness aptly illustrated in the fable of the dog who runs along a stream with a piece of meat in his mouth and, deceived by the reflection of the meat in the water, opens his mouth to snap at it and so loses both the meat and the reflection.[14]

You will ask, "If all who are in the church are priests, how do these whom we now call priests differ from laymen?" I answer: Injustice is done those words "priest," "cleric," "spiritual," "ecclesiastic," when they are transferred from all Christians to those few who are now by a

---

14. Luther was fond of Aesop's Fables, of which this is one.

mischievous usage called "ecclesiastics." Holy Scripture makes no distinction between them, although it gives the name "ministers," "servants," "stewards" to those who are now proudly called popes, bishops, and lords and who should according to the ministry of the Word serve others and teach them the faith of Christ and the freedom of believers. Although we are all equally priests, we cannot all publicly minister and teach. We ought not do so even if we could. Paul writes accordingly in I Cor. 4 [:1]: "This is how one should regard us, as servants of Christ and stewards of the mysteries of God."

That stewardship, however, has now been developed into so great a display of power and so terrible a tyranny that no heathen empire or other earthly power can be compared with it, just as if laymen were not also Christians. Through this perversion the knowledge of Christian grace, faith, liberty, and of Christ himself has altogether perished, and its place has been taken by an unbearable bondage of human works and laws until we have become, as the Lamentations of Jeremiah [1] say, servants of the vilest men on earth who abuse our misfortune to serve only their base and shameless will.

To return to our purpose, I believe that it has now become clear that it is not enough or in any sense Christian to preach the works, life, and words of Christ as historical facts, as if the knowledge of these would suffice for the conduct of life; yet this is the fashion among those who must today be regarded as our best preachers. Far less is it sufficient or Christian to say nothing at all about Christ and to teach instead the laws of men and the decrees of the fathers. Now there are not a few who preach Christ and read about him that they may move men's affections to sympathy with Christ, to anger against the Jews, and such childish and effeminate nonsense. Rather ought Christ to be preached to the end that faith in him may be established that he may not only be Christ, but be Christ for you and me, and that what is said of him and is denoted in his name may be effectual in us. Such faith is produced and preserved in us by preaching why Christ came, what he brought and bestowed, what benefit it is to us to accept him. This is done when that Christian liberty which he bestows is rightly taught and we are told in what way we Christians are all kings and priests and therefore lords of all and may firmly believe that whatever we have done is pleasing and acceptable in the sight of God, as I have already said.

What man is there whose heart, upon hearing these things, will not rejoice to its depth, and when receiving such comfort will not grow tender so that he will love Christ as he never could by means of any laws or works? Who would have the power to harm or frighten such a heart? If the knowledge of sin or the fear of death should break in upon it, it is ready to hope in the Lord. It does not grow afraid when it hears tidings of evil. It is not disturbed when it sees its enemies. This is so because it believes that the righteousness of Christ is its own and that its sin is not its own, but Christ's, and that all sin is swallowed up by the righteousness of Christ. This, as has been said above,[15] is a necessary consequence on account of faith in Christ. So the heart learns to scoff at death and sin and to say with the Apostle, "O death, where is thy victory? O death, where is thy sting? The sting of death is sin, and the power of sin is the law. But thanks be to God, who gives us the victory through our Lord Jesus Christ" [I Cor. 15:55-57]. Death is swallowed up not only in the victory of Christ but also by our victory, because through faith his victory has become ours and in that faith we also are conquerors.

Let this suffice concerning the inner man, his liberty, and the source of his liberty, the righteousness of faith. He needs neither laws nor good works but, on the contrary,

15. Cf. p. 287.

is injured by them if he believes that he is justified by them.

Now let us turn to the second part, the outer man. Here we shall answer all those who, offended by the word "faith" and by all that has been said, now ask, "If faith does all things and is alone sufficient unto righteousness, why then are good works commanded? We will take our ease and do no works and be content with faith." I answer: not so, you wicked men, not so. That would indeed be proper if we were wholly inner and perfectly spiritual men. But such we shall be only at the last day, the day of the resurrection of the dead. As long as we live in the flesh we only begin to make some progress in that which shall be perfected in the future life. For this reason the Apostle in Rom. 8 [:23] calls all that we attain in this life "the first fruits of the Spirit" because we shall indeed receive the greater portion, even the fulness of the Spirit, in the future. This is the place to assert that which was said above, namely, that a Christian is the servant of all and made subject to all. Insofar as he is free he does no works, but insofar as he is a servant he does all kinds of works. How this is possible we shall see.

Although, as I have said, a man is abundantly and sufficiently justified by faith inwardly, in his spirit, and so has all that he needs, except insofar as this faith and these riches must grow from day to day even to the future life; yet he remains in this mortal life on earth. In this life he must control his own body and have dealings with men. Here the works begin; here a man cannot enjoy leisure; here he must indeed take care to discipline his body by fastings, watchings, labors, and other reasonable discipline and to subject it to the Spirit so that it will obey and conform to the inner man and faith and not revolt against faith and hinder the inner man, as it is the nature of the body to do if it is not held in check. The inner man, who by faith is created in the image of God, is both joyful and happy because of Christ in whom so many benefits are conferred upon him; and therefore it is his one occupation to serve God joyfully and without thought of gain, in love that is not constrained.

While he is doing this, behold, he meets a contrary will in his own flesh which strives to serve the world and seeks its own advantage. This the spirit of faith cannot tolerate, but with joyful zeal it attempts to put the body under control and hold it in check, as Paul says in Rom. 7 [:22-23], "For I delight in the law of God, in my inmost self, but I see in my members another law at war with the law of my mind and making me captive to the law of sin," and in another place, "But I pommel my body and subdue it, lest after preaching to others I myself should be disqualified" [I Cor. 9:27], and in Galatians [5:24], "And those who belong to Christ Jesus have crucified the flesh with its passions and desires."

In doing these works, however, we must not think that a man is justified before God by them, for faith, which alone is righteousness before God, cannot endure that erroneous opinion. We must, however, realize that these works reduce the body to subjection and purify it of its evil lusts, and our whole purpose is to be directed only toward the driving out of lusts. Since by faith the soul is cleansed and made to love God, it desires that all things, and especially its own body, shall be purified so that all things may join with it in loving and praising God. Hence a man cannot be idle, for the need of his body drives him and he is compelled to do many good works to reduce it to subjection. Nevertheless the works themselves do not justify him before God, but he does the works out of spontaneous love in obedience to God and considers nothing except the approval of God, whom he would most scrupulously obey in all things.

In this way everyone will easily be able to learn for himself the limit and discretion, as they say, of his bodily castigations, for he will fast, watch, and labor as much as he finds sufficient to repress the lasciviousness and lust of his body. But those who presume to be justified by works do not regard the mortifying of the lusts, but only the works themselves, and think that if only they have done as many and as great works as are possible, they have done well and have become righteous. At times they even addle their brains and destroy, or at least render useless, their natural strength with their works. This is the height of folly and utter ignorance of Christian life and faith, that a man should seek to be justified and saved by works and without faith.

In order to make that which we have said more easily understood, we shall explain by analogies. We should think of the works of a Christian who is justified and saved by faith because of the pure and free mercy of God, just as we would think of the works which Adam and Eve did in Paradise, and all their children would have done if they had not sinned. We read in Gen. 2 [:15] that "The Lord God took the man and put him in the garden of Eden to till it and keep it." Now Adam was created righteous and upright and without sin by God so that he had no need of being justified and made upright through his tilling and keeping the garden; but, that he might not be idle, the Lord gave him a task to do, to cultivate and protect the garden. This task would truly have been the freest of works, done only to please God and not to obtain righteousness, which Adam already had in full measure and which would have been the birthright of us all.

The works of a believer are like this. Through his faith he has been restored to Paradise and created anew, has no need of works that he may become or be righteous; but that he may not be idle and may provide for and keep his body, he must do such works freely only to please God. Since, however, we are not wholly recreated, and our faith and love are not yet perfect, these are to be increased, not by external works, however, but of themselves.

A second example: A bishop, when he consecrates a

church, confirms children, or performs some other duty belonging to his office, is not made a bishop by these works. Indeed, if he had not first been made a bishop, none of these works would be valid. They would be foolish, childish, and farcical. So the Christian who is consecrated by his faith does good works, but the works do not make him holier or more Christian, for that is the work of faith alone. And if a man were not first a believer and a Christian, all his works would amount to nothing and would be truly wicked and damnable sins.

The following statements are therefore true: "Good works do not make a good man, but a good man does good works; evil works do not make a wicked man, but a wicked man does evil works." Consequently it is always necessary that the substance or person himself be good before there can be any good works, and that good works follow and proceed from the good person, as Christ also says, "A good tree cannot bear evil fruit, nor can a bad tree bear good fruit" [Matt. 7:18]. It is clear that the fruits do not bear the tree and that the tree does not grow on the fruits, also that, on the contrary, the trees bear the fruits and the fruits grow on the trees. As it is necessary, therefore, that the trees exist before their fruits and the fruits do not make trees either good or bad, but rather as the trees are, so are the fruits they bear; so a man must first be good or wicked before he does a good or wicked work, and his works do not make him good or wicked, but he himself makes his works either good or wicked.

Illustrations of the same truth can be seen in all trades. A good or a bad house does not make a good or a bad builder; but a good or a bad builder makes a good or a bad house. And in general, the work never makes the workman like itself, but the workman makes the work like himself. So it is with the works of man. As the man is, whether believer or unbeliever, so also is his work—good if it was done in faith, wicked if it was done in unbelief.

But the converse is not true, that the work makes the man either a believer or unbeliever. As works do not make a man a believer, so also they do not make him righteous. But as faith makes a man a believer and righteous, so faith does good works. Since, then, works justify no one, and a man must be righteous before he does a good work, it is very evident that it is faith alone which, because of the pure mercy of God through Christ and in his Word, worthily and sufficiently justifies and saves the person. A Christian has no need of any work or law in order to be saved since through faith he is free from every law and does everything out of pure liberty and freely. He seeks neither benefit nor salvation since he already abounds in all things and is saved through the grace of God because in his faith he now seeks only to please God.

Furthermore, no good work helps justify or save an unbeliever. On the other hand, no evil work makes him wicked or damns him; but the unbelief which makes the person and the tree evil does the evil and damnable works. Hence when a man is good or evil, this is effected not by the works, but by faith or unbelief, as the Wise Man says, "This is the beginning of sin, that a man falls away from God" [Cf. Sirach 10:14-15], which happens when he does not believe. And Paul says in Heb. 11 [:6], "For whoever would draw near to God must believe. . . ." And Christ says the same: "Either make the tree good, and its fruit good; or make the tree bad, and its fruit bad" [Matt. 12:33], as if he would say, "Let him who wishes to have good fruit begin by planting a good tree." So let him who wishes to do good works begin not with the doing of works, but with believing, which makes the person good, for nothing makes a man good except faith, or evil except unbelief.

It is ineed true that in the sight of men a man is made good or evil by his works; but this being made good or evil only means that the man who is good or evil is pointed out and known as such, as Christ says in Matt. 7 [:20], "Thus you will know them by their fruits." All this remains on the surface, however, and very many have been deceived by this outward appearance and have presumed to write and teach concerning good works by which we may be justified without even mentioning faith. They go their way, always being deceived and deceiving [II Tim. 3:13], progressing, indeed, but into a worse state, blind leaders of the blind, wearying themselves with many works and still never attaining to true righteousness [Matt. 15:14]. Of such people Paul says in II Tim. 3 [:5, 7]: "Holding the form of religion but denying the power of it . . . who will listen to anybody and can never arrive at a knowledge of the truth."

Whoever, therefore, does not wish to go astray with those blind men must look beyond works, and beyond laws and doctrines about works. Turning his eyes from works, he must look upon the person and ask how he is justified. For the person is justified and saved, not by works or laws, but by the Word of God, that is, by the promise of his grace, and by faith, that the glory may remain God's, who saved us not by works of righteousness which we have done [Titus 3:5], but by virtue of his mercy by the word of his grace when we believed [I Cor. 1:21].

From this it is easy to know how far good works are to be rejected or not, and by what standard all the teachings of men concerning works are to be interpreted. If works are sought after as a means to righteousness, are burdened with this perverse leviathan,[16] and are done under the false impression that through them one is justified, they are made necessary and freedom and faith are destroyed; and this addition to them makes them no longer good but truly damnable works. They are not free, and they blaspheme the grace of God, since to justify and to save by

16. Probably a reminiscence of Leviathan, the twisting serpent, in Isa. 27:1.

faith belongs to the grace of God alone. What the works have no power to do they nevertheless—by a godless presumption through this folly of ours—pretend to do and thus violently force themselves into the office and glory of grace. We do not, therefore, reject good works; on the contrary, we cherish and teach them as much as possible. We do not condemn them for their own sake but on account of this godless addition to them and the perverse idea that righteousness is to be sought through them; for that makes them appear good outwardly, when in truth they are not good. They deceive men and lead them to deceive one another like ravening wolves in sheep's clothing [Matt. 7:15].

But this leviathan, or perverse notion concerning works, is unconquerable where sincere faith is wanting. Those work-saints cannot get rid of it unless faith, its destroyer, comes and rules in their hearts. Nature of itself cannot drive it out or even recognize it, but rather regards it as a mark of the most holy will. If the influence of custom is added and confirms this perverseness of nature, as wicked teachers have caused it to do, it becomes an incurable evil and leads astray and destroys countless men beyond all hope of restoration. Therefore, although it is good to preach and write about penitence, confession, and satisfaction, our teaching is unquestionably deceitful and diabolical if we stop with that and do not go on to teach about faith.

Christ, like his forerunner John, not only said, "Repent" [Matt. 3:2; 4:17], but added the word of faith, saying, "The kingdom of heaven is at hand." We are not to preach only one of these words of God, but both; we are to bring forth out of our treasure things new and old, the voice of the law as well as the word of grace [Matt. 13:52]. We must bring forth the voice of the law that men may be made to fear and come to a knowledge of their sins and so be converted to repentance and a better life. But we must not stop with that, for that would only amount to wounding and not binding up, smiting and not healing, killing and not making alive, leading down into hell and not bringing back again, humbling and not exalting. Therefore we must also preach the word of grace and the promise of forgiveness by which faith is taught and aroused. Without this word of grace the works of the law, contrition, penitence, and all the rest are done and taught in vain.

Preachers of repentance and grace remain even to our day, but they do not explain God's law and promise that a man might learn from them the source of repentance and grace. Repentance proceeds from the law of God, but faith or grace from the promise of God, as Rom. 10 [:17] says: "So faith comes from what is heard, and what is heard comes by the preaching of Christ." Accordingly man is consoled and exalted by faith in the divine promise after he has been humbled and led to a knowledge of himself by the threats and the fear of the divine law. So we read in Psalm 30 [:5]: "Weeping may tarry for the night, but joy comes with the morning."

Let this suffice concerning works in general and at the same time concerning the works which a Christian does for himself. Lastly, we shall also speak of the things which he does toward his neighbor. A man does not live for himself alone in this mortal body to work for it alone, but he lives also for all men on earth; rather, he lives only for others and not for himself. To this end he brings his body into subjection that he may the more sincerely and freely serve others, as Paul says in Rom. 14 [:7-8], "None of us lives to himself, and none of us dies to himself. If we live, we live to the Lord, and if we die, we die to the Lord." He cannot ever in this life be idle and without works toward his neighbors, for he will necessarily speak, deal with, and exchange views with men, as Christ also, being made in the likeness of men [Phil. 2:7], was found in form as a man and conversed with men, as Baruch 3 [:37] says.

Man, however, needs none of these things for his righteousness and salvation. Therefore he should be guided in all his works by this thought and contemplate this one thing alone, that he may serve and benefit others in all that he does, considering nothing except the need and the advantage of his neighbor. Accordingly the Apostle commands us to work with our hands so that we may give to the needy, although he might have said that we should work to support ourselves. He says, however, "that he may be able to give to those in need" [Eph. 4:28]. This is what makes caring for the body a Christian work, that through its health and comfort we may be able to work, to acquire, and lay by funds with which to aid those who are in need, that in this way the strong member may serve the weaker, and we may be sons of God, each caring for and working for the other, bearing one another's burdens and so fulfilling the law of Christ [Gal. 6:2]. This is a truly Christian life. Here faith is truly active through love [Gal. 5:6], that is, it finds expression in works of the freest service, cheerfully and lovingly done, with which a man willingly serves another without hope of reward; and for himself he is satisfied with the fullness and wealth of his faith.

Accordingly Paul, after teaching the Philippians how rich they were made through faith in Christ, in which they obtained all things, thereafter teaches them, saying, "So if there is any encouragement in Christ, any incentive of love, any participation in the Spirit, any affection and sympathy, complete my joy by being of the same mind, having the same love, being in full accord and of one mind. Do nothing from selfishness or conceit, but in humility count others better than yourselves. Let each of you look not only to his own interests, but also to the interests of others" [Phil. 2:1-4]. Here we see clearly that the Apostle has prescribed this rule for the life of Christians, namely, that we should devote all our works to the welfare of others, since each has such abundant riches in his faith that all his other works and his whole life are a surplus with which he can by voluntary benevolence serve and do good to his neighbor.

As an example of such life the Apostle cites Christ, saying, "Have this mind among yourselves, which you have in Christ Jesus, who though he was in the form of God, did not count equality with God a thing to be grasped, but emptied himself, taking the form of a servant, being born in the likeness of men. And being found in human form he humbled himself and became obedient unto death" [Phil. 2:5-8]. This salutary word of the Apostle has been obscured for us by those who have not at all understood his words, "form of God," "form of a servant," "human form," "likeness of men," and have applied them to the divine and the human nature. Paul means this: Although Christ was filled with the form of God and rich in all good things, so that he needed no work and no suffering to make him righteous and saved (for he had all this externally), yet he was not puffed up by them and did not exalt himself above us and assume power over us, although he could rightly have done so; but, on the contrary, he so lived, labored, worked, suffered, and died that he might be like other men and in fashion and in actions be nothing else than a man, just as if he had need of all these things and had nothing of the form of God. But he did all this for our sake, that he might serve us and that all things which he accomplished in this form of a servant might become ours.

So a Christian, like Christ his head, is filled and made rich by faith and should be content with this form of God which he has obtained by faith; only, as I have said, he should increase this faith until it is made perfect. For this faith is his life, his righteousness, and his salvation: it saves him and makes him acceptable, and bestows upon him all things that are Christ's, as has been said above, and as Paul asserts in Gal. 2 [:20] when he says, "And the life I now live in the flesh I live by faith in the Son of God." Although the Christian is thus free from all works, he ought in this liberty to empty himself, take upon himself the form of a servant, be made in the likeness of men, be found in human form, and to serve, help, and in every way deal with his neighbor as he sees that God through Christ has dealt and still deals with him. This he should do freely, having regard for nothing but divine approval.

He ought to think: "Although I am an unworthy and condemned man, my God has given me in Christ all the riches of righteousness and salvation without any merit on my part, out of pure, free mercy, so that from now on I need nothing except faith which believes that this is true. Why should I not therefore freely, joyfully, with all my heart, and with an eager will do all things which I know are pleasing and acceptable to such a Father who has overwhelmed me with his inestimable riches? I will therefore give myself as a Christ to my neighbor, just as Christ offered himself to me; I will do nothing in this life except what I see is necessary, profitable, and salutary to my neighbor, since through faith I have an abundance of all good things in Christ."

Behold, from faith thus flow forth love and joy in the Lord, and from love a joyful, willing, and free mind that serves one's neighbor willingly and takes no account of gratitude or ingratitude, of praise or blame, of gain or loss. For a man does not serve that he may put men under obligations. He does not distinguish between friends and enemies or anticipate their thankfulness or unthankfulness, but he most freely and most willingly spends himself and all that he has, whether he wastes all on the thankless or whether he gains a reward. As his Father does, distributing all things to all men richly and freely, making "his sun rise on the evil and on the good" [Matt. 5:45], so also the son does all things and suffers all things with that freely bestowing joy which is his delight when through Christ he sees it in God, the dispenser of such great benefits.

Therefore, if we recognize the great and precious things

which are given us, as Paul says [Rom. 5:5], our hearts will be filled by the Holy Spirit with the love which makes us free, joyful, almighty workers and conquerors over all tribulations, servants of our neighbors, and yet lords of all. For those who do not recognize the gifts bestowed upon them through Christ, however, Christ has been born in vain; they go their way with their works and shall never come to taste or feel those things. Just as our neighbor is in need and and lacks that in which we abound, so we were in need before God and lacked his mercy. Hence, as our heavenly Father has in Christ freely come to our aid, we also ought freely to help our neighbor through our body and its works, and each one should become as it were a Christ to the other that we may be Christs to one another and Christ may be the same in all, that is, that we may be truly Christians.

Who then can comprehend the riches and the glory of the Christian life? It can do all things and has all things and lacks nothing. It is lord over sin, death, and hell, and yet at the same time it serves, ministers to, and benefits all men. But, alas, in our day this life is unknown throughout the world; it is neither preached about nor sought after; we are altogether ignorant of our own name and do not know why we are Christians or bear the name of Christians. Surely we are named after Christ, not because he is absent from us, but because he dwells in us, that is, because we believe in him and are Christ's one to another and do to our neighbors as Christ does to us. But in our day we are taught by the doctrine of men to seek nothing but merits, rewards, and the things that are ours; of Christ we have made only a taskmaster far harsher than Moses.

We have a pre-eminent example of such a faith in the blessed Virgin. As is written in Luke 2 [:22], she was purified according to the law of Moses according to the custom of all women, although she was not bound by that law and did not need to be purified. Out of free and willing

305

love, however, she submitted to the law like other women that she might not offend or despise them. She was not justified by this work, but being righteous she did it freely and willingly. So also our works should be done, not that we may be justified by them, since, being justified beforehand by faith, we ought to do all things freely and joyfully for the sake of others.

St. Paul also circumcised his disciple Timothy, not because circumcision was necessary for his righteousness, but that he might not offend or despise the Jews who were weak in the faith and could not yet grasp the liberty of faith. But, on the other hand, when they despised the liberty of faith and insisted that circumcision was necessary for righteousness, he resisted them and did not allow Titus to be circumcised Gal. 2 [:3]. Just as he was unwilling to offend or despise any man's weak faith and yielded to their will for a time, so he was also unwilling that the liberty of faith should be offended against or despised by stubborn, work-righteous men. He chose a middle way, sparing the weak for a time, but always withstanding the stubborn, that he might convert all to the liberty of faith. What we do should be done with the same zeal to sustain the weak in faith, as in Rom. 14 [:1]; but we should firmly resist the stubborn teachers of works. Of this we shall say more later.

Christ also, in Matt. 7 [:24-27], when the tax money was demanded of his disciples, discussed with St. Peter whether the sons of the king were not free from the payment of tribute, and Peter affirmed that they were. Nonetheless, Christ commanded Peter to go to the sea and said, "Not to give offense to them, go to the sea and cast a hook, and take the first fish that comes up, and when you open its mouth you will find a shekel; take that and give it to them for me and for yourself." This incident fits our subject beautifully, for Christ here calls himself and those who are his children sons of the king, who need nothing; and yet he freely submits and pays the tribute. Just as necessary and helpful as this work was to Christ's righteousness or salvation, just so much do all other works of his or his followers avail for righteousness, since they all follow after righteousness and are done only to serve others and to give them an example of good works.

Of the same nature are the precepts which Paul gives in Rom. 13 [:1-7], namely, that Christians should be subject to the governing authorities and be ready to do every good work, not that they shall in this way be justified, since they already are righteous through faith, but that in the liberty of the Spirit they shall by so doing serve others and the authorities themselves and obey their will freely and out of love. The works of all colleges,[17] monasteries, and priests should be of this nature. Each one should do the works of his profession and station, not that by them he may strive after righteousness, but that through them he may keep his body under control, be an example to others who also need to keep their bodies under control, and finally that by such works he may submit his will to that of others in the freedom of love. But very great care must always be exercised so that no man in a false confidence imagines that by such works he will be justified or acquire merit or be saved; for this is the work of faith alone, as I have repeatedly said.

Anyone knowing this could easily and without danger find his way through those numberless mandates and precepts of pope, bishops, monasteries, churches, princes, and magistrates upon which some ignorant pastors insist as if they were necessary to righteousness and salvation, calling them "precepts of the church," although they are nothing of the kind. For a Christian, as a free man, will say, "I will fast, pray, do this and that as men command, not because it is necessary to my righteousness or salvation; but that I may show due respect to the pope, the bishop, the com-

17. The word "college" here denotes a corporation of clergy supported by a foundation and performing certain religious services.

munity, a magistrate, or my neighbor, and give them an example. I will do and suffer all things, just as Christ did and suffered far more for me, although he needed nothing of it all for himself, and was made under the law for my sake, although he was not under the law." Although tyrants do violence or injustice in making their demands, yet it will do no harm as long as they demand nothing contrary to God.

From what has been said, everyone can pass a safe judgment on all works and laws and make a trustworthy distinction between them and know who are the blind and ignorant pastors and who are the good and true. Any work that is not done solely for the purpose of keeping the body under control or of serving one's neighbor, as long as he asks nothing contrary to God, is not good or Christian. For this reason I greatly fear that few or no colleges, monasteries, altars, and offices of the church are really Christian in our day—nor the special fasts and prayers on certain saints' days. I fear, I say, that in all these we seek only our profit, thinking that through them our sins are purged away and that we find salvation in them. In this way Christian liberty perishes altogether. This is a consequence of our ignorance of Christian faith and liberty.

This ignorance and suppression of liberty very many blind pastors take pains to encourage. They stir up and urge on their people in these practices by praising such works, puffing them up with their indulgences, and never teaching faith. If, however, you wish to pray, fast, or establish a foundation in the church, I advise you to be careful not to do it in order to obtain some benefit, whether temporal or eternal, for you would do injury to your faith which alone offers you all things. Your one care should be that faith may grow, whether it is trained by works or sufferings. Make your gifts freely and for no consideration, so that others may profit by them and fare well because of you and your goodness. In this way you shall be truly good and Christian. Of what benefit to you are the good works which you do not need for keeping your body under control? Your faith is sufficient for you, through which God has given you all things.

See, according to this rule the good things we have from God should flow from one to the other and be common to all, so that everyone should "put on" his neighbor and so conduct himself toward him as if he himself were in the other's place. From Christ the good things have flowed and are flowing into us. He has so "put on" us and acted for us as if he had been what we are. From us they flow on to those who have need of them, so that I should lay before God my faith and my righteousness that they may cover and intercede for the sins of my neighbor which I take upon myself, and so labor and serve in them as if they were my very own. That is what Christ did for us. This is true love and the genuine rule of a Christian life. Love is true and genuine where there is true and genuine faith. Hence the Apostle says of love in I Cor. 13 [:5] that "it does not seek its own."

We conclude, therefore, that a Christian lives not in himself, but in Christ and in his neighbor. Otherwise he is not a Christian. He lives in Christ through faith, in his neighbor through love. By faith he is caught up beyond himself into God. By love he descends beneath himself into his neighbor. Yet he always remains in God and in his love, as Christ says in John I [:51], "Truly, truly, I say to you, you will see heaven opened, and the angels of God ascending and descending upon the Son of man."

Summary of the two Christian loves.

Enough now of freedom. As you see, it is a spiritual and true freedom and makes our hearts free from all sins, laws and commands, as Paul says, I Tim. 1 [:9], "The law is not laid down for the just." It is more excellent than all other liberty, which is external, as heaven is more excellent than earth. May Christ give us this liberty both to understand and to preserve. Amen.

Finally, something must be added for the sake of those for whom nothing can be said so well that they will not spoil it by misunderstanding it. It is questionable whether they will understand even what will be said here. There are very many who, when they hear of this freedom of faith, immediately turn it into an occasion for the flesh and think that now all things are allowed them. They want to show that they are free men and Christians only by despising and finding fault with ceremonies, traditions, and human laws; as if they were Christians because on stated days they do not fast or eat meat when others fast, or because they do not use the accustomed prayers, and with upturned nose scoff at the precepts of men, although they utterly disregard all else that pertains to the Christian religion. The extreme opposite of these are those who rely for their salvation solely on their reverent observance of ceremonies, as if they would be saved because on certain days they fast or abstain from meats, or pray certain prayers; these make a boast of the precepts of the church and of the fathers, and do not care a fig for the things which are of the essence of our faith. Plainly, both are in error because they neglect the weightier things which are necessary to salvation, and quarrel so noisily about trifling and unnecessary matters.

How much better is the teaching of the Apostle Paul who bids us take a middle course and condemns both sides when he says, "Let not him who eats despise him who abstains, and let not him whom abstains pass judgment on him who eats" [Rom. 14:3]. Here you see that they who neglect and disparage ceremonies, not out of piety, but out of mere contempt, are reproved, since the Apostle teaches us not to despise them. Such men are puffed up by knowledge. On the other hand, he teaches those who insist on the ceremonies not to judge the others, for neither party acts toward the other according to the love that edifies. Wherefore we ought to listen to Scripture which teaches that we should not go aside to the right or to the left [Deut. 28:14] but follow the statutes of the Lord which are right, "rejoicing the heart" [Ps. 19:8]. As a man is not righteous because he keeps and clings to the works and forms of the ceremonies, so also will a man not be counted righteous merely because he neglects and despises them.

Our faith in Christ does not free us from works but from false opinions concerning works, that is, from the foolish presumption that justification is acquired by works. Faith redeems, corrects, and preserves our consciences so that we know that righteousness does not consist in works, although works neither can nor ought to be wanting; just as we cannot be without food and drink and all the works of this mortal body, yet our righteousness is not in them, but in faith; and yet those works of the body are not to be despised or neglected on that account. In this world we are bound by the needs of our bodily life, but we are not righteous because of them. "My kingship is not of this world" [John 18:36], says Christ. He does not, however, say, "My kingship is not here, that is, in this world." And Paul says, "Though we live in the world we are not carrying on a worldly war" [II Cor. 10:3], and in Gal. 2 [:20], "The life I now live in the flesh I live by faith in the Son of God." Thus what we do, live, and are in works and ceremonies, we do because of the necessities of this life and of the effort to rule our body. Nevertheless we are righteous, not in these, but in the faith of the Son of God.

Hence the Christian must take a middle course and face those two classes of men. He will meet first the unyielding, stubborn ceremonialists who like deaf adders are not willing to hear the truth of liberty [Ps. 58:4] but, having no faith, boast of, prescribe, and insist upon their ceremonies as means of justification. Such were the Jews of old, who were unwilling to learn how to do good. These he must resist, do the very opposite, and offend them boldly lest by their impious views they drag many with them into error. In the presence of such men it is good to eat meat, break the fasts, and for the sake of the liberty of faith do other things which they regard as the greatest of sins. Of them we must say, "Let them alone; they are blind guides." According to this principle Paul would not circumcise Titus when the Jews insisted that he should [Gal. 2:3], and Christ excused the apostles when they plucked ears of grain on the sabbath [Matt. 12:1-8]. There are many similar instances. The other class of men whom a Christian will meet are simple-minded, ignorant men, weak in the faith, as the Apostle calls them, who cannot yet grasp the liberty of faith, even if they were willing to do so [Rom. 14:1]. These he must take care not to offend. He must yield to their weakness until they are more fully instructed. Since they do and think as they do, not because they are stubbornly wicked, but only because their faith is weak, the fasts and other things which they consider necessary must be observed to avoid giving them offense. This is the command of love which would harm no one but would serve all men. It is not by their fault that they are weak, but by that of their pastors who have taken them captive with the snares of their traditions and have wickedly used these traditions as rods with which to beat them. They should have been delivered from these pastors by the teachings of faith and freedom. So the Apostle teaches us in Romans 14: "If food is a cause of my brother's falling, I will never eat meat" [Cf. Rom. 14:21 and I Cor. 8:13]; and again, "I know and am persuaded in the Lord Jesus that nothing is unclean in itself; but it is unclean for any one who thinks it unclean" [Rom. 14:14].

For this reason, although we should boldly resist those teachers of traditions and sharply censure the laws of the popes by means of which they plunder the people of God, yet we must spare the timid multitude whom these impious tyrants hold captive by means of these laws until they are set free. Therefore fight strenuously against the wolves, but for the sheep and not also against the sheep. This you will do if you inveigh against the laws and the lawgivers and at the same time observe the laws with the weak so that they will not be offended, until they also recognize tyranny and understand their freedom. If you wish to use your freedom, do so in secret, as Paul says, Rom. 14 [:22], "The faith that you have, keep between yourself and God"; but take care not to use your freedom in the sight of the weak. On the other hand, use your freedom constantly and consistently in the sight of and despite the tyrants and the stubborn so that they also may learn that they are impious, that their laws are of no avail for righteousness, and that they had no right to set them up.

Since we cannot live our lives without ceremonies and works, and the perverse and untrained youth need to be restrained and saved from harm by such bonds; and since each one should keep his body under control by means of such works, there is need that the minister of Christ be far-seeing and faithful. He ought so to govern and teach Christians in all these matters that their conscience and faith will not be offended and that there will not spring up in them a suspicion and a root of bitterness and many will thereby be defiled, as Paul admonishes the Hebrews [Heb. 12:15]; that is, that they may not lose faith and become defiled by the false estimate of the value of works and think that they must be justified by works. Unless faith is at the same time constantly taught, this happens easily and defiles a great many, as has been done until now through the pestilent, impious, soul-destroying traditions of our popes and the opinions of our theologians. By these snares numberless souls have been dragged down to hell, so that you might see in this the work of Antichrist.

In brief, as wealth is the test of poverty, business the test of faithfulness, honors the test of humility, feasts the test of temperance, pleasures the test of chastity, so ceremonies are the test of the righteousness of faith. "Can a man," asks

313

Solomon, "carry fire in his bosom and his clothes and not be burned?" [Prov. 6:27]. Yet as a man must live in the midst of wealth, business, honors, pleasures, and feasts, so also must he live in the midst of ceremonies, that is, in the midst of dangers. Indeed, as infant boys need beyond all else to be cherished in the bosoms and by the hands of maidens to keep them from perishing, yet when they are grown up their salvation is endangered if they associate with maidens, so the inexperienced and perverse youth need to be restrained and trained by the iron bars of ceremonies lest their unchecked ardor rush headlong into vice after vice. On the other hand, it would be death for them always to be held in bondage to ceremonies, thinking that these justify them. They are rather to be taught that they have been so imprisoned in ceremonies, not that they should be made righteous or gain great merit by them, but that they might thus be kept from doing evil and might more easily be instructed to the righteousness of faith. Such instruction they would not endure if the impulsiveness of their youth were not restrained.

Hence ceremonies are to be given the same place in the life of a Christian as models and plans have among builders and artisans. They are prepared, not as a permanent structure, but because without them nothing could be built or made. When the structure is complete the models and plans are laid aside. You see, they are not despised, rather they are greatly sought after; but what we despise is the false estimate of them, since no one holds them to be the real and permanent structure.

If any man were so flagrantly foolish as to care for nothing all his life long except the most costly, careful, and persistent preparation of plans and models and never to think of the structure itself, and were satisfied with his work in producing such plans and mere aids to work, and boasted of it, would not all men pity his insanity and think that something great might have been built with what he

314

has wasted? Thus we do not despise ceremonies and works but we set great store by them; but we despise the false estimate placed upon works in order that no one may think that they are true righteousness, as those hypocrites believe who spend and lose their whole lives in zeal for works and never reach that goal for the sake of which the works are to be done, who, as the Apostle says, "will listen to anybody and can never arrive at a knowledge of the truth" [II Tim. 3:7]. They seem to wish to build, they make their preparations, and yet they never build. Thus they remain caught in the form of religion and do not attain unto its power [II Tim. 3:5]. Meanwhile they are pleased with their efforts and even dare to judge all others whom they do not see shining with a like show of works. Yet with the gifts of God which they have spent and abused in vain they might if they had been filled with faith, have accomplished great things to their own salvation and that of others.

Since human nature and natural reason, as it is called, are by nature superstitious and ready to imagine, when laws and works are prescribed, that righteousness must be obtained through laws and works; and further, since they are trained and confirmed in this opinion by the practice of all earthly lawgivers, it is impossible that they should of themselves escape from the slavery of works and come to a knowledge of the freedom of faith. Therefore there is need of the prayer that the Lord may give us and make us *theodidacti*, that is, those taught by God [John 6:45], and himself, as he has promised, write his law in our hearts; otherwise there is no hope for us. If he himself does not teach our hearts this wisdom hidden in mystery [I Cor. 2:7], nature can only condemn it and judge it to be heretical because nature is offended by it and regards it as foolishness. So we see that it happened in the old days in the case of the apostles and prophets, and so godless and blind popes and their flatterers do to me and to those who are like me. May God at last be merciful on them and to us and cause his face to shine upon us that we may know his way upon earth [Ps. 67:1-2], his salvation among all nations, God, who is blessed forever [II Cor. 11:31]. Amen.

Type used in this book
Body, 10 on 12 Caledonia
Display 14 Bernhard